LIFE IN THE S

LIFE IN THE SICK-ROOM

Harriet Martineau

edited by Maria H. Frawley

broadview literary texts

National Library of Canada Cataloguing in Publication

Martineau, Harriet, 1802-1876
    Life in the sick-room / Harriet Martineau ; edited by Maria Frawley.

(Broadview literary texts)
Includes bibliographical references.
ISBN 1-55111-265-5

1. Invalids—Conduct of life.   2. Martineau, Harriet, 1802-1876—Health.
I. Frawley, Maria H., 1961- .   II. Title.   III. Series.

BJ1571.M37 2003   170'.87'7   C2002-905699-3

Broadview Press Ltd. is an independent, international publishing house, incorporated in 1985. Broadview believes in shared ownership, both with its employees and with the general public; since the year 2000 Broadview shares have traded publicly on the Toronto Venture Exchange under the symbol BDP.

We welcome comments and suggestions regarding any aspect of our publications—please feel free to contact us at the addresses below or at broadview@broadviewpress.com.

North America
PO Box 1243, Peterborough, Ontario, Canada K9J 7H5
3576 California Road, Orchard Park, NY, USA 14127
Tel: (705) 743-8990; Fax: (705) 743-8353
email: customerservice@broadviewpress.com

UK, Ireland, and continental Europe
Thomas Lyster Ltd., Units 3 & 4a, Old Boundary Way
Burscough Road, Ormskirk
Lancashire, L39 2YW
Tel: (01695) 575112; Fax: (01695) 570120
email: books@tlyster.co.uk

Australia and New Zealand
UNIREPS, University of New South Wales
Sydney, NSW, 2052
Tel: 61 2 9664 0999; Fax: 61 2 9664 5420
email: info.press@unsw.edu.au

www.broadviewpress.com

Broadview Press Ltd. gratefully acknowledges the financial support of the Government of Canada through the Book Publishing Industry Development Program for our publishing activities.

This book is printed on acid-free paper containing 20% post-consumer fibre.
Series editor: Professor L.W. Conolly
Advisory editor for this volume: Professor Eugene Benson
Text design and composition by George Kirkpatrick

PRINTED IN CANADA

MISS MARTINEAU
(By courtesy of the National Portrait Gallery, London.)

Contents

Appendix G: Additional Examples of Sickroom Literature

Acknowledgements

I began this project while at Elizabethtown College and give thanks to Joyce Ney for her help in the earliest stages of preparing this edition. A General University Research grant from the University of Delaware provided the support for me to travel to London to access the manuscript of *Life in the Sick-Room* at the Fawcett Library and to work in Harriet Martineau archives in Britain. Special thanks go to Anna Greening, Jennifer Haynes, and the wonderful staff at the Fawcett Library in London for facilitating my work with the manuscript. Archivists at the Bodleian Library and the Dr. Williams' Library also provided essential help in working with materials relevant to this project. Christine Penney and Martin Killeen at the University of Birmingham Library were generous with their time in helping me track down information related to their wonderful collection, *The Papers of Harriet Martineau 1802-1876*. I want also to express my appreciation to Richard Makepeace Martineau and to Imogen Harriet Martineau for their generous communication and for their willingness to grant permission to have a photograph taken of the manuscript. Catherine Flood from the Mary Evans Picture Library worked efficiently to facilitate photographic reproduction. Permission to quote from Martineau's correspondence has been granted by the Bodleian Library, the British Library, and the University Library, and will be cited at specific points within this edition.

Thanks of a different sort go to the many students who have helped me track down information about Harriet Martineau; I am especially grateful to Cheryl Horton, Kathryn Miele, and Jason Weinberg for their efforts. I am grateful, also, to the many colleagues with whom I have discussed Martineau and her identity as an invalid, especially Sally Mitchell, Patrick Leary, Alison Winter, Deborah Logan, and Alexis Easley. Members of VICTORIA, the internet discussion list, provided detailed information on numerous issues related to Martineau, her contemporaries, and Victorian medicine. I thank all those with whom I have worked at Broadview Press for their patience and encouragement.

Finally, I thank my family for their help over the years. My parents, Barton and Sabrena Hinkle, have always encouraged me in my work. My husband, Bill Frawley, has been both generous and patient with his help. My children, Christopher and Emma Frawley, have kept me sane and happy.

Introduction

When in 1855 Harriet Martineau (1802-76) embarked on her autobiography, she began with the characteristically Victorian declaration that she had been long compelled by a sense of duty to record her life and that she "could not die in peace till this work was done." [1] Evidently Martineau had twice before in her life attempted the feat, "once in 1831, and again about ten years later, during [her] long illness in Tynemouth" (I, 1). "While I was in health, there was always so much to do that was immediately wanted, that, as usually happens in such cases, that which was not immediately necessary was deferred," Martineau continued (I, 1). If Harriet Martineau was like many of her fellow Victorians in so vigorously attaching an ideal of duty to the record of her life, her association of writing with ill-health was peculiarly her own.[2] Sickness was not only the linchpin of her self-understanding, her guiding frame of reference, it was the lens through which she wanted her readers to see and understand her life and career. Her two-volume autobiography begins with an account of her status as "a delicate child" (I, 7) and details a range of medical problems, including deafness, that she traces to an inadequate wet-nurse. It goes on to describe "long years of indigestion by day and night-mare terrors," (I, 8). "Never was poor mortal cursed with a more beggarly nervous system," Martineau notes as she recounts the "world of suffering" that left her "infirm and ill-developed" (I, 8-9, 102). The autobiography recounts numerous subsequent episodes of failing health, suffering, pain, and feebleness and ends when she receives what she takes to be a terminal diagnosis, evidently receiving confirmation from two physicians that her heart

---

1 *Harriet Martineau's Autobiography.* Edited by Maria Weston Chapman. Volume One. Fourth Edition. (Boston: Houghton, Osgood, and Company, 1879) 1. Martineau wrote the autobiography in 1855, but it was not published until after her death over twenty years later. All references are to this edition and hereafter will be cited parenthetically in the text by volume and page number.
2 In "Making the most of martyrdom: Harriet Martineau, autobiography and death," Trev Lynn Broughton persuasively argues that the entire autobiography is framed by "the liminal view from the Sick Room." *Literature & History* 2, 2 (Autumn 1993): 30.

was "too feeble for its work" (II, 102).[1] "When I returned to my lodgings, and was preparing for dinner, a momentary thrill of something like painful emotion passed through me,—not at all because I was going to die, but at the thought that I should never feel health again" (II, 102). Always anxious to control her public reputation, Martineau prepared her own obituary,[2] then lived for more than twenty more years at her beloved home, The Knoll, in Ambleside, active in her writing even while continuing throughout many of these years to prepare for death.

Life in the Sick-Room, first published in 1844, occupies a crucial place in Harriet Martineau's history and career, particularly given her life-long preoccupation with sickness and health. Already well-known as a journalist and author of the *Illustrations of Political Economy* series when she became seriously ill in 1839, Martineau would go on after roughly five years of confinement to a long and distinguished writing career, producing an eclectic array of works such as *Eastern Life, Present and Past* (1848), *British Rule in India: A Historical Sketch* (1857), *Household Education* (1849), *Health, Husbandry and Handicraft* (1861), and *A Complete Guide to the English Lakes* (1855), and regularly writing for the *Daily News* as well as popular and prestigious monthly and quarterly periodicals. Reflecting on Martineau's considerable abilities, George Eliot once described her as a "*trump*—the only English woman that possesses thoroughly the art of writing."[3]

Written during the "long illness in Tynemouth," a period that her autobiography repeatedly invokes, *Life in the Sick-Room* is Martineau's most sustained examination of life as experienced by a sufferer. Its ten chapters cover topics such as "Sympathy to the Invalid," "Nature to the Invalid," "Temper," and "Becoming Inured." Martineau clearly wanted her readers to understand the

---

1   Martineau's autobiography identifies the two physicians as Dr. Latham and Dr. Watson. Martineau was in frequent consultation with Dr. Peter Mere Latham, a specialist in diseases of the heart, and considered him a trusted and valuable medical advisor. For samples of Martineau's correspondence with Dr. Latham, see Appendix C.

2   This obituary, retitled by the *Daily News* as "An Autobiographic Memoir," appears in Appendix D.

3   George Eliot to Mr. and Mrs. C. Bray and Sara Hennell, 2 June 1852. This letter is reprinted in *The George Eliot Letters*. Ed. Gordon S. Haight. 9 Volumes (London and New Haven: Yale University Press, 1954-1978): II, 32.

subjective experience of illness—i.e., what the long-suffering *felt* and how they experienced life in the sick-room—but her book is not purely didactic. Yet in it, passages that describe the invalid's experiences generally and that instruct healthy readers on how to respect the invalid's feelings co-mingle with those that evoke her own personal experiences; ruminations about life in the sick-room lead her on to myriad other topics, including the status of biography, the nature of privacy and the privilege of correspondence, the pleasures of reading, and the inventions and adventurers of her day. Part memoir, part treatise, *Life in the Sick-Room* is a hybrid text that illustrates a particularly Victorian approach to pathography[1] even as it resists traditional literary classification.[2]

Publishing her book under the pseudonym of "An Invalid," Martineau claimed in her autobiography that she "never wrote any thing so fast as that book" (I, 457). "It went off like sleep. I was hardly conscious of the act, while writing or afterwards,—so strong was the need to speak," she wrote (I, 457). The manuscript of *Life in the Sick-Room* corroborates Martineau's comment, as it is written in small, neat handwriting somewhat uncharacteristic of Martineau's other manuscripts and reveals relatively little revision or alteration. Preparing her manuscript for her publisher, Edward Moxon, Martineau did little more than make a few stylistic corrections, clarifying a point or two, and changing some phrases to make her points as broadly applicable as possible—so that the phrase "our time" might be crossed out and changed to "each age," for example. Authoring the book anonymously as "an invalid," and at times directing her remarks to a readership of "fellow-sufferers" and "unknown comrades in suffering," a readership she had addressed earlier in her 1834 "Letter to the Deaf,"

---

1   For more on this type of writing, see Anne Hunsaker Hawkins' *Reconstructing Illness: Studies in Pathography*. (West Lafayette, IN: Purdue University Press, 1995).

2   While most of Martineau's contemporaries contented themselves with vague accolades, calling it "a delightful book," more recently critics have sought to categorize *Life in the Sick-Room*. In "Mothering and Mesmerism in The Life of Harriet Martineau," Diana Postlethwaite describes it as "an autobiographic meditation on invalidism." *Signs* (Spring 1989): 585. In "Harriet Martineau and the Reform of the Invalid in Victorian England," Alison Winter calls it a "normative treatise." *Historical Journal* 38, 3 (1995): 597. Anka Ryall designates it a "self-help book for fellow sufferers" in "Medical Body and Lived Experience: The Case of Harriet Martineau." *Mosaic* 33, 4 (December 2000): 39.

Martineau reveals the extent to which her project was influenced by the culture of invalidism that took hold and flourished in nineteenth-century England.[1] Florence Nightingale, Elizabeth Barrett Browning, Charles Darwin, Alfred Tennyson, and Robert Louis Stevenson are among the most celebrated writers and intellectuals of the period to be publicly acknowledged as invalids at various points in their lives, but they were surrounded by hundreds of lesser-known men and women who either were, or believed themselves to be, invalids. "What small community cannot array a host of invalids? What family is without one or more?" asked *The Christian Examiner* in its 1845 review of *Life in the Sick-Room*.[2] One need only look to newspapers, magazines, and popular fiction of the period to find wide-ranging evidence of the invalid's cultural omnipresence—in advertisements for new inventions such as an "invalid bedstead," announcements of the availability of special "life assurance" or asylums for invalids, and illustrations of the crippled or bedridden. Hymnals, prayer-books, cookbooks, travel guides, and advice manuals designed for invalids proliferated during the period. The valetudinarians, malingerers, hypochondriacs, and consumptives who frequent nineteenth-century fiction are indicative of the invalid's status as a recognizable and ubiquitous figure of nineteenth-century social and medical life.

A variety of social and historical forces converged in nineteenth-century England to enable invalidism to assume this cultural status. Evangelicalism, for example, validated suffering as God-given and linked protracted illness to the spiritual transformation crucial to conversion, enabling the afflicted to see themselves as pupils of God.

Industrialization contributed to the culture of invalidism as well, for it spawned categories of work that helped to produce new beliefs about physical and mental performance, capacity, and exertion that, in turn, generated new medical categories, many of

---

1   For additional information about the experience of and fascination with ill health in nineteenth-century England, see Athena Vrettos' *Somatic Fictions: Imagining Illness in Victorian Culture* (1995); Janet Oppenheim's *"Shattered Nerves": Doctors, Patients, and Depression in Victorian England* (1991); and Roy Porter and Dorothy Porter's *In Sickness and In Health: The British Experience 1650-1850* (1988).

2   See Appendix B for this and other contemporary reviews of Martineau's book.

them linked to the idea of "overwork" and nearly all freighted with additional assumptions about gender differences. Women in particular were subject to deeply-entrenched medical beliefs that linked health to the reproductive system and associated the female body and mind with fragility, weakness of will, and susceptibility to hysteria, beliefs that fueled controversy over the impact of work and its converse, idleness, on the well-being of women.[1] The emergence of scientific medicine resulted in new diagnostic technologies if not in substantial therapeutic advances. Alternative medicines, treatments, and health regimens such as hydropathy, homeopathy, and mesmerism flourished throughout the eighteenth century and into the nineteenth century, in part because orthodox medicine, gradually becoming both more professionalized and more scientific, became less patient-centered. As Roy Porter puts it, "The ensuing vacuum, left by the demise of patient-centred medicine, came to be filled by fringe sects that continued to make some sense of sickness."[2] Just as the meanings attached to being a patient changed over the course of the century—and in different ways, depending on factors such as class, gender, and age—so too did the symbolic significance of being pronounced—or pronouncing oneself—incurable.

Published in January of 1844 and selling out by the end of the following month, *Life in the Sick-Room* emerged out of and reflects this complex cultural heritage in numerous ways.[3] Contemplating her sickroom years, Martineau explained in her autobiography: "I was patient in illness and pain because I was proud of the distinction, and of being taken into such special pupilage by God; and I hoped for, and expected early death till it was too late to die early" (I, 440). While not strictly Evangelical in

---

1 For an excellent overview of these issues, see Janet Oppenheim's "Neurotic Women" in *"Shattered Nerves": Doctors, Patients, and Depression in Victorian England* (New York and Oxford: Oxford University Press, 1991) 181-232.

2 See *Health for Sale: Quackery in England 1660-1850* (Manchester University Press, 1989) 132.

3 Noting that the original print-run was for 1,250 copies, Alison Winter makes the important point that "the contemporary impression of *Sick-room*'s popularity should, however, be placed in the context of the low sales of Martineau's works during her illness" (Winter, 1995, 604, n.32). Always believing in a wide audience for Martineau's book, her publisher Edward Moxon would later re-release *Life in the Sick-Room* in a smaller, cheaper edition.

orientation—indeed, one of Martineau's early biographers, Vera Wheatley, aptly calls *Life in the Sick-Room* "the swan-song of her Unitarian orthodoxy"[1]—the book is writ through with tributes to the ways invalidism enables the sufferer to more fully apprehend God: "Nothing but experience can convey a conception of the intense reality in which God appears supreme, Christ and his gospel divine, and holiness the one worthy aim and chief good, when our frame is refusing its offices, and we can lay hold on no immediate outward support and solace," Martineau writes. Martineau's rhetoric and posturing in *Life in the Sick-Room* illustrate, as critics have remarked, the way patriarchal stereotypes of the female body and feminine submission could be deployed in the service of Christian ideals of resignation and fortitude.

Martineau's autobiography reveals the extent to which evolving medical understanding of the relationship between work and one's mental health influenced her retreat to Tynemouth as well. She attributed her illness both to the "excessive anxiety of mind" and "extreme tension of nerves" induced by caring for an increasingly infirm mother when already in a state of "reduced health" herself and to being "overworked, fearfully, in addition to the pain of mind [she] had to bear" (I, 441-42). Reflecting changes in medicine in still another way, *Life in the Sick-Room* exposes Martineau's receptivity to alternative medical treatments, what many in her day would have regarded as quackery. Of mesmerism, for example, she writes: "who believes that it could be revived, again and again at intervals of centuries, if there were not something in it?"

The question itself reveals something of the intellectual curiosity that Harriet Martineau cultivated throughout her life, a curiosity perhaps intensified by the partial deafness that she lived with from early adulthood. One of eight children born to Thomas and Elizabeth Martineau, a manufacturing family of Norwich, Martineau grew up in a Unitarian home that she found deficient in providing adequate emotional support and sustenance. Although her two opportunities to receive formal school-

---

1 Vera Wheatley, *The Life and Work of Harriet Martineau* (London: Secker & Warburg, 1957) 233.

ing in Norwich and Bristol were brief, she supplemented this education with regular study at home, often with her younger brother, James. She published her first article at the age of twenty. Appearing in a Unitarian magazine, the *Monthly Repository*, this essay, "Female Writers on Practical Divinity," was quickly followed by another titled "On Female Education." *Devotional Exercises for the Use of Young Persons* was published the following year. Subsequent essays would later earn Martineau prize money from the Central Unitarian Association. When her father died in 1826 and the family business failed in 1829, Martineau's desire to support herself through writing intensified, and W. J. Fox, the new editor of the *Monthly Repository*, encouraged her to contribute regularly to that journal. In her autobiography, Martineau credits Fox's correspondence, criticism, and editorial help with being "the cause of the greatest intellectual progress [she] ever made before the age of thirty" (I, 106-07). Martineau moved to London to live with relatives and further satisfy her writing ambitions. Although plagued by some difficulties with her mother, who restricted the time she could spend in London, Martineau worked hard and within several years had achieved her goal of publishing a nine-volume series on political economy — what Carlyle famously called "the dismal science." By the time Martineau traveled to America in 1834, her *Illustrations of Political Economy* (1832-34) had sold more than 10,000 copies, giving her considerable financial independence and literary celebrity. She was, as R. H. Horne wrote, a "Spirit of the Age," and, as the *Dictionary of National Biography* would later put it, "one of the 'lions' of the day."[1]

Illustrations of Political Economy is significant not simply because it marks a turning point in Martineau's authorial career and the beginning of her literary celebrity, but also because it reveals her trademark interest in and commitment to popularizing ideas, making difficult or little-known concepts accessible to a broad spectrum of ordinary readers.[2] In her self-written obituary,

---

1   Horne wrote an adulatory essay on Martineau and Anna Jameson for his book *A New Spirit of the Age* (London: Smith, Elder and Co., 1844) 65-82.

2   *Political Economy and Fiction in the Early Works of Harriet Martineau* by Claudia Orazem provides comprehensive discussion of this theme. Anglo-American Studies Series.

Martineau wrote that "she could popularize, while she could neither discover nor invent" and claimed that "auxiliary usefulness" was "the aim of Harriet Martineau's history."[1] Despite the disparaging tone that underlies her self-assessment, Martineau was clearly driven by a belief in the importance of this kind of work, seeing it as particularly empowering for women and ultimately as a kind of "civic agency."[2] Whether informing her readers about the experiences of the deaf, the consequences of slavery and/or the ramifications of the Civil War in the United States, sanitary conditions in India, or health in the home, nearly all of Martineau's writing evidences this drive to popularize and thereby educate. *Life in the Sick-Room* is no exception.

When Martineau commenced writing *Life in the Sick-Room*, she had been staying in her lodgings in Tynemouth for several years, having moved there in March of 1840 after a short period in her sister's home in Newcastle-upon-Tyne, where she was under the care of her brother-in-law, the physician Thomas Greenhow. Drawing largely on the account provided in her autobiography, Martineau's biographers have reconstructed the major events leading to her retreat to Tynemouth and the years spent there. Although beginning to experience a decline in energy and other signs of physical deterioration, Martineau traveled with a small group of friends to Europe in 1839, where she evidently collapsed while in Italy and was diagnosed by a Venetian physician as suffering from a prolapse of the uterus and polypous tumours. She returned to England to consult with Greenhow and begin a series of treatments that included the surgical removal of the tumours and various kinds of drug therapy, including morphine dosing and the application of iodine ointment. Evidently anticipating no easy recovery or cure, Martineau eventually removed herself from the Greenhow home, taking lodgings in

---

   New York: Peter Lang, 1999. See also the chapter "A career launched" in Shelagh Hunter's *Harriet Martineau: The Poetics of Moralism* (Aldershot, England: Scolar Press, 1995) 7-58.

1 For a thorough assessment of the implications of this rhetoric for our understanding of Martineau's position in patriarchal culture, see the chapters on Martineau in Deirdre David's *Intellectual Women and Victorian Patriarchy: Harriet Martineau, Elizabeth Barrett Browning, George Eliot.* (New York: Cornell University Press, 1987).

2 The phrase is Anka Ryall's in "Medical Body and Lived Experience: The Case of Harriet Martineau." *Mosaic* 33/4 (December 2000): 37.

Tynemouth that she could furnish to suit her needs. She decorated her rooms with flowers, plants, and her favorite paintings and books and made frequent use of a telescope a friend gave her to take in the view from a window overlooking the valley below. Although G.A. Simcox would later write in the *Fortnightly Review* that Martineau went to Tynemouth "with the instinct of wild creatures that creep apart to die," her efforts to create a positive environment in which to think, write, and visit with others belie that judgment.[1] Noting that "unlike the typical sick-room, [Martineau's] was a place in which the invalid became *more* independent, rather than less so," Alison Winter more accurately describes the room as "a testimony to her social and intellectual networks."[2] But however "independent" her life as an invalid, Martineau stayed there—a self-described "prisoner to the couch"[3]—for five years; only after a series of experiments with mesmerism did she recover and resume an active life outside the confines of her home.

Numerous biographers and critics have addressed the vexed question of what plagued Martineau during these years and what, exactly, accounts for the recovery she seemed to enjoy for a decade or so after her experiments with mesmerism. While some relate Martineau's problems exclusively to her tumour and account for her temporary recovery by reference to a shift in the location or change in the position of the tumours, others identify her illness as being largely psychological, "an unconscious attempt on her part to evade family responsibilities, particularly for her mother."[4] R.K. Webb begins his chapter on Martineau's Tynemouth years with the disclaimer that "It should be said at once that Miss Martineau was really ill. Her invalidism was not simply hysteria or hypochondria or an excuse to escape, however much all of them may have entered into the situation."[5] Most critics sensibly agree that felt emotional burdens and exhaustion from

---

1   "Miss Martineau." *Fortnightly Review* CXXIV (April 1877): 531.

2   "Harriet Martineau and the Reform of the Invalid in Victorian England," 603.

3   Martineau uses this phrase in her self-written obituary, portions of which are reprinted in Appendix D. The phrase, or some variation of it, was popular with invalid authors.

4   "Harriet Martineau." In Olive Banks' *The Biographical Dictionary of British Feminists* (New York: New York University Press, 1985): 124.

5   *Harriet Martineau: A Radical Victorian* (London: Heinemann, 1960) 193.

work combined with the prolapsed uterus and ovarian cyst to incapacitate Martineau. However ample the body of material accessible to scholars today about Martineau's situation, retrospective diagnosis is inevitably fraught with problems, and what seems most significant to an understanding of *Life in the Sick-Room* is an appreciation of the fact that Martineau believed herself to be suffering from an incurable condition that made exertion and activity difficult, if not impossible, *and* that she had received some official medical confirmation of this incurability. If at various points in her life Martineau sought to contest medical authority, she desired and sought out its legitimizing powers as well, as her correspondence with various physicians about her case makes clear.

No matter what the exact nature of Martineau's physical and psychological condition while at Tynemouth, there can be little doubt that her case would not have engendered so much debate were it not for the fact that she undertook mesmerism and believed herself cured. In 1844, at the suggestion of several friends and, ironically, Greenhow himself, Martineau agreed to be mesmerized by Spencer Timothy Hall, an "itinerant phreno-mesmerist."[1] Although the first attempt was unsuccessful, Martineau's maid-servant Jane Arrowsmith imitated what she had seen and succeeded in helping Martineau, who then embarked on repeated mesmeric treatments both with Arrowsmith and other healers, mostly women. Within a few months, Martineau believed herself to be cured. Responding to rumors circulating about her recovery, she wrote "Six Letters on Mesmerism" for the *Athenaeum* in 1844, later publishing them together as a book.[2] Martineau's efforts to verify her experiences and preserve her integrity could do little to mitigate the impact of the pamphlet published immediately afterwards by her brother-in-law. Titled "A Medical Report of the Case of Miss H—— M————," it includes graphic gynecological details—discussing, for example,

---

1   The phrase is Roger Cooter's, in "Dichotomy and Denial: Mesmerism, Medicine and Harriet Martineau," an excellent analysis of the various issues at stake for medical historians and feminists in the case of Harriet Martineau. In *Science and Sensibility: Gender and Scientific Enquiry, 1780-1945*. Ed. Marina Benjamin (Oxford: Basil Blackwell, 1991) 147.
2   The first of these *Letters on Mesmerism* is reprinted in Appendix F.

Martineau's menstrual history and describing discharges from and irregularities in her vagina—all in order to discredit her claims for a mesmeric recovery.[1] Martineau was shocked and distressed, emphasizing in her autobiography that his account had appeared "not in a Medical Journal, where nobody but the profession would ever have seen it, and where [she] should never have heard of it,—but in a shilling pamphlet—not even written in Latin—but open to all the world!" (I, 477). She discontinued contact with Greenhow. Despite the turmoil, she embraced her recovery, building a new home for herself in Ambleside (with William Wordsworth and Matthew Arnold as neighbors nearby) and immersing herself in work. With her new friend Henry George Atkinson, she authored *Letters on the Laws of Man's Nature and Development* (1851).

The controversy over the nature of Martineau's illness and recovery—and the debate about the role of her own imagination in both—never entirely went away. Taking stock of the situation in an April 1877 essay on Martineau, a reviewer for *Blackwood's Edinburgh Magazine* wrote: "The case made a great noise at the time, and it seems extremely unreasonable that a sick person should not be permitted to cure herself or achieve a cure in any way that is practicable. Any treatment in the world which made a sufferer well, and restored an invalid to active life, must have had an excellent claim upon the belief of that invalid, if of no one else, and the assaults upon her in this case seem most foolish and unreasonable" (492). Expressing that sentiment more cautiously was Samuel Smiles, who in his essay on Martineau for his *Brief Biographies* wrote that "whether from the potency of the remedy or the force of the patient's imagination, certain it was that she was shortly after restored to health" (509). The medical community was, predictably, not so accommodating to Martineau's position. Indeed, just months after her death in 1876, Thomas Spencer Wells, a highly regarded surgeon, delivered a lecture titled "Remarks on the Case of Miss Martineau," that was based in part on autopsy findings; it, in turn, prompted a series of contributions

---

1 See Appendix C. For an analysis of Greenhow's report and of later post-mortem studies of Martineau, see Anka Ryall's "Medical Body and Lived Experience: The Case of Harriet Martineau" in *Mosaic* 33, 4 (December 2000): 35-53.

on the matter to the influential *British Medical Journal*. Perhaps most significantly, Greenhow himself, who would quote liberally from it throughout his self-justifying article "Termination of the Case of Miss Martineau," first publicized the post-mortem report. As Anka Ryall summarizes, "For Greenhow, who in the wake of the *Autobiography* again felt the need to vindicate himself, the result of the post-mortem proved that, even if he had originally targeted the wrong female organ, his diagnosis had been basically correct, while Martineau's own account contained, as he phrases it, '*little fact* and *much imagination*.'"[1] Ryall finds in her study of the medical establishment's response to Harriet Martineau evidence that "the main issue was the eminence of Martineau herself" and her brazen challenge to medical "science" and authority, a position shared by other scholars.[2]

Given the extraordinary publicity that Harriet Martineau's case attracted, medical historians and feminists alike not surprisingly have found much of interest in this episode of her life. Yet the attention to her confrontation with medical authority through the mesmeric experiences and its concomitant ability to shed light on our understanding of the position of women in early Victorian England has overshadowed certain features of Martineau's story equally deserving of critical attention. After the decade of excellent health that followed upon her mesmeric treatments, Harriet Martineau again began to suffer debilitating symptoms of disease, and, though not as incapacitated and immobile as during the Tynemouth years, she resumed the life of an invalid, staying mostly confined to her home in Ambleside and peppering her voluminous correspondence with frequent reference to her failing health and various attempts to secure relief. Valerie Sanders summarizes: "From 1855, fuelled with beef tea and the odd teaspoon of brandy before meals, she created for herself the perfect hospice, managed by her nieces and devoted maidservants, who wrote letters at her dictation, and filtered the flow of sometimes unwanted

---

1   "Medical Body and Lived Experience," 41.

2   Roger Cooter, for example, writes that "the potential of this historical episode rests on more than just the body in question, however; it rests, too, on the stature of the woman herself" (145). Alison Winter includes a comprehensive analysis of this issue as it relates to Martineau and other female invalids in chapter nine of *Mesmerized: Powers of Mind in Victorian Britain* (Chicago: University of Chicago Press, 1998) 213-45.

visitors. By the time she died, in 1876, she had made her invalidism into a profession, a fine art, through which she had won her freedom" (83).

During these years Martineau enjoyed frequent and friendly consultation with physicians, among them Dr. Peter Latham and Sir Thomas Watson. Indeed, her letters to and from Dr. Latham provide abundant evidence of mutual, reciprocal respect between doctor and patient, both contributing to an ongoing process of diagnosis and treatment. This correspondence is a trenchant reminder of the need to not too readily assume that patients like Martineau were ultimately powerless in the face of medical authority or that doctors invariably distanced themselves from and objectified their patients, treating them not as persons but as "disease material" to study. It was during this same period of invalidism that Martineau's friendship with fellow invalid Florence Nightingale blossomed. "I too have 'no future' & must do what I can without delay," Nightingale wrote to Martineau in 1858, revealing just one of the ways that invalidism fostered, rather than restricted, work for these women.[1] Writing to Martineau in 1858, their correspondence is enlightening in revealing the extent to which the ideas Martineau put forth in *Life in the Sick-Room* were shared by Nightingale and were compatible with her *Notes on Nursing*. In fact, when Martineau reviewed *Notes on Nursing* for the influential *Quarterly Review* in 1860, she opportunistically included discussion of *Life in the Sick-Room* in the review, even going so far as to list it with *Notes on Nursing* at the top of the review — and this despite the fact that it had been published sixteen years earlier![2] Nightingale and Martineau found solace in each other's brief accounts of their health woes, occasionally hinting at their sympathy but more often bolstering one another in their mutual commitment to work. Helping to get Nightingale's position on a range of matters into print, Martineau garnered for her self the satisfaction of becoming something akin to a nurse herself. Her frequent contributions to the popular middle-class

---

1   Florence Nightingale to Harriet Martineau. 4 December 1858. BL Add 45788. For additional examples of the Nightingale/Martineau correspondence, consult Appendix E.

2   Excerpts from this review can be found in Appendix E.

magazine *Once a Week* (with titles such as "The Baker: His Health," "The Steel-Grinder: His Health," and "The Governess: Her Health") testify to the authority she sought to assume as an expert on health matters, moving from more personal accounts such as her "Letter to the Deaf" and *Letters on Mesmerism* to speak to broader public health issues. Perhaps most notably, in 1864 she spear-headed the publication of a series of articles on the Contagious Disease Acts in the *Daily News* and her name appeared at the head of a list of over one hundred influential women who signed an "Appeal to the Women of England" expressing opposition to the Acts.[1] Aligning herself with Nightingale enabled her to adopt and adapt the role of surrogate nurse to the nation.

Given the fact that Martineau would spend her final two decades reliving the life of an invalid, it is interesting to note that when in 1855 she wrote her autobiography she made it a point to distance herself from the views she had articulated in *Life in the Sick-Room*. At the heart of her disavowal were widely different views about Christianity that had evolved over the course of those eleven years.[2] Seeing *Life in the Sick-Room* as evidencing both a "conventional Christian outlook" and the "beginning of her deconversion in its most serious form," Valerie Sanders believes that her travels to Biblical lands, undertaken just after she was cured, "helped complete her loss of faith" (192-93). Martineau's contemporary Douglas Jerrold famously quipped, "There is no God, and Harriet is his prophet."[3] In any event, Martineau began her retrospective view of her Tynemouth years with the following comment: "I am aware that the religious world, proud of its Christian faith as the 'Worship of Sorrow,' thinks it a duty and a privilege to dwell on the morbid conditions of human life; but my experience of wide extremes of health and sickness, of happiness and misery, leads me to a very different con-

---

1   The Contagious Diseases Bill passed, despite the opposition, but was later repealed. For discussion of this bill and of its significance to Martineau's career, see Gillian Thomas's "Harriet Martineau," 174.

2   Martineau's "disavowal" was not so complete as to prevent her from coupling *Life in the Sick-Room* with Nightingale's *Notes on Nursing* for review in the *Quarterly Review* in 1860. See Appendix E.

3   Quoted by R.K. Webb, 299.

clusion" (I, 439). She went on to deplore the tendency of religious literature to "generate vanity and egotism about bodily pain and early death" (I, 440) and to express regret that her own "Christian superstition, now at last giving way before science" had combined with "youthful vanity" to encourage her to believe herself dying. Worse still in her mind was the "dismal self-consciousness" (I, 459) she associated with the book, which led her to write:

> I can only now say that I am ashamed, considering my years and experience of suffering, that my state of mind was so crude, if not morbid, as I now see it to have been. I say this, not from any saucy elevation of health and prosperity, but in an hour of pain and feebleness, under a more serious and certainly fatal illness than that of 1843, and after ten intervening years of health and strength, ease and prosperity. All the facts in the book, and some of the practical doctrine of the sick-room, I could still swear to: but the magnifying of my own experience, the desperate concern as to my own ease and happiness, the moaning undertone running through what many people have called the stoicism, and the total inability to distinguish between the metaphysically apparent and the positively true, make me, to say the truth, heartily despise a considerable part of the book. (I, 458-59)

Whatever its flaws, *Life in the Sick-Room* did not strike most of its first readers as unparalleled evidence of an unbridled ego or as the ramblings of an unrepentant whiner. Martineau's autobiography refers to the letters that she "afterwards received from invalids" affirming her views. Fellow recluse (and one with whom Martineau had enjoyed some correspondence about their respective experiences with invalidism[1]) Elizabeth Barrett was evidently flattered by the assumption of many that she was the book's

---

1 In her first letter to Elizabeth Barrett, Martineau wrote: "These few words may perhaps not come amiss from one who has for friends some who are yours,— who has, like you, lost health, & become inured to the want of it, & who, like you, almost forgets to wish for ease & vigour in the keen sense of enjoyments which bear no relation to the body & its welfare." Quoted in Appendix I of *The Brownings' Correspondence*. Volume 4. Eds. Philip Kelley & Ronand Hudson (Winfield, KS: Wedgestone Press, 1986) 326.

unnamed dedicatee.[1] To Samuel Smiles it was "one of her most delightful books" (499); G. A. Simcox called it a "beautiful little volume" (532); and Florence Fenwick Miller described it as "a most interesting record of the high thoughts and feelings by which so melancholy an experience as years of suffering, of an apparently hopeless character, can be elevated, and made productive of benefit to the sufferer's own nature" (122). The *Dublin University Magazine* called it a "wise and thoughtful book—the offspring of a lofty mind" (573). To the *Chamber's Edinburgh Journal*, Martineau's was a book "which all her friends must receive with a deep, though it may be a melancholy interest," one that would cause them "to admire the heroic good intentions and aspirations of the gifted author" (107). The *Westminster Review* predicted that it would be "the most enduring" of Martineau's productions (609). The *Christian Examiner* praised it for its "profound reflection on the science of human nature" (158). Even the reviews written when Martineau's identity as its author was as yet unverified were by-and-large favorable. Calling its readers' attention to "the wise teachings, the hallowed breathings of a tried and purified spirit, which comes forth of the furnace, firm as the Faith and Truth on which it rests," *Tait's Edinburgh Magazine* gushed that "we have rarely perused a volume more calculated to impress sympathetic and reflective minds than these Essays of an Invalid" (131). Striking a sour note amidst the clamor of praise was the *British Foreign and Medical Review*, which directed its readers' attentions to the book's "revelations" of "the morbidity of mind of a nervous invalid" (472) and excoriated the "morbid self-consciousness" everywhere evident.

Far different standards and interests will direct what readers today think about *Life in the Sick-Room*. Not only does Martineau's book illuminate certain dimensions of nineteenth-century medical history and literary history, but it serves as an excellent example of the Victorian investment in forms of life writing that drew on, but did not limit themselves to, the overtly biographical or autobiographical and that adapted these modes to

---

1   See Valerie Pichanick's discussion of their relationship in *Harriet Martineau: The Woman and Her Work, 1802-76* (Ann Arbor, MI: University of Michigan Press) 129.

the speculative and practical postures sometimes associated with "sage writing."[1] Whereas much Victorian narrative—including many forms of life writing—is structured around paradigms of crisis and recovery, Martineau's book, by virtue of its concern with invalidism and the experience of long suffering, resists and even undercuts that pattern. When Harriet Martineau first corresponded with her publisher, Edward Moxon, about the possibility of publishing *Life in the Sick-Room*, she thought of herself as making a true, important, and necessary contribution to her society. As Shelagh Hunter has argued, by so often directing her remarks to fellow invalids, Martineau sought to turn "personal loss to public service in a particularly intimate way."[2] Edward Moxon corroborated Martineau's sense of the project's originality, assuring her, for example, that the subject was one "so deeply interesting as not to require the assistance of a name to bring it into notice," and that the title was "a very good one and has not ... been used before." "You are conferring a great benefit on mankind," he told his gratified author.[3] Describing her purpose in *Life in the Sick-Room* to her friend Mrs. Romilly just months later, Martineau wrote: "... it seems as if my business in life has been, & is to be, to suffer for other people's *information*,—to be a sort of pioneer in the regions of pain, to make the way somewhat easier,—or at least more direct to those who come after."[4] Even the *British and Foreign Medical Review* in its largely hostile account of Martineau's book grudgingly allowed that her book "differs materially from the majority which fall under our notice" (473).

However original or distinctive *Life in the Sick-Room*, it should ultimately be seen as of a piece with many other documents that Victorians authored about their experiences with extended illness. Such texts are many and varied; they range from diaries, letters, and other works unintended for publication such as Charles

---

1 For more on the Victorian phenomena of "life writing" and "sage writing" see the chapters on those subjects authored by Timothy Pelatson and Linda H. Peterson, respectively. Both appear in *A Companion to Victorian Literature & Culture*. Ed. Herbert F. Tucker (Oxford: Blackwell, 1999).

2 See *Harriet Martineau: The Poetics of Moralism*, 192.

3 Edward Moxon to Harriet Martineau. HM1127 and HM1128. Excerpts reprinted by permission of the Birmingham University Library.

4 HM to Mrs. Romilly, 9 March 1844, MS Autobr, d.21 Bodleian. Reprinted with the permission of the Bodleian Library.

Darwin's "health diary" to an enormous and varied array of public documents, many written at roughly the same historical moment as Martineau's book. These works included Bulwer Lytton's "Confessions and Observations of a Water Patient" (1845), consolatory texts such as the anonymously authored *Companion for the Sick Bed* (1836) and *The Invalid's Book: Pieces in Poetry and Prose* (1838), travel essays such as "A Letter to an Invalid about to Visit Madeira" (1834), literary collections such as *Occasional Poems: by an Invalid* (1848), religious manuals such as *Devotions for the Sick Room and For Times of Trouble*, and other full-length studies such as *Letters from a Sick Room* (1845), published in America where the culture of invalidism also flourished.[1] One of the textual landmarks of Martineau's authorial career, *Life in the Sick-Room* clearly reflects far more than Martineau's personal preoccupations and her private experience as a "prisoner to the couch." Engaging in a particular kind of cultural work, it speaks to all of us interested in coming to terms with the early Victorian milieu. In other ways, it seems to transcend its historical moment, its elaboration of psychological dimensions of illness serving as a prelude not only to the emergence of medical sociology in the twentieth century but to the kind of theorizing about illness undertaken by Virginia Woolf in her 1926 essay "On Being Ill" and, far more recently, by Susan Sontag in *Illness as Metaphor*. Like Woolf, who wrote that "only the recumbent ... know what, after all, Nature is at no pains to conceal,"[2] Martineau believed that invalidism had equipped her and all of her fellow sufferers with powers of perspective unknown to the healthy. Like Susan Sontag, who described illness as "the night-side of life, a more onerous citizenship," Martineau fully felt the burden of those powers.[3]

---

1   For some selections from these texts, please consult Appendix G.
2   "On Being Ill." Reprinted in *Collected Essays by Virginia Woolf*. Volume Four (London: Hogarth Press, 1967) 198.
3   Susan Sontag. *Illness as Metaphor* (New York: Vintage Books, 1979) 3.

Harriet Martineau: A Brief Chronology

1802 Born at Norwich to Thomas Martineau and Elizabeth Rankin Martineau.

1806 James Martineau born.

1818 Attends school in Bristol. Deafness appears.

1822-23 Publishes "Female Writers of Practical Divinity" and "On Female Education" in the *Monthly Repository*.

1823 Publishes *Devotional Exercises for the Use of Young Persons*.

1826 Thomas Martineau, Harriet's father, dies in June.

1829 Financial failure of the Martineau family.

1832-34 Publishes *Illustrations of Political Economy*.

1832 Moves to London.

1834 Publishes "Letter to the Deaf" in *Tait's Edinburgh Magazine*.

1834-36 Travels in America.

1837-39 Publishes *Society in America, Retrospect of Western Travel, How to Observe: Morals and Manners*, and a novel, *Deerbrook*.

1839-44 Becomes ill; moves to Tynemouth.

1841 Publishes *The Hour and the Man*.

1844 Publishes *Life in the Sick-Room*. Experiments with mesmerism and publishes "Letters on Mesmerism" in *The Athenaeum*.

1845 Thomas Greenhow publishes "Medical Report of the Case of Miss H—— M———."

1845 Meets Henry G. Atkinson.

1845-46 After recovery, buys property and builds house, The Knoll, in Ambleside.

1846 Travels to Egypt and Palestine.

1848 Publishes *Eastern Life, Present and Past*.

1849-50 Publishes *Household Education* and *A History of England during the Thirty Years' Peace*.

1851 Publishes with Atkinson *Letters on the Laws of Man's Nature and Development*.

1851 Publishes *Letters from Ireland*.

1852-69 Writes leaders for the *Daily News*.

1853 Translates and publishes *The Positive Philosophy of August Comte.*

1853-57 Writes editorials dealing with the Divorce and Matrimonial Causes Acts.

1855 Becomes ill; writes autobiography and obituary; niece Maria Martineau lives with her as companion until Maria's death in 1864. Niece Jane Martineau lives with her as companion until 1873.

1857 Publishes *British Rule in India.*

1858-68 Corresponds regularly with Florence Nightingale.

1861 Publishes *Health, Husbandry, and Handicraft,* a compilation of *Once a Week* articles.

1866 Signs petition to Parliament on woman's suffrage.

1869 Campaigns against the Contagious Diseases Act; Publishes *Biographical Sketches.*

1876 Dies at Ambleside.

Tynemouth From the Sickroom Window

A Note on the Text

This edition is based on the first edition of Harriet Martineau's *Life in the Sick-Room*, which was published by Edward Moxon in 1844. There are no substantive differences between this edition and the manuscript of *Life in the Sick-Room*, which is held at the Fawcett Library in London. Although one of Martineau's early biographers, Florence Fenwick Miller, refers to a chapter on euthanasia that was not published, no such chapter appears with the manuscript itself, nor have I discovered reference to it in the many letters written between Martineau and Edward Moxon that I have consulted.[1] I have preserved Martineau's spellings and punctuation as they appear in the first edition.

As described in the introduction, the manuscript of Martineau's book is written in small and uncharacteristically neat handwriting. Preparing the manuscript for publication, Martineau changed some of her expressions to broaden the applicability of her comments or to achieve better clarity, substituting words such as "season" for "day," for example, or changing "wakeful" to "sleepless" and "perceive" to "observe." These changes were followed by Edward Moxon in his printing from the manuscript. Eliza L. Follen's introduction to the American edition of *Life in the Sick-Room*, which was published by Leonard C. Bowles and William Crosby of Boston in 1844, is included in Appendix A.

---

1 Fenwick Miller bases her assumption of a "missing chapter on Euthanasia" on a letter Martineau wrote to Henry Atkinson dated 19 November 1872 that includes the following sentence: "I wonder whether the chapter I wrote about this for the 'Sick Room' book will ever see the light" (123). Fenwick Miller reports that she could "get no tidings of this missing chapter on Euthanasia," and I, too, have been unable to locate it.

Manuscript of *Life in the Sick-Room*
(By courtesy of the Mary Evans Picture Library)

LIFE IN THE SICK-ROOM

"Quand on se porte bien, on ne comprend pas comment on pourrait faire si on était malade; et quand on l'est, on prend médecine gaiement: le mal y résout. On n'a plus les passions et les désirs des divertissements et des promenades, que la santé donnait, et qui sont incompatibles avec les nécessités de la maladie. La nature donne alors des passions et des désirs conformes a l'état présent. Ce ne sont que les craintes que nous nous donnons nous-mêmes, et non pas la nature, qui nous troublent; parcequ'elles joignent a l'état où nous sommes les passions de l'état où nous ne sommes pas." — Pascal[1]

---

1   "When we are well we wonder how we should manage if we were ill. When we are ill we happily take medicine: the illness takes care of that; we no longer have the passions and desires for distractions and outings prompted by good health, and which are incompatible with the demands of illness. Nature then prompts the passions and desires appropriate to our present state. It is only the fears that we inspire in ourselves, and not by nature, which disturb us, because they link the state in which we are with the passions of the state in which we are not." Blaise Pascal, *Pensees*, XXXV, #529. My translation is taken from Blaise Pascal, *Pensees and Other Writings*. Translated by Honor Levi (Oxford: Oxford University Press, 1995) 125.

LIFE IN THE SICK-ROOM.

ESSAYS.
BY
AN INVALID.

"For they breathe truth that breathe their words in pain."
— Shakespere.[1]

"The saddest birds a season find to sing."
— Robert Southwell.[2]

---

1   William Shakespeare (1564-1616), *King Richard II*, Act II, Scene I.
2   Robert Southwell (1561-95), "Times goe by turns."

CONTENTS

TO————

"Passion I see is catching; for mine eyes;
   Seeing those beads of sorrow stand in thine,
   Began to water."

                              Shakspere.[1]

"When we our betters see bearing our woes,
   We scarcely think our miseries our foes;
   Who alone suffers suffers most i' the mind,
   Leaving free things and happy shows behind.
   But then the mind much sufferance doth o'erskip,
   When grief hath mates, and bearing fellowship."

                              Shakspere.[2]

As I write this, I cannot but wonder when and how you will read
it, and whether it will cause a single throb at the idea that it may
be meant for you. You have been in my mind during the passage
of almost all the thoughts that will be found in this book. But for
your sympathy — confidently reckoned on, though never asked —
I do not know that I should have had courage to mark their pro-
cession, and record their order. I have felt that if I spoke of these
things at all, it must be to some fellow-sufferer — to some one
who had attained these experiences before me or with me; and,
having you for my companion throughout, (however unconsciously to yourself), I have uttered many things that I could hardly otherwise have spoken: for one may speak far more freely with
a friend, though in the hearing of others, than when singly
addressing a number. Most frequently, however, I have forgotten
that others could hear, and have conversed as with you alone.

   It matters little, in this view, that we have never met — that
each of us does not know, except by the eye of the mind, with
what outward face the other has encountered the unusual lot
appointed to both. While I was as busy as any one on the sunny
plain of life, I heard of you laid aside in the shadowy recess where
our sunshine of hope and joy could never penetrate to you; and it

---

1   William Shakespeare (1564-1616), *Julius Caesar*, Act III, Scene I.
2   William Shakespeare, *King Lear*, Act III, Scene VI.

was with reverence, and not pity, that I inquired of those who could tell whether you had separate lights of heaven, such as there are for retreats like yours. When I was myself withdrawn into such a recess, if I learned to pity more than before, it was with a still enhanced reverence for your older experience. As the evils of protracted unhealthiness came upon me, one after another, I knew that they had all visited you long ago; and I felt as if they brought me a greeting from you. For me, at least, you have not suffered in vain. Would there might be anything in this volume which might enable you to say the same to me!

At all events, there is something sweet and consoling in the fellowship. Though we would, if we could, endure anything to set the other free — though we would thankfully take upon us any suffering that nature could bear for the thought that no one else was qualified to conceive of our troubles, — yet, as this cannot be, we may make the most of the comfort of our companionship. In our wakeful night seasons, when the healthy and the happy are asleep, we may call to each other from our retreats, to know each how the other fares; and, whether we are at the moment dreary or at peace, it may be that there are angels abroad, (perhaps the messengers of our own sympathies), who may bear our mutual greetings, and drop them on their rounds. Often has this been my fancy, when the images close about me have been terrific enough; and when, in the very throng of these horrors, I have cast about for some charm or talisman wherewith to rid myself of them, and some voice of prayer has presently reached me from a temple on the furthest horizon of my life — or some sweet or triumphant hymn of submission or praise has floated to my spirit's ear from the far shores of my childhood — I have hoped, in the midst of the heaven thus brought down about me, that the same consolations were visiting you, who in the same need would, I knew, make the same appeal.

But there are times when the sense of fellowship is dearer still. You know, doubtless, as well as I, the emptiness of the consolation when our pitying friends, in all love and sincerity, remind us of what we did by our efforts when we were well and active, and what we are doing still for the world, by preserving a decent quietness in the midst of our troubles. You know, as well as I, how withering would be the sense of our own nothingness, if we tried to take comfort from our own dignity and usefulness. You know, as well as I, how very far we can see from our place on the verge of life, over its expanse, and how ridiculous, if it were not shocking, would be any complacency on the ground of our having followed the instincts of our nature to work, while work was possible,—the issues of such divinely-appointed instrumentality being wholly brought out and directed by Him who framed and actuated us. You know, as I do, how useful it is to human beings to have before their eyes spectacles of all experiences; and we are alike willing, having worked while we could, now to suffer as we may, to help our kind in another mode. We feel it some little service to be appointed to,—having become accustomed to our footing on the shaking plank over the deep dark river,—to lead on and uphold with a steady hand some who may be appointed to follow, and perhaps to pass us upon it.

But while agreeing in this, our happiest fellowship must be, I think, in seeing, with a clearness we could never otherwise have attained, the vastness and certainty of the progression with which we have so little to do. I do not believe it is possible for persons in health and action to trace, as we can, the agencies for good that are going on in life and the world. Or, if they can, it seems as if the perception were accompanied by a breathless fear,—a dread of being, if not crushed, whirled away somewhere, hurried along to new regions for which they are unprepared, and to which, however good, they would prefer the familiar. You and I, and our fellow-sufferers, see differently, whether or not we see further. We know and feel, to the very centre of our souls, that there is no hurry, no crushing, no devastation attending Divine processes. While we see the whole system of human life rising and rising into a higher region and a purer light, we perceive that every atom is as much cared for as the whole. While we use our new insight to show us how things are done,—and gravely smile to see that it is by every man's overrating the issues of his immediate pursuit, in order that he may devote all his energies to it, (without which nothing would ever be done,) we smile with another feeling presently, on perceiving how an industry and care from above are compensating to every man his mistake by giving him collateral benefits when he misses the direct good he sought,—by giving him and his helpers a wealth of ideas, as often as their schemes turn out, in their professed objects, profitless. When we see men straining every nerve to reach the tempting apples which are to prove dust and ashes in their jaws, we see also, by virtue of our position, the flying messenger who is descending with the ambrosia which is to feed their immortal part. We can tell, that while revolutions are grandly operating, by which life and the world will in time change their aspect,—while a progress is advancing to which it is now scarcely conceivable that we should ever have dreamed of putting our hands,—there is not one of our passing thoughts that is not ordained,—not a sigh of weariness unheeded,—not an effort of patience that is not met halfway by divine pity,—not a generous emotion of triumph in the world's improvement that is not hallowed by the divine sympathy ever living and breathing round about us. This our peculiar privilege, of seeing and feeling something of the simultaneous vastness, and minuteness of providential administration, is one in which we most enjoy sympathy;—at least, I do:—and in this, therefore, do I find your undoubted fellowship most precious.

Here then I end my greeting,—except in as far as the whole book is truly conversation with you. I shall not direct it to your hands, but trust to the most infallible force in the universe,— human sympathy,—to bring these words under your eye. If they should have the virtue to summon thoughts which may, for a single hour, soften your couch, shame and banish your foes of depression and pain, and set your chamber in holy order and something of cheerful adornment, I may have the honor of being your nurse, though I am myself laid low, — though hundreds of miles are between us, and though we can never know one another's face or voice.

Yours,

ESSAYS.

CHAPTER ONE

THE TRANSIENT AND THE PERMANENT
IN THE SICK-ROOM.

"Lasting! what's lasting?
The earth that swims so well, must drown in fire,
And Time be last to perish at the stake.
The heavens must parch; the universe must smoulder.
Nothing but thoughts can live, and such thoughts only
As god-like are, making God's recreation."

I. Knowe.[1]

"Affliction worketh patience: and patience, experience; and
experience, hope."

St. Paul.[2]

"All places that the eye of Heaven visits
Are to a wise man ports and happy havens."

Shakespere.[3]

THE sick-room becomes the scene of intense convictions; and
among these, none, it seems to me, is more distinct and powerful
than that of the permanent nature of good, and the transient
nature of evil. At times I could almost believe that long sickness
or other trouble is ordained to prove to us this very point — a
point worth any costliness of proof.

The truth may pass across the mind of one who has suffered
briefly — may occur to him when glancing back over his experi-

---

1   I have been unable to locate a source for this passage or to identify I. Knowe, which
may be a pseudonym, possibly one Martineau herself adopted for the purposes of this
volume only.
2   Romans 5:4.
3   William Shakespeare (1564-1616), *King Richard II*, Act I, Scene III.

ence of a short sharp illness or adversity. He may say to himself that his temporary suffering brought him lasting good, in revealing to him the sympathy of his friends, and the close connexion of human happiness with things unseen; but this occasional recognition of the truth is a very different thing from the abiding and unspeakably vivid conviction of it, which arises out of a condition of protracted suffering. It may look like a paradox to say that a condition of permanent pain is that which, above all, proves to one the transient nature of pain; but this is what I do affirm, and can testify.

The apparent contradiction lies in the words "permanent pain"—that condition being made up of a series of pains, each of which is annihilated as it departs; whereas all real good has an existence beyond the moment, and is indeed indestructible.

A day's illness may teach something of this to a thoughtful mind; but the most inconsiderate can scarcely fail to learn the lesson, when the proof is drawn out over a succession of months and seasons. With me, it has now included several New Year's Days; and what have they taught me? What any future New Year's retrospect cannot possibly contradict, and must confirm: though it can scarcely illustrate further what is already as clear as its moon and stars.

During the year looked back upon, all the days, and most hours of the day, have had their portion of pain—usually mild—now and then, for a few marked hours of a few marked weeks, severe and engrossing; while, perhaps, some dozen evenings, and half-dozen mornings, are remembered as being times of almost entire ease. So much for the body. The mind, meantime, though clear and active, has been so far affected by the bodily state as to lose all its gaiety, and, by disuse, almost to forget its sense of enjoyment. During the year, perhaps, there may have been two surprises of light-heartedness, for four hours in June, and two hours and a half in October, with a few single flashes of joy in the intermediate seasons, on the occurrence of some rousing idea, or the revival of some ancient association. Over all the rest has brooded a thick heavy cloud of care, apparently causeless, but not for that the less real. This is the sum of the pains of the year, in relation to illness. Where are these pains now? — Not only gone, but annihilated.

They are destroyed so utterly, that even memory can lay no hold upon them. The fact of their occurrence is all that even memory can preserve. The sensations themselves cannot be retained, nor recalled, nor revived; they are the most absolutely evanescent, the most essentially and completely destructible of all things. Sensations are unimaginable to those who are most familiar with them. Their concomitants may be remembered, and so vividly conceived of, as to excite emotions at a future time: but the sensations themselves cannot be conceived of when absent. This pain, which I feel now as I write, I have felt innumerable times before; yet, accustomed as I am to entertain and manage it, the sensation itself is new every time; and a few hours hence I shall be as unable to represent it to myself as to the healthiest person in the house. Thus are all the pains of the year annihilated. What remains?

All the good remains.

And how is this? whence this wide difference between the good and the evil?

Because the good is indissolubly connected with ideas — with the unseen realities which are indestructible. This is true, even of those pleasures of sense which of themselves would be as evanescent as bodily pains. The flowers sent to me by kind neighbors have not perished, — that is, the idea and pleasure of them remain, though every blossom was withered months ago. The game and fruit, eaten in their season, remain as comforts and luxuries, preserved in the love that sent them. Every letter and conversation abide, — every new idea is mine forever; all the knowledge, all the experience of the year, is so much gain. Even the courses of the planets, and the changes of the moon, and the hay-making and harvest, are so much immortal wealth — as real a possession as all the pain of the year was a passing apparition. Yes, even the quick bursts of sunshine are still mine. For one instance, which will well illustrate what I mean, let us look back so far as the Spring, and take one particular night of severe pain, which made all rest impossible. A short intermission, which enabled me to send my servant to rest, having ended in pain, I was unwilling to give further disturbance, and wandered, from mere misery, from my bed and my dim room, which seemed full of pain, to the next apartment, where some glimmer through the thick window-curtain showed that there was light abroad. Light indeed! as I found on looking forth. The sun, resting on the edge of the sea, was hidden from me by the walls of the old priory: but a flood of rays poured through the windows of the ruin, and gushed over the waters, strewing them with diamonds, and then across the green down before my windows, gilding its furrows, and then lighting up the yellow sands on the opposite shore of the harbor, while the market-garden below was glittering with dew and busy with early bees and butterflies. Besides these bees and butterflies, nothing seemed stirring, except the earliest riser of the neighborhood, to whom the garden belongs. At the moment, she was passing down to feed her pigs, and let out her cows; and her easy pace, arms a-kimbo, and complacent survey of her early greens, presented me with a picture of ease so opposite to my own state, as to impress me ineffaceably. I was suffering too much to enjoy this picture at the moment: but how was it at the end of the year? The pains of all those hours were annihilated—as completely vanished as if they had never been; while the momentary peep behind the window-curtain made me possessor of this radiant picture for evermore. This is an illustration of the universal fact. That brief instant of good has swallowed up long weary hours of pain. An inexperienced observer might, at the moment, have thought the conditions of my gain heavy enough; but the conditions being not only discharged, but annihilated long ago, and the treasure remaining forever, would not my best friend congratulate me on that sunrise? Suppose it shining on, now and forever, in the souls of a hundred other invalids or mourners, who may have marked it in the same manner, and who shall estimate its glory and its good!

It is clear that the conviction I speak of arises from the supposition—indispensable and, I believe, almost universal,—that pain is the chastisement of a Father; or, at least, that it is, in some way or other, ordained for, or instrumental to good. The experience of men leaves this belief uncontested, and incontestable. Otherwise, evil and pain would be, in their effects on sufferers, long-lived, if not as immortal as good. If we believed our sufferings to be inflicted by cruelty or malice, our pains would immediately take a permanent existence by becoming connected with our passions of fear, revenge, &c.; though still—as is known to students of the human soul,—the evil, however long sustained, must be finally absorbed in the good. We, of our age and state of society, however, have to do with none who believe pain to be inflicted by the malignity of a superior being. Those who are not so happy as to recognise in it a mere disguise of blessings otherwise unattainable, receive it, under some of the various theories of necessary imperfection, as something unavoidable, and therefore to be received placidly, if not gratefully. These would admit, as cheerfully as the adorers of a chastening Father, the richness of my wealth, as I lie, on New Year's Eve, surrounded by the treasures of the departing year,— the kindly Year which has utterly destroyed for me so much that is terrible and grievous, while he leaves with me all the new knowledge and power, all the teachings from on high, and the love from far and near, and even the frailest-seeming blossom of pleasure that, in any moment, he has cast into my lap.

Thus has a succession of these friendly years now visited me and gone: and, as far as we can see, thus will every future one repeat the lesson. If any person disputes, no one can disprove, the result, wrought out, as it is, by natural experience. It is no contradiction, that some are soured by suffering. Their pains, like mine, are gone; and with them, as with others, it is ideas which remain; and ideas are essentially good, a part of the indestructible inner life which must, from its very nature, sooner or later part with its evil, through experience of the superabounding good of the universe. If one so soured by pain dies in this mood, the ideal part of him is that which remains to be carried into a fresh scene, where the mood cannot be fed by the experience which nourished it here. If he lives long enough to change his mood, there is every probability that the benignant influences which are perpetually at work throughout life and nature will dissolve and disperse his troubles, as the eastern lights, the breath of morning and the chirp of birds, steal in upon the senses of the troubled sleeper, and thence possessing themselves of his reason, convince him that the miseries of the night season were but a dream.

True and consoling as it may be for him, and for those about him, to find thus that "trouble may endure for a night, but joy cometh in the morning,"[1] they have not fully learned the lessons of the sick-room if they are not aware that, while the troubles of

---

1 Psalms 30:5.

that night season are thus sure to pass away, its product of thoughts and experiences must endure, till the stars which looked down upon the scene have dissolved in their courses. The constellations formed in the human soul, out of the chaos of pain, must have a duration compared with which, those of the firmament are but as the sparkles showered over the sea by the rising sun. To one still in this chaos,—if he do but see the creative process advancing,—it can be no reasonable matter of complaint, that his course is laid the while through such a region; and he will feel almost ashamed of even the most passing anxiety as to how soon he may be permitted to emerge.

CHAPTER TWO

SYMPATHY TO THE INVALID

"The essence of friendship is entireness; a total magnanimity and trust. It must not surmise or provide for infirmity. It treats its object as a god, that it may deify both."

Emerson.[1]

"Our hands in one, we will not shrink
From life's severest due: —
Our hands in one, we will not blink
The terrible and true."

Milnes.[2]

IF all sorrow teaches us that nothing is more universal than sympathy, long and irremediable sickness proves plainly, that nothing is more various than its kinds and degrees; or, it may be, than the manifestations of the sympathetic grief which is shared by all. In a sharp sickness of a few days or weeks, all good and kind people act and speak much alike; are busy and ingenious in hastening the recovery, and providing relief meantime. It is when death is not to be looked for, nor yet health, that the test is applied; that, on either hand, the genius and the awkwardness of consolation present themselves, with a vast gradation between these extremes. It is easy and pleasant to be grateful for all, and to appreciate the love and pity which inspire them; but it is impossible to relish all equally, or to give the same admiration to that which flows forth fully and freely, and that sympathy which is suppressed, restricted, or in any way changed before it reaches its object.

O! what a heavenly solace to the soul is free sympathy in its hour of need! There is but one that can vie with it; and that one is, in truth, an enhancement of the same emotions. Communion with

---

1 Ralph Waldo Emerson (1803-82), "Friendship."
2 Richard Monckton Milnes (1809-85), "Friendship and Love."

> "Mercy, carried infinite degrees
> Beyond the tenderness of human hearts,"[1]

is, indeed, the supreme, incommunicable delight which must be only referred to, because no sense of it can be conveyed by language; but, because it is of kindred nature, though separated by immeasurable distance, the solace of human sympathy ranks next to this. What a springing of the heart, like that on the discovery of a new truth, or entrance on a new enterprise in youth, attends the revelation to a sufferer of some stroke of genius in the consolations of one of the many who grieve for his affliction!

Many give their best thoughts to provide alleviations — whether in the form of medicines, or dainties for the mind or palate, for the eye or ear; and sweet is the enjoyment of the kindness which provides, whether the luxuries themselves can be relished or not. Some kind soul does a better service still, by affording opportunity for the sufferer to minister to other afflicted ones; to relieve some distress of poverty, or other want. This is sweet; but there are times when the personal trial needs some solace nearer and more direct than this. Then is the hour when the pain of sympathy in the hearts of friends impels them to cast about for relief, and tempts them to speak of hope to the sufferer who has no hope, or none compatible with the kind of consolation they attempt. Going back to the days when I, myself, was the sympathiser, I remember how strong is the temptation to imagine, and to assure the sick one, that his pain will not last; that the time will come when he will be well again; that he is already better; or, if it be impossible to say that, that he will get used to his affliction, and find it more endurable. How was it that I did not see that such offers of consolation must be purely irritating to one who was not feeling better, nor believing that he should ever be better, nor in a state to be cheered by any speculation as to whether his pain would, or would not become more endurable with time! Exactly in proportion to the zeal with which such considerations were pressed, must have been the sufferer's clearness of perception of the disguised selfishness which dictated the topics and the words.

---

1   William Wordsworth (1770-1850), *The Excursion*, Book 4 (1814).

I was, (as I half suspected at the time, from my sense of restraint and uneasiness,) trying to console myself, and not my friend; indulging my own cowardice, my own shrinking from a painful truth, at the expense of the feelings of the sufferer for whom my heart was aching. I, who had no genius for consolation, at least in cases of illness, have been silently corrected by the benignest of reproofs,—by the experience of this genius in my own season of infirmity.

The manifestations of sympathetic feeling are as various as of other feelings; but the differences are marked by those whom they concern, with a keenness proportioned to the hunger of their heart. The sick man has even sometimes to assure himself of the grief of his friends, by their silence to him on circumstances which he cannot but feel most important. Their letters, extending over months and years, perhaps contain no mention of his trial, no reference to his condition, not a line which will show to his executors that the years over which they spread were years of illness. Though he can account for this suppression in the very love of his friends, yet it brings no particular consolation to him. Others, perhaps, administer praise;—praise, which is the last thing a humbled sufferer can appropriate;—praise of his patience or fortitude, which perhaps arrives at the moment when his resolution has wholly given way, and tears may be streaming from his eyes, and exclamations of anguish bursting from his lips. Such consolations require forbearance, however it may be mingled with gratitude. Far different was my emotion, when one said to me, with a face like the face of an angel, "Why should we be bent upon your being better, and make up a bright prospect for you? I see no brightness in it; and the time seems past for expecting you ever to be well." How my spirits rose in a moment at this recognition of the truth!

And again—when I was weakly dwelling on a consideration which troubled me much for some time, that many of my friends gave me credit for far severer pain than I was enduring, and that I thus felt myself a sort of impostor, encroaching unwarrantably on their sympathies, "O! never mind!" was the reply. "That may be more than balanced hereafter. You will suffer more, with time— or you will seem to yourself to suffer more; and then you will have less sympathy. We grow tired of despairing, and think less and less of such cases, whether reasonably or not; and you may have less sympathy when you need it more. Meantime, you are not answerable for what your friends feel; and it is good for them—natural and right—whether you think it accurate or not."

These words put a new heart into me, dismissed my scruples about the over-wealth of the present hour, and strengthened my soul for future need—the hour of which has not, however, yet arrived. It is a comfortable season, if it may but last, when one's friends have ceased to hope unreasonably, and not "grown tired of despairing."

Another friend, endowed both my nature and experience with the power I speak of, gave me strength for months—for my whole probation—by a brave utterance of one word, "Yes." In answer to a hoping consoler, I told a truth of fact which sounded dismal, though because it was fact I spoke it in no dismal mood; and the genius at my side, by a confirmatory "yes," opened to my view a whole world of aid in prospect from a soul so penetrating and so true.

I know it is pleaded that there are sufferers not strong enough to bear the truth—who like to be soothed with hopes, well or ill grounded; who find immediate comfort in being told that they will throw off their pain and be at ease. If there be such, I have never known them; and I doubt their existence. I believe that the tendency to make the worst of bodily complaints, on which so many satires (some just) are founded, is much aggravated, if not generally caused, by the tendency in the healthy and happy to disallow pain and a sad prospect. Children, weak and unpractised sufferers as they are, are found not to be consolable in the manner proposed. We all know the story of the little boy in the street, crying from the smart of a fall, who, when assured by a good-natured passenger that he should not cry, because he would be well to-morrow, answered, "Then I won't cry to-morrow."

The weakest sufferers are precisely those who are least able to appropriate the future and its good things. If this be true of the weak, and if the strong find it irritating to be medicined with soft fictions, or presented with anything but sound truth, the popular method of consolation appears to be excluded altogether. If my own life were to be lived over again, I should, from the strength of this conviction, convert most of its words of intended consolation into a far more consolatory condolence. Never again should the suffering spirit turn from me, as I fear it has often done — if too gentle to be irritated — yet sickening at hollow words of promise, when instant fellow-feeling was what was needed; and mournfully thinking, though too kind to say it, "'the heart knoweth its own bitterness,' and mine must endure alone." The fair retribution has not followed, for never thus have I been left to feel.

I am here reminded of a sort of consolation, often offered, which I do not at all understand. I do not quarrel with it, however, for it may suit others less insensible to its claims. Sequestered sufferers, whose term of activity is over, and who apparently have only to endure as they may, and learn and enjoy what they can, till they receive their summons to enter on a new career, are referred for solace to their consciences — to their consciousness of services rendered to society, and duty done in active days. I strongly doubt whether Conscience was ever appointed to the function of Consoler. I more than doubt; I disbelieve it. According to my own experience, the utmost enjoyment that conscience is capable of is a negative state, that of ease. Its power of suffering is strong; and its natural and best condition I take to be one of simple ease; but for enjoyment and consolation, I believe we must look to other powers and susceptibilities of our nature.

It is inconceivable to me that our moral sense can ever be gratified by anything in our own moral state. It must be more offended by our own sins and weaknesses than by all the other sin and weakness in the world, in proportion as the evil is more profoundly known to it, and more nakedly disgusting, because it is stripped of the allowances and palliations which are admissible in all other cases. And this disgust is not compensated for by a corresponding satisfaction in our own good; for the very best good we can ever recognise in ourselves falls so far short of our own conceptions, so fails to satisfy the requisitions of the moral sense, that it can afford no gratification. A conscience which can enjoy itself on its own resources, must be of a very low degree — I should say of a spurious nature. In the highest state of health that I can conceive of—health spiritual and physical—I believe the function of the moral sense to be to delight itself in good wherever it is to be found, (and no wise person will look for it within himself,) to keep watch and ward against evil, and to cherish lowliness at home by its incessant consciousness of the imperfection there; an imperfection so keenly felt by an enlightened and accurate conscience, as to cause a wholesome going abroad for interests and gratifications, so that ease may be found in self-forgetfulness. The necessity which so many feel of a relief from their disappointed conscience—of adventitious merits on which to rely in the failure of their own—of a saving interposition between their own imperfections and the requisitions of God and duty; this prevalent need is an unanswerable rebuke to the presumption which talks of "the happiness of an approving conscience."[1] If it is thus in the season of vigor, health, and self-command, how inexpressibly absurd is the mistake of bringing such a topic as consolation to the sick and sequestered!—to the sick, whose whole heart is faint, and the mental frame disordered, more or less, in proportion as the body is jaded and the nerves unstrung; and to the sequestered, who perforce devour their own hearts, and find them the bitterest food! Why, one of the most painful trials of long sickness and seclusion is, that all old pains, all past moral sufferings, are renewed and magnified; that in sleepless nights, and especially on waking in the morning, every old sin and folly, and even the most trifling error, rises up anew, however long ago repented of and forgiven, and, in the activity of ordinary life, forgotten. Any sort of ghost is more easily laid than this kind. Though their "brains were out"[2] long years ago, they continue to come—they present themselves in defiance of all—even the most sacred, exorcisms; so that it becomes one of the duties of the sick to bear their presence with composure, and cease to struggle for their exclusion. In the midst of this experience, to have one's friends come, and desire one to look back upon one's past life for complacency and self-gratulation, in order to assure one's self how well one has used one's powers and opportunities—how much

---

1   Thomas Carlyle (1795-1881), *Sartor Resartus* (1833-4).
2   William Shakespeare (1564-1616), *Macbeth*, Act III, Scene IV.

one has done for society—how lofty and honourable a life one has led—and so forth,— O! what words can express the absurdity! If the consoler could but see the invisible array which comes thronging into the sick-room from the deep regions of the past, brought by every sound of nature without, by every movement of the spirit within; the pale lips of dead friends whispering one's hard or careless words, spoken in childhood or youth—the upbraiding gaze of duties slighted and opportunities neglected—the horrible apparition of old selfishness and pusillanimities—the disgusting foolery of idiotic vanities; if the consoler could catch a momentary glimpse of this phantasmagoria of the sick-room, he would turn with fear and loathing from the past, and shudder, while the inured invalid smiles, at such a choice of topics for solace.

Then it might become the turn of the invalid to console—to explain how these are but phantoms—how solace does abound, though it comes from every region rather than the kingdom of conscience—and how, while the past is dry and dreary enough, there are streams descending from the heaven-bright mountain-tops of the future, for ever flowing down to our retreat, pure enough for the most fastidious longing, abundant enough for the thirstiest soul. The consoler may then learn for life how easily all personal complacencies may be dispensed with, while the sufferer can tell of a true "refuge and strength," and "present help," and of this "river that gladdens the city of God,"[1] and flows to meet us as we journey towards it.

But, the anxious consoler may say, Is it right so to banish these complacencies? If you really have served the world, however imperfectly in your own eyes—if you have sown thoughts in minds, and called forth affections in hearts—ought you to deny the facts, or that they are good?

By no means. If you assure me of these things as facts, you bring me good news. But I should feel it as good news—perhaps better—if the service had been rendered by anybody else; for the simple reason that the good would then be to me unmixed, which now it is not, nor can ever be. Call upon me, whenever

---

1   All three phrases are from Psalm 46:1-4.

you will, to rejoice that men have gained an idea — that the aged or children have been amused or strengthened — or that society has been relieved from an abuse, by any one's means. Rouse me from the depression of pain, wake me up from sleep for the better refreshment of this news, and I will rejoice; but do not think to enhance your tidings by telling me that these things are my doing. The only effect of that is, to remind me how much better the service might have been done. Surely we both believe that all truth and goodness are destined to arise sooner or later among men. To be visited with new or good ideas is a blessing: to be appointed to communicate them is an honour: but these blessings and honours are a ground for personal humility, not complacency. It is to me impossible to connect the idea of merit with any such destiny. There is nothing we have so little hand in as our own ideas; there is no occupation less voluntary than that of uttering them. And so will every servant of his race say of his own species of service. He will rejoice that something new and good is acquired or attained by his race; and he must naturally be thankful for the honor and enjoyment appointed to him as the medium: but he can find no ground for personal complacency in the matter. He will be utterly careless whether men know, a hundred years hence, through whom they received the benefit, or whether his name has been for ninety years lost to all but his intimate friends. If he were offered the choice between this reputation and the fact of his having conquered one unkind emotion, or made one single effort of endurance, he would eagerly prefer the secret genuine good to the blazoned apparent one.

"There is something extremely absurd and ridiculous," says the holy Hartley, "in supposing a person to be perpetually feasting his own mind with, and dwelling upon, the praises that already are, or which he hopes will hereafter be, given to him. And yet, unless a man does this (which besides would evidently incapacitate him for deserving or obtaining praise), how can he fill up the thousandth part of his time with the pleasures of ambition?"[1] Even

---

1   David Hartley, M.A. (1705-57), *Observations on Man, His Frame, His Duty, and His Expectations* (1749). Part II, Section IV. "On the Regard due to the Pleasures of Honour, and the Pains of Shame, informing the Rule of Life."

more absurd is to me the image of a lonely sufferer, trying not only to fill up his time, but to soothe his pains of body, and calm his anguish of spirit, by drawing delight from the remembrance of his own little contrivings and doings in the world. I would recommend, in preference, the project of drawing sunbeams from cucumbers, as a solace on the rack.

If it is asked, after all this, "who can console? How is it possible to please and soothe the sufferer?" I answer, that nothing is easier—nothing is more common—nothing more natural to simple-minded people. Never creature had more title than I to speak confidently of this, from experience which melts my heart day by day. "Speaking the truth in love," is the way. One who does this cannot but be an angel of consolation. Everything but truth becomes loathed in a sick-room. The restless can repose on nothing but this: the sharpened intellectual appetite can be satisfied with nothing less substantial; the susceptible spiritual taste can be gratified with nothing less genuine, noble, and fair.

Then the question arises, what sort of truth? Why, that which is appropriate to the one who administers. To each a separate gift may be appointed. Only let all avoid every shadow of falsehood. Let the nurse avow that the medicine is nauseous. Let the physician declare that the treatment will be painful. Let sister, or brother, or friend, tell me that I must never look to be well. When the time approaches that I am to die, let me be told that I am to die, and when. If I encroach thoughtlessly on the time or strength of those about me, let me be reminded; if selfishly, let me be remonstrated with. Thus to speak the truth in love is in the power of all. Higher service is a talent in the hands of those who have a genius for sympathy—a genius less rare, thank God! than other kinds.

The archangel of consolation is the friend who, at a fitting moment, reminds me of my high calling. Not the clergyman, making his stated visit for the purpose; not the zealous watcher for souls, who fears for mine on the ground of difference of doctrine; not the meddler, who takes charge of my spiritual relations whether I will or no: none such are, by virtue of these offices, effectual consolers. But if the friend of my brighter days—with whom I have travelled, sung, danced, consulted about my work, enjoyed books and society—the friend, now far off, busy in robust health of body and spirit, sends me a missive which says, "You languish — you are sick at heart. But put this sickness from your heart, and your pains under your feet. You have known before that there is a divine joy in endurance. Prove it now. Lift up your head amidst your lot, and wait the issue — not submissively, but heroically. Live out your season, not wistfully looking out for hope, or shrinking from fear: but serenely and immoveably (because in full understanding with God), ENDURE;" if such an appeal comes, and at any hour (for there is no hour of sickness with which it is not congenial,) what an influx of life does it bring! What a heavenly day, week, year, succeeds! How the crippled spirit leaps up at the miraculous touch, and springs on its way, praising God in his very temple! And again, when a thoughtful, conscientious spirit, guided by an analytical intellect, utters from a distance, not as an appeal, but as in soliloquy — "With an eternity before us, it cannot matter much, if we would but consider it, whether we are laid aside for such or such a length of time; whether we can be busy for others at this moment, or must wait so many months or years: and as for ourselves, how can we tell but that we shall find the experience we are gaining worth any cost of suffering?" When such a thought comes under my eye, as if I overheard some spirit in the night-wind communing with itself, I feel a strong and kindly hand take my heart and steep it in patience. Again, a kind visitor, eloquent by using few words or none on matters nearest at heart, takes down from my shelves a Fenelon or other quietist,[1] and with silent finger points to the saying, inexhaustible in truth, that it is what we *are* that matters — not what we *do*; and here, in one moment, do I find a boundless career opened to me within the four walls of my room. Again — a tender spirit, anxious under responsibility, says, "If you could but fully feel, as you will one day feel, the privilege of having your life and lot settled for you — your spirit free, your mind at leisure — no hurry, no conflicts nor misgivings about duty — you would

---

1 Quietism refers to the Christian doctrine associating perfection with the passivity of the soul and renunciation of any human effort that might interfere with divine action. The French theologian and archbishop Francois de Salgnac de La Mothe (1651-1715) sought answers to his spiritual questions through the Quietest school of prayer.

easily conceive that there are some who would gladly exchange with you, and pour into your lap willingly all the good things that you seem to be without. I dare say we are very philosophical for you about your sufferings; but where I do sympathize with you, is in regard to this clearness and settledness of your life's duty and affairs." To this again, my whole being cries "amen!" Here are a few of the heavenly messages which have come to me through human hearts. When below these are ranged the innumerable ministrations of help, of smiles and tears, of solid comforts and beguiling luxuries, it does indeed seem impossible that I should be in any degree dubious or hard to please in the contemplation and reception of human sympathy. What I have said of its most perfect forms, I have said from my own knowledge.

Under this head of sympathy occurs the important practical consideration, what should be the arrangements of a permanent invalid, in regard to companionship?

In most cases, this is no matter of choice, but a point settled by domestic circumstances; where it is not, however, I cannot but wish that more consideration was given to the comfort of being alone in illness. This is so far from being understood, that, though the cases are numerous of sufferers who prefer, and earnestly endeavour to procure solitude, they are, if not resisted, wondered at, and humoured for a supposed peculiarity, rather than seen to be reasonable; whereas, if they are listened to as the best judges of their own comforts, it may be found that they have reason on their side.

In a house full of relations, it may be unnatural for an invalid to pass many hours alone; but where, as is the case with numbers who belong to the middle and working classes of society, all the other members of the family have occupations and duties — regular business in life — without the charge of the invalid, it does appear to me, and is felt by me through experience, to be incomparably the happiest plan for the sick one to live alone. By experience it is found to be not only expedient, but important in regard to happiness. In pictures of the sick-room, drawn by those who are at ease and happy, the group is always of the sufferer supported and soothed by some loving hand and tender voice, and every pain shared by sympathy. This may be an approach to truth in the case of short sharp illness, where the sufferer is taken by surprise, and has his whole lesson to learn; but a very different account would often be given by an invalid whose burden is for life, and who has learned the truths of the condition. We, of that class, find it best and happiest to admit our friends only in our easiest hours, when we can enjoy their society, and feel ourselves least of a burden; and it is indispensable to our peace of mind to be alone when in pain. Where welfare of body is out of the question, peace of mind becomes an object of supreme importance; and this is unattainable when we see any whom we love suffering, in our sufferings, even more than we do: or when we know that we have been the means of turning any one's day of ease and pleasure into sorrow. The experience of years qualifies me to speak about this; and I declare that I know of no comfort, at the end of a day of suffering, comparable to that of feeling that, however it may have been with one's self, no one else has suffered,—that one's own fogs have dimmed nobody's sunshine: and when this grows to be the nightly comfort of weeks, months, and years, it becomes the most valuable element in the peace of the sufferer, and lightens his whole lot. If not in the midst of pain, he feels in prospect of it, and after it, that it really matters very little whether and how much he suffers, if nobody else is pained by it. It becomes a habit, from the recurrence of this feeling, to write letters in one's best mood; to give an account of one's self in one's best hours; to present one's most cheerful aspect abroad, and keep one's miseries close at home, under lock and key.

The objection commonly brought to this system is, that it is injurious to one's loving and anxious friends. But I do not find it so. So loving and anxious are my friends, that they do not need the wretched stimulus of seeing me suffer. All that can be done for me is done; and it would be no consolation, but a great aggravation to me, that they should suffer gratuitously. Their general love, and care and concern for me, are fully satisfying to me; and I know that I have only to call and they will come. But I feel with inexpressible comfort what a difference there is between their general concern for my state, and the pain of days, now separately spent by them in ease and joy, which would be more dreary to them than to me, if I let them share my dreariness. A trifling incident, which occurred the other day, gave me strong satisfaction, as proving that where my method can be made a system, it works well,—promoting the cheerfulness, without impairing the sympathies, of even the youngest of those for whom I have a welcome only at certain seasons. Two little friends were with me—one greatly admiring various luxuries about me, and thence proceeding to reckon up a large amount of privileges and enjoyments in my possession and prospect, when his companion said, with a sigh and tenderness of tone, musical to my soul, "Ah! but then, there is the unhealthiness! that spoils everything!" To which the other mournfully assented. What more could these children know by having their hearts wounded by the spectacle of suffering? And if they may be spared the pain, larger minds and more ripened hearts must require it even less.

I need not say that this plan of solitude in pain supposes sufficient and kindly attendance; but, for a permanence, (though I know it to be otherwise in short illnesses,) there is no attendance to be compared with that of a servant. In as far as the help is mechanical, it tends to habituate the sufferer to his lot, and the relation is sustained with the least expenditure of painful feeling on both sides,—with the least anxiety, as well as pain of sympathy.

There is sufficient kindliness excited in the attendant by the appeal to her feelings, while there is no call for the agony which a congenial friend must sustain; and, on the other side, there is no overwhelming sense of obligation to the nurse, but a satisfactory consciousness of, at least, partial requital. It is no small item in the account of this method, that the promotion of the happiness of the attendant is a cheerful, natural, and salutary pursuit to the invalid; a daily duty imposed when so many others are withdrawn; a fragment of beneficent power left in the scene of its wreck. To dignify her by putting one's self under express and frequent obligations to her,—to rejoice her by enjoying relief or pleasure devised by her ingenuity,—to spare her health, promote her little fortunes, encourage her best tastes and aspirations, and draw out for her, as well as for one's self, the lessons of the sickroom; to study these things befits the mutual relation, and cheers the life of the sufferer, while the connexion is not so close as to involve the severer pains of sympathy.

In a sick-room, where health is never again to enter, it is well and easily understood that commemorative seasons, anniversaries, &c., are far from being, as elsewhere, among the gayest. In truth, they are often mournful enough; but I am confident that they are most cheerily spent alone. No heart leal[1] to its kind can bear to let them pass unnoticed. It is an intolerable selfishness to abolish them, as far as in one lies, because they have ceased to gladden us; this would be as paltry as to turn one's back on an old companion, formerly all merriment and smiles, because he comes to us in mourning or in tears; or, let us say, abstracted and thoughtful. But it does not succeed to make small attempts to keep the day, for the sake of one or two companions, putting up Christmas holly over the fireplace, where there is only one to sit, and having Christmas fare brought to the couch, to be sent away again. But when one is alone, the matter is very different, and becomes far gayer. There is nothing, then, to prevent my being in the world again for the day; no human presence to chain me to my prison. When my servant is dismissed to make merry with the rest, and I am alone with my holly sprigs and the memories of old years, I can flit at will among the family groups that I see gathered round many fire-sides. If the morning is sunny, I actually see, with my telescope, the gay crowds that throng the opposite shore after church; and the sight revives the dimmed image of crowded streets, and brings back to my ear the almost forgotten sound of "the church-going bell."[2] When it grows dark, and my lamp burns so steadily as to give of itself a deep impression of stillness; when there is no sound but of the cinder dropping on the hearth, or of the turning of the leaf as I read or write, there is something of a holiday feeling in pausing to view and listen to what is going on in all the houses where one has an interest. By means of that inimitable telescope we carry about in us, (which acts as well in the pitch-dark night as at noon, and defies distance and house-walls,) I see in turn a Christmas tree, with its tapers glittering in a room full of young eyes, or the games and the dance, or the cozy little party of elderly folk round

---

1   Chiefly Scottish, meaning loyal or true.
2   William Cowper (1731-1800), "Verses, Supposed to be written by Alexander Selkirk, During His Solitary Abode in the Island of Juan Fernandez" (1782).

the fire or the tea-table; and I hear, not the actual jokes, but the laughter, and "the sough of words without the sense," and can catch at least the soul of the merriment. If I am at ease, I am verily among them: if not, I am thankful not to be there; and, at all events have, from life-long association, caught so much of the contagious spirit of sociability, that, when midnight comes, I lie down with an impression of its having been an extraordinary day,—a social one, though, (as these are the days when one is sure *not* to see one's doctor,) the face of my maid is, in reality, the only one that has met my eyes. O yes! on these marked days, however it may be on ordinary ones, our friends may take our word for it that we are most cheery alone.

There is one day of the year of which everybody will believe this,—one's birthday. Regarded as a birthday usually and naturally is, in ordinary circumstances, there must be something melancholy in it when attempted to be kept in the sick-room of a permanent invalid: but this melancholy is lost when one is alone. It is true, one's mind goes back to the festivals of the day in one's childhood, and to the mantling feelings of one's youth, when each birthday brought us a step further into the world which lay in its gay charms all before us;[1] and we find the gray hairs and thin hands of to-day form an ugly contrast with the images conjured up. But, in another view,—a view which can be enjoyed only in silence and alone,—what a sanctity belongs to these gray hairs and other tokens of decay! They and the day are each tokens (how dear!) seals (how distinct!) of promise of our selection for a not distant admittance to a station whence we may review life and the world to better advantage than even now. If, with every year of contemplation, the world appears a more astonishing fact, and life a more noble mystery, we cannot but be reanimated by the recurrence of every birthday which draws us up higher into the region of contemplation, and nearer to the gate within which lies the disclosure of all mysteries which worthily occupy us now, and doubtless a new series of others adapted to our then ennobled powers. This is a birthday experience which it requires leisure and solitude fully to appropriate: and it yet leaves liberty for the

---

1   An allusion to *Paradise Lost*, Book XII, by John Milton (1608-74).

human sympathies which belong to the season. Post time is looked to for its sure freight of love and pity and good wishes from a few — or not a few — whose affections keep them even more on the watch than ourselves for one's own holy day. Letters are one's best company on that day,—and best if they are one's only company.

There is one point on which I can speak only as every one may,—from observation and thought,—but on which I have a very decided impression, notwithstanding;—as to the conduct which would be dictated by the truest sympathy in a case which not unfrequently occurs. I have known instances of persons, most benevolent and thoughtless of themselves through life, becoming *exigeans*[1] and oppressive in their last days, merely through want of information as to what they are doing. One attendant is usually preferred to all others by a dying person: and I have seen the favorite nurse worn out by the incessant service required day and night by the sufferer, in ignorance how time passes,—even in mistake of the night for the day. I have known the most devoted and benevolent of women call up her young nurse from a snatch of sleep at two in the morning to read aloud, when she had been reading aloud for six or seven hours of the preceding day. I have known a kind-hearted and self-denying man require of two or three members of his family to sit and talk and be merry in his chamber, two or three hours after midnight: — and both for want of a mere intimation that it was night, and time for the nurse's rest. How it makes one shudder to think of this being one's own case! The passing doubt whether one can trust one's friends, when the season comes, to save one from such tyrannical mistakes, is a doubt sickening to the heart. Nothing is clearer *now*, when we are in full possession of ourselves, than that the most sympathising friend is one who cherishes our amiability and reasonableness to the last,— who preserves our perfect understanding with those about us through all dimness of the eyes and wandering of the brain. If I could not trust my friends to save me from involuntary encroachment at the last, I had rather scoop myself a hole in the sand of the desert, and die alone, than be

---

1   A form of exigeant, which means "exacting."

tended by the gentlest hands, and soothed by the most loving voices in the choicest chamber.

It is doubtless easiest to comply at the moment of such exactions, at any sacrifice of subsequent health and nerve: but it should be remembered that the sacrifice is not of health alone. The posthumous love must suffer;—or if not the love, the respect for the departed. It is impossible to love one who appears in a selfish aspect,—though it be the merest mask, most briefly worn,—so well as the countenance that never concealed its benevolence for a moment. Let then the timely thought of the future,—a provident care for the memory of the dying friend, suggest the easy prudence which may obviate encroachment. Let the bewildered sufferer be frequently and cheerfully told the hour,—and informed that such an one is going to rest, to be replaced by another for so many hours. A little forethought and resource may generally prevent the great evil I speak of: and if not, true sympathy requires that there should be a cheerful word of remonstrance—or let us call it rectification. So may it be with me, if so lingering a departure be appointed! Thus would every one say beforehand; and it seems to me a sin against every one's moral rights not to take him at his word.

CHAPTER THREE

NATURE TO THE INVALID

"O mighty love! Man is one world and hath
Another to attend him!"

George Herbert.[1]

"Let us find room for this great guest in our small houses."

Emerson.[2]

"Shut not so soon! The dull-eyed night
Has not as yet begun
To make a seizure of the light,
Or to seal up the sun."

Herrick.[3]

WHEN an invalid is under sentence of disease for life, it becomes a duty of first-rate importance to select a proper place of abode. This is often overlooked; and a sick prisoner goes on to live where he lived before, for no other reason than because he lived there before. Many a sufferer languishes amidst street noises, or passes year after year in a room whose windows command dead walls, or paved courts, or some such objects; so that he sees nothing of Nature but such sky and stars as show themselves above the chimney-tops. I remember the heart-ache it gave me to see a youth, confined to a recumbent posture for two or three years, lying in a room whence he could see nothing, and dependent therefore on the cage of birds by his bed-side, and the flowers his friends sent him, for the only notices of Nature that reached him, except the summer's heat and winter's cold. There was no sufficient reason why he should not have been placed where he could overlook fields, or even the sea.

---

1 George Herbert (1593-1633), "Man."
2 Ralph Waldo Emerson (1803-82), "Heroism."
3 Robert Herrick (1591-1674), "To Daisies, not to shut so soon."

If a healthy man, entering upon a temporary imprisonment, hangs his walls with a paper covered with roses, and every one sympathises in this forethought for his mind's health, much more should the invalid, (who, though he must be a prisoner, has yet liberty of choice where his prison shall be,) provide for sustaining and improving his attachment to Nature, and for beguiling his sufferings by the unequalled refreshments she affords. He will be wise to sacrifice indolence, habit, money and convenience, at the outset, to place himself where he can command the widest or the most beautiful view that can be had without sacrificing advantages more essential still. There are few things more essential still: but there are some;— such as medical attendance, and a command of the ordinary conveniences of life.

What is the best kind of view for a sick prisoner's windows to command? I have chosen the sea, and am satisfied with my choice. We should have the widest expanse of sky, for night scenery. We should have a wide expanse of land or water, for the sake of a sense of liberty, yet more than for variety; and also because then the inestimable help of a telescope may be called in. Think of the difference to us between seeing from our sofas the width of a street, even if it be Sackville-street, Dublin, or Portland Place, in London, and thirty miles of sea view, with its long boundary of rocks, and the power of sweeping our glance over half a county, by means of a telescope! But the chief ground of preference of the sea is less its space than its motion, and the perpetual shifting of objects caused by it. There can be nothing in inland scenery which can give the sense of life and motion and connexion with the world like sea changes. The motion of a waterfall is too continuous,— too little varied,— as the breaking of the waves would be, if that were all the sea could afford. The fitful action of a windmill,— the waving of trees, the ever-changing aspects of mountains are good and beautiful: but there is something more life-like in the going forth and return of ships, in the passage of fleets, and in the never-ending variety of a fishery.

But then, there must not be too much sea. The strongest eyes and nerves could not support the glare and oppressive vastness of an unrelieved expanse of waters. I was aware of this in time, and fixed myself where the view of the sea was inferior to what I should have preferred, if I had come to the coast for a summer visit. Between my window and the sea is a green down, as green as any field in Ireland; and on the nearer half of this down, hay-making goes forward in its season. It slopes down to a hollow, where the Prior of old preserved his fish, there being sluices formerly at either end, the one opening upon the river, and the other upon the little haven below the Priory, whose ruins still crown the rock. From the Prior's fish-pond, the green down slopes upwards again to a ridge; and on the slope are cows grazing all summer, and half way into the winter. Over the ridge, I survey the harbor and all its traffic, the view extending from the light-houses far to the right, to a horizon of sea to the left. Beyond the harbor lies another county, with, first, its sandy beach, where there are frequent wrecks — too interesting to an invalid, — and a fine stretch of rocky shore to the left; and above the rocks, a spreading heath, where I watch troops of boys flying their kites; lovers and friends taking their breezy walk on Sundays; the sportsman with his gun and dog; and the washerwomen converging from the farm-houses on Saturday evenings, to carry their loads, in company, to the village on the yet further height. I see them, now talking in a cluster, as they walk, each with her white burden on her head, and now in file, as they pass through the narrow lane; and finally they part off on the village green, each to some neighboring house of the gentry. Behind the village and the heath, stretches the rail-road; and I watch the train triumphantly careering along the level road, and puffing forth its steam above hedges and groups of trees, and then laboring and panting up the ascent, till it is lost between two heights, which at last bound my view. But on these heights are more objects; a windmill, now in motion and now at rest; a lime-kiln, in a picturesque rocky field; an ancient church-tower, barely visible in the morning, but conspicuous when the setting sun shines upon it; a colliery, with its lofty wagon-way, and the self-moving wagons running hither and thither, as if in pure wilfulness; and three or four farms, at various degrees of ascent, whose yards, paddocks, and dairies I am better acquainted with than their inhabitants would believe possible. I know every stack of the one on the heights. Against the sky I see the stacking of corn and hay in the season, and can detect the slicing away of the provender, with an accurate eye, at the distance of several miles. I can follow the sociable farmer in his summer-evening ride, pricking on in the lanes where he is alone, in order to have more time for the unconscionable gossip at the gate of the next farm-house, and for the second talk over the paddock-fence of the next, or for the third or fourth before the porch, or over the wall, when the resident farmer comes out, pipe in mouth, and puffs away amidst his chat, till the wife appears, with a shawl over her cap, to see what can detain him so long; and the daughter follows, with her gown turned over head (for it is now chill evening), and at last the sociable horseman finds he must be going, looks at his watch, and, with a gesture of surprise, turns his steed down a steep broken way to the beach, and canters home over the sands, left hard and wet by the ebbing tide, the white horse making his progress visible to me through the dusk. Then, if the question arises which has most of the gossip spirit, he or I, there is no shame in the answer. Any such small amusement is better than harmless — is salutary — which carries the spirit of the sick prisoner abroad into the open air, and among country people. When I shut down my window, I feel that my mind has had an airing.

But there are many times when these distant views cannot be sought; when we are too languid for any objects that do not present themselves near at hand. Here, too, I am provided. I overlook gardens, and particularly a well-managed market-garden, from which I have learned, and enjoyed, not a little. From the radish-sowing in early spring, to the latest turnip and onion cropping, I watch the growth of everything, and hence feel an interest in the frosts and rain, which I should otherwise not dream of. A shower is worth much to me when the wide potato-beds, all dry and withering in the morning, are green and fresh in the evening light; and the mistress of the garden, bringing up her pails of frothing milk from the cow-house, looks about her with complacency, and comes forth with fresh alacrity to cut the young lettuces which are sent for, for somebody's supper of cold lamb.

The usual drawback of a sea-side residence is the deficiency of trees. I see none (except through the telescope) but one shabby sycamore, which grows between my eye and the chimney of the baths in the haven. But this is not a pure disadvantage. I may see less beauty in summer, but I also see less dreariness in winter.

The winter beauty of the coast is a great consideration. The snow does not lie; at least rarely for more than a very few hours; and then it has no time to lose its lustre. When I look forth in the morning, the whole land may be sheeted with glittering snow, while the myrtle-green sea swells and tumbles, forming an almost incredible contrast to the summer aspect of both, and even to the afternoon aspect; for before sunset the snow is gone, except in the hollows; all is green again on shore, and the waves are lilac, crested with white. My winter pleasures of this kind were, at first, a pure surprise to me. I had spent every winter of my life in a town; and here, how different it is! The sun shines into my room from my hour of rising till within a few minutes of dusk, and this, almost by settled custom, till February, our worst month. The sheeny sea, swelling in orange light, is crossed by fishing-boats, which look black by contrast, and there is none of the deadness of winter in the landscape; no leafless trees, no locking up with ice; and the air comes in through my open upper sash brisk, but sunwarmed. The robins twitter and hop in my flower-boxes, outside the window; and the sea-birds sit on the water, or cluster on the spits of sand left by the tide. Within-doors, all is gay and bright with flowering narcissus, tulips, crocus, and hyacinths. And at night, what a heaven! What an expanse of stars above, appearing more steadfast, the more the Northern Lights dart and quiver! And what a silvery sheet of moonlight below, crossed by vessels more black than those which looked blackest in the golden sea of the morning! It makes one's very frame shiver with a delicious surprise to look, (and the more, the oftener one looks,) at a moonlit sea through the telescope; at least, it is so with one who can never get near the object in any other way. I doubt whether there be any inland spectacle so singular and stirring, except that which is common to both, a good telescopic view of the planets. This transcends all. It is well to see, by day, the shadows of walkers on the wet sands; the shadows of the sails of a windmill on the sward; the shadow of rocks in a deep sea cave; but far beyond this is it to see the shadow of the disk of Saturn on his rings. How is it that so many sick prisoners are needlessly deprived of all these sights; shut up in a street of a town? What is there there, that can compensate them for what they lose?

There is some set-off to the winter privileges I have spoken of, in an occasional day of storms; perhaps two or three in each season. These are very dreary while they last; though, considering the reaction, the next fine day, salutary on the whole. On these days, the horror of the winds is great. One's very bed shakes under them; and some neighbor's house is pretty sure to be unroofed. The window-cushions must be removed, because nothing can keep out the rain, not even the ugly array of cloths laid over all the sashes. The rain and spray seem to ooze through the very glass. The wet comes through to the ceiling, however perfect the tiling. The splash and dash against the panes are wearing to the nerves. Balls of foam drive, like little balloons, over the garden; and, sooner or later in the day, we see the ominous rush of men and boys to the rocks and the ridge, and we know that there is mischief. We see either a vessel laboring over the bar, amidst an universal expectation that she will strike; or we see, by a certain slope of the masts, that she is actually on the rocks; or she drives wilfully over to the sands, in spite of all the efforts of steam-tugs and her own crew; and then come forth the life-boats, which we cannot help watching, but which look as if they must themselves capsize, and increase the misery instead of preventing it. Then, when the crew are taken from the rigging, and carried up to the port, ensues the painful sight of the destruction of the vessel; parties, or files of women, boys, and men, passing along the ridge or the sands with the spoils; bundles of sailcloth, armsful of spars, shoulder-loads of planks; while, in the midst, there is sure to be a report, false or true, of a vessel having foundered, somewhere near at hand. On such days, it is a relief to bar the shutters at length, and close the curtains, and light the lamp, and, if the wind will allow, to forget the history of the day. Still more thankful are we to go to bed — I can hardly say to rest — for invalids are liable to a return in the night of the painful impressions of noon, with exaggerations, unless the agitation has been such as to wear them out with fatigue. But, as I said, such days are very few. Two or three such in a year, and two or three weeks of shifting seafog in spring, are nearly all the drawbacks we have; nearly the only obscurations of Nature's beauties.

How different are "the seasons, and their change,"[1] to us, and to the busy inhabitants of towns! How common is it for townspeople to observe, that the shortest day is past without their remembering it was so near! or the equinox, or even the longest day! Whereas, we sick watchers have, as it were, a property in the changes of the seasons, and even of the moon. It is a good we would not sell for any profit, to say to ourselves, at the end of March, that the six months of longest days are now before us; that we are entering upon a region of light evenings, with their soft lulling beauties; and of short nights, when, late as we go to rest, we can almost bid defiance to horrors, and the depressions of darkness. There is a monthly spring of the spirits too, when the young moon appears again, and we have the prospect of three weeks' pleasure in her course, if the sky be propitious. I have often smiled in detecting in myself this sense of property in such shows; in becoming aware of a sort of resentment, of feeling of personal grievance, when the sky is not propitious; when I have no benefit of the moon for several nights together, through the malice of the clouds, or the sea-haze in spring. But, now I have learned by observation where and when to look for the rising moon; what a superb pleasure it is to lie watching the sea-line, night after night, unwilling to shut the window, to leave the window-couch, to let the lamp be lighted, till the punctual and radiant blessing comes, answering to my hope, surpassing my expectation, and appearing to greet me with express and consolatory intent! Should I actually have quitted life without this set of affections, if I had not been ill? I believe it. And, moreover, I believe that my interest in these spectacles of Nature has created a new regard to them in others. I see a looking out for the rising moon among the neighbors, who have possessed the same horizon-line all their lives, but did not know its value till they saw what it is to me. I observe the children from the cottage swinging themselves up to obtain a peep over the palings, when they see me on the watch in the window;

---

1   John Milton (1608-74), *Paradise Lost*, Book IV, line 640.

and an occasional peep at a planet, through my telescope, appears to dress the heavens in quite a new light to such as venture to take a look.

They do not know, however, anything of my most thrilling experience of these things—for it happens when they are all at rest. I keep late hours, (for the sake of husbanding my seasons of ease;) and now and then I have nerve enough to look abroad for my last vision of the day, an hour after midnight, when the gibbous moon,—having forsaken the sea,—slowly surmounts the priory ruins on the high rock, appearing in the black-blue heaven like a quite different planet from that which I have been watching,—and from that which I shall next greet, a slender crescent in the light western sky, just after sunset. To go from this spectacle to one's bed, is to recover for the hour one's health of soul, at least: and the remembrance of such a thrill is a cordial for future sickly hours which strengthens by keeping.

I have a sense of property too in the larks which nestle in all the furrows of the down. It is a disquietude to see them start up and soar, with premature joy, on some mild January day, before our snows and storms have begun, when I detect in myself a feeling of duty to the careless creatures,—a longing to warn them, by my superior wisdom, that they must not reckon yet on spring. And on April mornings, when the shadows are strong in the hollows, and some neighbor's child sends me in a handful of primroses from the fields, I look forth, as for my due, to see the warblers spring and fall, and to catch their carol above the hum and rejoicing outcry of awakening Nature. If the yellow butterflies do not come to my flower-box in the sunny noon, I feel myself wronged. But they do come,—and so do the bees: and there are times when the service is too importunate,—when the life and light are more than I can bear, and I draw down the blind, and shut myself in with my weakness, and with thoughts more abstract. But when, in former days, had simple, natural influences such power over me? How is it that the long-suffering sick, already deprived of so much, are ever needlessly debarred from natural and renovating pleasures like these?

Watch the effect upon them of a picture, or a print of a breezy tree,—of a gushing stream,—of a group of children swinging on a gate in a lane. If they do not (because they cannot) express in words the thirst of their souls for these images, observe how their eyes wistfully follow the portfolio or volume of plates which ministers this scenery to them. Observe how, in looking at portraits, their notice fastens at once on any morsel of back-ground which presents any rural objects. Observe the sad fondness with which they cherish flowers,—how reluctantly it is admitted that they fade. Mark the value of presents of bulbs,—above the most splendid array of plants in flower, which kind people love to send to sick prisoners. Plants in bloom are beautiful and glorious; but the pleasure to a prisoner is to see the process of growth. It is less the bright and fragrant flower that the spirit longs for, than the spectacle of vegetation.

Blessings on the inventors and improvers of fern-houses![1] We feel towards them a mingling of the gratitude due to physicians, and appropriate to the Good People. We find under their glass-bells fairy gifts, and prescriptions devised with consummate skill. In towns, let the sick prisoner have a fern-house as a compensation for rural pleasures; and in the country as an addition to them.

Blessings on the writers of voyages and travels; and not the less for their not having contemplated our case in describing what they have seen! A school-boy's or a soldier's eagerness after voyages and travels is nothing to that of an invalid. We are insatiable in regard to this kind of book. To us it is scenery, exercise, fresh air. The new knowledge is quite a secondary consideration. We are weary of the aspect of a chest of drawers,—tired of certain marks on the wall, and of many unchangeable features of our apartment; so that when a morning comes, and our eyes open on these objects, and we foresee the seasons of pain or bodily distress, or mental depression, which we know must come round as regularly as the hours, we loathe the prospect of our day. Things clear up a little when we rise, and we think we ought to be writing a letter to such-a-one, which has been on our conscience for some time. While the paper and ink are being brought, we put out our

---

1 A glass case used to house ferns. For more information on the Victorian fascination with ferns, see David Allen's *The Victorian Fern Craze: A History of Pteridomania* (London: Hutchinson & Co., 1969).

hand for that book,—arrived or laid in sight this morning. It is a Journal of Travels to the Polar Sea, or over the Passes of the Alps,—or in the Punjab,—or in Central or South America. Here the leaves turn over rapidly;—there we linger, and read one paragraph again and again, dwelling fondly on some congregation of images, to be seen by our bodily eyes no more:—on we go till stopped by the fluttering and distress,—the familiar pain, or the leaden down-sinking of the spirits, and wonder that our trying time has come so soon, before the letter is written. It has not come soon;—it is only that some hours of our penance have been beguiled,—that we have been let out of our prison for a holiday, and are now brought back to our schooling. But the good does not end here. We see everything with different eyes,— the chest of drawers,—the walls,—the bookshelves, and the pattern of the rug. We have been seeing the Northern Lights and icebergs: we have been watching for avalanches, or for the sunrise from Etna, or gazing over the Pampas, or peering through the primeval forest; and fragments of these visions freshen the very daylight to us.

Blessings, above all, on Christopher North![1] We cannot but wonder whether he ever cast a thought upon such as we are when breasting the breeze on the moors, or pressing up the mountain-side, or watching beside the trout-stream; or summoning the fowls of heaven, and passing them in review into his Aviary;—or, especially, whether he had any thought of recreating us when he sent forth his "Recreations" within reach of our hands. If he did not think of sick prisoners in issuing his vital, breezy book, he has missed a pleasure worthy of a heart like his.[2] He pities the town-dwellers who might relish nature and will not: but his pity for them must be destitute of the zest which pity derives from a consciousness of helpfulness. He can hardly help those to country privileges who will not help themselves. But has he remembered the chamber-dwellers,—the involuntary plodders within narrow bounds,—few in comparison with the other

---

1   Christopher North, pseudonym of John Wilson (1785-1854), Scottish reviewer and essayist who often wrote about adventures in exotic lands.
2   Martineau refers to *The Recreations of Christopher North* (Edinburgh: Blackwood, 1842).

class, it is true, but, if estimated by emotion—by experience in which his heart can sympathise, not less entitled to his regards?

Whether he thought of us or not, he has recreated us. Whether he is now conscious of the fact or not, his spirit has come, many a time while his tired body slept, and opened our prison-doors, and led us a long flight over mountain and moor, lake and lea, and dropped us again on our beds, refreshed and soothed, to dream at least of having felt the long-lost sensation of health once more. Blessings on him then, as the kindest of the friendly ghosts who use well their privilege of passing in and out of all secret and sorrowful places, as they go to and fro on the earth! If he has ministered to us with more or less deliberate intent, he needs not to be told with what heartiness we drink his health in the first full draught of the spring west wind—how cordially we pledge him in the sparkling thunder-shower, or the brimming harvest-moon.

O! if every one who sorrows for us would help us to assert our claim to Nature's nursing, we should soon have our solace and our due. We have not all the vigour and spirit,—nor even the inclination, in our morbid state, to turn our faces to the fountain of solace—the fresh waters which cool the spirit when fretted by its tormenting companion. We cannot infallibly keep alive in our weak selves the love of Nature which would lead us to repose ourselves upon her, and forget the evils which even she cannot cure. But this should be done for us. When our sentence is passed, clear and irreversible, the next thing is to make it as lenient as possible in its operation; and especially by seeing that it is through no oversight that, if the outward man must decay, the inward man is not renewed day by day. This renewal, say some, must be by grace. Well, Nature is God's grace, meant to abound to all,—and not least to those whom, by his chastening, he may be humbly supposed to love.

CHAPTER FOUR

LIFE TO THE INVALID

"There is a pause, near death, when men grow bold
Toward all things else."

Robert Landor.[1]

"Man will come to see that the world is the perennial miracle which the soul worketh, and be less astonished at particular wonders; he will learn that there is no profane history;
that all history is sacred; that the universe is represented in
an atom, in a moment of time. He will weave no longer a
spotted life of shreds and patches, but he will live with a
divine unity. He will cease from what is base and frivolous
in his own life, and be content with all places, and any service he can render. He will calmly front the morrow in the
negligency of that trust which carries God with it, and so
hath already the whole future in the bottom of the heart."

Emerson.[2]

CAN we not all remember the time when, on first taking to heart
Milton, and afterwards Akenside,[3] —(before knowing anything of
Dante,) we conceived the grandest moment of possible existence
to be that of a Seraph, poised on balanced wings, watching the
bringing out of a world from chaos, its completion in fitness,
beauty and radiance, and its first motion in its orbit, when sent
forth by the creative hand on its everlasting way? How many a
young imagination has dwelt on this image till the act appeared to
be almost one of memory,— till the vision became one of the
persuasives to entertain the notion of human pre-existence, in
which we find one or another about us apt to delight! To me, this

---

1   Robert Landor (1781-1869), "The Impious Feast," Book II.
2   Ralph Waldo Emerson (1803-1882), "Heroism."
3   Mark Akenside (1721-70) was a poet, physician, and satirist best known for *The
    Pleasures of Imagination* (1744).

conception was, in my childhood, one of eminent delight; and when, years afterwards, I was involved in more than the ordinary toil and hurry of existence, I now and then recurred to the old image, with a sort of longing to exchange my function,—my share of the world-building in which we all have to help, for the privilege of the supposed seraph. Was there nothing prophetic, or at least provident, in this? Is not sequestration from the action of life a different thing to me from what it would have been if there had been no preparation of the imagination? Though I, and my fellows in lot, must wait long for the seraphic powers which would enable us fully to enjoy and use our position, we have the position; and it is for us to see how far we can make our privilege correspond to the anticipation.

Nothing is more impossible to represent in words, even to one's self in meditative moments, than what it is to lie on the verge of life and watch, with nothing to do but to think, and learn from what we behold. Let any one recall what it is to feel suddenly, by personal experience, the full depth of meaning of some saying, always believed in, often repeated with sincerity, but never till now *known*. Every one has felt this, in regard to some one proverb, or divine scriptural clause, or word of some right royal philosopher or poet. Let any one then try to conceive of an extension of this realisation through all that has ever been wisely said of man and human life, and he will be endeavouring to imagine our experience. Engrossing, thrilling, overpowering as the experience is, we have each to bear it alone; for each of us is surrounded by the active and the busy, who have a different gift and a different office;—and if not, it is one of those experiences which are incommunicable. If we endeavour to utter our thoughts on the folly of the pursuit of wealth, on the emptiness of ambition, on the surface nature of distinctions of rank, &c. we are only saying what our hearers have had by heart all their lives from books,—through a long range of authors, from Solomon to Burns. Spoken moralities really reach only those whom they immediately concern;—and they are such as are saying the same things within their own hearts. We utter them under two conditions:—sometimes because we cannot help it; and sometimes under a sense of certainty that a human heart somewhere is needing the sympathy for which we yearn.

You, my fellow-sufferer, now lying on your couch, the newspaper dropping from your hand, while your eyes are fixed on the lamp, are you not smiling at the thought that you have preserved, up to this time, more or less of that faith of your childhood—that everything that is in print is true? Before we had our present leisure for reflection, we read one newspaper,—perhaps occasionally one on the other side. We found opposition of views; but this was to be expected from diversities of minds and position. Now the whole press is open to us, and we see what is said on all sides. What an astonishing result! We hear that Cabinet Ministers are apt to grow nervous about newspaper commentaries on their conduct. To us this seems scarcely possible, seeing, as we do, that, though every paper may be useful reading for the suggestions and other lights it affords, every one is at fault, as a judge. Every one forgets, actually or politically, that it is in possession of only partial information, generally speaking; we find no guarding intimation to the reader, that there may be information behind which might alter the aspect of the question. Such notice may be too much to expect of diurnal literature; but the confusion made by the positiveness of all parties, proceeding on their respective faulty grounds of fact—a positiveness usually proportioned to the faultiness of the grounds—is such as might, one would think, relieve Cabinet Ministers who have their work at heart, from any very anxious solicitude about the judgments of the press, in regard to unfinished affairs. Meantime, what a work is done! Amidst the flat contradictions of fact, and oppositions of opinion,—amidst the passion which sets men's wits to work to conceive of and propose all imaginable motives and results, what an abundance of light is struck out! From a crowd of falsehoods, what a revelation we have of the truth, which no one man, nor party of men, could reveal!—of the wants, wishes, and ideas of every class or coterie of society that can speak for itself, and of some that cannot!

Observe the process to which all this conduces. Before we were laid aside, we read, as everybody read, philosophical histories, in which the progress of society was presented; we read of the old times, when the chieftain, whatever his title, dwelt in the castle on the steep, while his retainers were housed in a cluster of dwellings under the shadow of his protection. We read of the indispensable function of the Priest, in the castle, and of the rise of his order;

and then of the Lawyer and *his* order. We read of the origin of Commerce, beginning in monopoly; and then of the gradual admission of more and more parties to the privileges of trade, and their settling themselves in situations favourable for the purpose, and apart from the head monopolists. We read of the indispensable function of the Merchant, and the rise of *his* order. We read of the feuds and wars of the aristocratic orders, which, while fatally weakening them, left leisure for the middle and lower classes to rise and grow, and strengthen themselves, till the forces of society were shifted, and its destinies presented a new aspect. We read of the sure, though sometimes intermitting, advance of popular interests, and reduction of aristocratic power and privileges, throughout the general field of civilisation. We read of all these things, and assented to what seemed so very clear — so distinct an interpretation of what had happened up to our own day. At the same time, busy and involved as we were in the interests of the day, how little use did we make of the philosophic retrospect, which might and should have been prophetic! You, I think, dreaded in every popular movement a whirlwind of destruction — in every popular success a sentence of the dissolution of society. You believed that such a man, or such a set of men, could give stability to our condition, and fix us, for an unassignable time, at the point of the last settlement, or what you assumed to be the latest. I, meanwhile, believed that our safety or peril, for a term, depended on the event of this or that movement, the carrying of this or that question. I was not guilty of fearing political ruin. I did with constancy believe in the certain advance of popular interests, and demolition of all injurious power held by the few; but I believed that more depended on single questions than was really involved in such, and that separate measures would be more comprehensive and complete than a dispassionate observer thinks possible. In the midst of all this, you and I were taken apart; and have not our eyes been opened to perceive, in the action of society, the continuation of the history we read so long ago? I need scarcely allude to the progress of popular interests, and the unequalled rapidity with which some great questions are approaching to a settlement. We have a stronger tendency to speculate on the movements of the minds engaged in the transaction of affairs, than on the rate of advance of the affairs themselves. With much that is mortifying and sad, and something that is amusing, how much is there instructive! And how clear, as in a bird's-eye view of a battle, or as in the analysis of a wise speculative philosopher, is the process!

We see everybody that is busy doing what we did—overrating the immediate object. There is no sin in this, and no harm, however it proves incessantly the fallibility of human judgments. It is ordered by Him who constituted our minds and our duties, that our business of the hour should be magnified by the operation of our powers upon it. Without this, nothing would ever be done; for every man's energy is no more than sufficient for his task; and there would be a fatal abatement of energy, if a man saw his present employment in the proportion in which it must afterwards appear to other affairs,—the limitation and weakness of our powers causing us to apprehend feebly the details of what we see, when we endeavour to be comprehensive in our views. The truth seems to lie in a point of view different from either. I doubt whether it is possible for us to overrate the positive importance of what we are doing, though we are continually exaggerating its value in relation to other objects of our own, while it seems pretty certain that we entertain an inadequate estimate of interests that we have dismissed, to make room for new ones.

Next, we see the present operation of old liberalising causes so strong as to be irresistible; men of all parties—or, at least, reasonable men of all parties—so carried along by the current of events, that it is scarcely now a question with any one what is the point towards which the vessel of the State is to be carried next, but how she is to be most safely steered amidst the perils which beset an ordained course. One party mourns that no great political hero rises up to retard the speed to a rate of safety; and another party mourns that no great political hero presents himself to increase while guiding our speed by the inspiration of his genius; while there are a few tranquil observers who believe that, glorious as would be the advent of a great political hero at any time, we could never better get on without one, because never before were principles so clearly and strongly compelling their own adoption, and working out their own results. They are now the masters, and not the servants, of Statesmen; and inestimable as would be the boon of a great individual will, which should work in absolute congeniality with these powers, we may trust, for our safety and progress, in their dominion over all lesser wills.

Next, we perceive, (and we ask whether some others can be as blind to it as they appear to be,) that a great change has taken place in the morals—at least, in the conventional morals, of Statesmanship. Consistency was once; and not long ago, a primary virtue in a Statesman,—consistency, not only in general principle and aims, through a whole public life, but in views of particular questions. Now it has become far otherwise. The incurable bigots of political society are the only living politicians, except a very small number of so-called ultra-liberals, who can boast of unchanged views. Perhaps every public man of sense and honour has changed his opinions, on more or fewer questions, since he entered public life. It cannot be otherwise in a period of transition, in a monarchy where the popular element is rising, and the rulers are selected from the privileged classes alone. The virtue of such functionaries now is, not that their opinions remain stationary, and that their views remain consistent through a whole life, but that they can live and learn.

And there are two ways of doing this—two kinds of men who do it. One kind of man has all his life believed that certain popular principles are for the good of society; he now learns to extend this faith to measures which he once thought ultra and dangerous, and embraces these measures with an earnest heart, for their own value. Another sort of man has predilections opposed to these measures, laments their occurrence, and wishes the old state of affairs could have been preserved; but he sees that it is impossible,—he sees the strength of the national will, and the tendency of events so united with these measures, that there is peril in resistance. He thinks it a duty to make a timely proposal and grant of them, rather than endanger the general allegiance and tranquillity by delay, refusal, or conflict.

Now, though we may have our preferences in regard to such public men, we cannot impute guilt to either kind. We see that it is unjust to impute moral or political sin in either case. The great point of interest to you and me is to observe how such new necessities and methods work in society.

The incurables of the privileged classes of course act after their kind. They are full of astonishment and feeble rage. The very small number of really philosophical liberals — once ultras, but now nearly overtaken by the times — see tranquilly the fulfilment of their anticipations, and anticipate still — how wisely, time will show. Of the two intermediate parties, the question is, which appears most able to live and learn? From the start the liberals had originally, it would seem that they must hold the more dignified position of the two. But, judging them out of their own mouths, what can we think and say?

To us it appears a noble thing to apprehend truth early, not merely as a guess, but as a ground of opinion and action. A man who is capable of this is secure that his opinions will be embraced by more and more minds, till they become the universal belief of men. It is natural to him to feel satisfaction as the fellowship spreads — both because fellowship is pleasant to himself, and because the hour thereby draws nearer and nearer for society to be fully blessed with the truth which was early apparent to him. When this truth becomes indisputable and generally diffused, and its related action takes place, his satisfaction should be complete.

What an exception to this natural process, this healthy enjoyment, do we witness in the political transactions of the time! Whatever may be thought of the consistency of the most rapidly progressive party, what can be said of the philosophy of the more early liberal? At every advance of their former opponents, they are exasperated. They fight for every tardily-apprehended political truth as for a private property. They not only complain — "You thought the contrary in such a year!" "Here are the words you spoke in such a year; the reverse of what you say now!" but they cry, on every declaration of conversion to one of their long-avowed opinions, "Hands off! That is *my* truth; I got it so many years ago, and you shan't touch it!" To you and me (to whom it is much the same thing to look back and to look abroad), it irresistibly occurs to ask whether it was thus in former transition-states of society; whether, for instance, assured and long-avowed Christians exclaimed, on occasion of the conversion of enlightened heathens — "You extolled Jupiter in such a year, and now you disparage him." "Remember what you said of Diana no longer ago than such a year!" "Do you think we shall admit you to our Christ? He is ours these ten years!" Those of us who believe and feel that the development of moral science (of which political is one department) is as progressive as that of physical, cannot but glance at the aspect of such conduct in relation to the discovery of a new chemical agency, or important heavenly body; and then ... But enough of such illustration. Nobody doubts the absurdity, when fairly set down; though the number of grown men who have, within three years, committed it daily in newspapers, clubs, markets, and the Houses of Parliament, is so great as to be astonishing, till we discern the causes, proximate and final, of such unphilosophical discourse and demeanour.

While in this conflict grave and responsible leaders grow factious — while men of purpose forget their march onward in sideskirmishes — while reformers lose sight of the imperishable quality of their cause, and talk of hopeless corruption and inevitable destruction — how do affairs appear to us, in virtue merely of our being out of the strife?

We see that large principles are more extensively agreed upon than ever before — more manifest to all eyes, from the very absence of a hero to work them, since they are every hour showing how irresistibly they are making their own way. We see that the tale of the multitude is told as it never was told before — their health, their minds and morals, pleaded for in a tone perfectly new in the world. We see that the dreadful sins and woes of society are the results of old causes, and that our generation has the honor of being responsible for their relief, while the disgrace of their existence belongs, certainly not to our time, and perhaps to none. We see that no spot of earth ever before contained such an amount of infallible resources as our own country at this day; so much knowledge, so much sense, so much vigour, foresight, and benevolence, or such an amount of external means. We see the progress of amelioration, silent but sure, as the shepherd on the upland sees in the valley the advance of a gush of sunshine from between two hills. He observes what the people below are too busy to mark: how the light attains now this object and now that — how it now embellishes yonder copse, and now gilds that stream, and now glances upon the roofs of the far-off hamlet — the signs and sounds of life quickening along its course. When we remember that this is the same sun that guided the first vessels of commerce over the sea—the same by whose light Magna Charta was signed in Runnymede[1]—that shone in the eyes of Cromwell after Naseby[2] fight—that rose on 800,000 free blacks in the West Indies on a certain August morning[3] —and is now shining down into the dreariest recesses of the coal-mine, the prison, and the cellar—how can we doubt that darkness is to be chased away, and God's sunshine to vivify, at last, the whole of our world?

Is it necessary, some may ask, to be sick, and apart, to see and believe these things? Events seem to show that for some—for many—sequestration from affairs is necessary to this end; for there are not a few who, in the hubbub of party, have let go their faith, and have not to this moment found it again. If there are some in the throng who can at once act and anticipate faithfully, we may thank God for the blessing. But they are sadly few.

I have said how clearly appears to us the fact and the reason of every man's exaggerating at the moment the importance of the work under his hand. Not less clear is the ordination, as old and as continuous as human action, by which men fail, more or less, of obtaining their express objects, while all manner of unexpected good arises in a collateral way. It is usual to speak of the results of the labors of alchemists in this view, everybody seeing that while we still pick out our gold from the ground, we owe much to the alchemists that they never thought of. But the same is true of almost every object of human pursuit, and even of belief. No doubt we invalids keep up our likeness to our kind, in this respect, as far as we are able to act at all; but we have more time than others to contemplate the working of the plan on a large scale. Look at the projects, the discoveries, the quackeries of the day!

With regard to the projects, however, I am at present disposed

---

1 Signed on the Island of Runnymede in 1215, the Magna Charta sought to prohibit arbitrary royal acts and to distinguish between kingship and tyranny. However limited its success, it symbolizes sovereignty of the rule of law.

2 Decisive battle of the English Civil War, fought on 14 June 1645 and won by Cromwell's forces.

3 Martineau likely refers to the establishment of the first black republic in Haiti after the revolt against Napoleon led by Toussaint L'Ouverture in the 1790s. Toussaint L'Ouverture is the subject of Martineau's book *The Hour and the Man* (1841), also written during her sickroom years at Tynemouth.

to make one partial exception—to acknowledge, as far as I can at present see, one case of singularity. I mean with regard to the New Postage.[1] The general rule proves true in one half of it, that many great and yet unascertained benefits are arising, of which the projector did not dream; so that a volume might be filled with anecdotes, curious to the spectator and delightful to the benevolent. But, thus far, it does not appear that any fallacy has mixed itself with the express expectations of the projector. I do not speak of the failure of his efforts to get his whole plan adopted. That will soon be a matter of small account—a disappointment and vexation gone by—a temporary trial of patience, forgotten except by the record. I mean that he has advanced no propositions which he does not seem perfectly able to prove, uttered no promises which do not appear certain to be fulfilled. This project is perhaps the noblest afloat in our country and time, considering the moral interests it involves. It is, perhaps, scarcely possible to exaggerate the force and extent of its civilising and humanising influences, especially in regard to its spreading the spirit of Home over all the occupations and interests of life, in defiance of the separating powers of distance and poverty; and it will be curious if this enterprise, besides keeping the school-child at his mother's bosom, the apprentice, the governess, and the maid-servant, at their father's hearth—and us sick or aged people entertained daily with the flowers, music, books, sentiment and news of the world we have left—should prove an exception to all others in performing all its express promises. At present, I own, this appears no matter of doubt.

As for the discoveries or quackeries of the time, (and who will undertake to say in what instances they are not, sooner or later, compounded?) how clear is the collateral good, whatever may be the express failure? Those who receive all the sayings of the Coryphæus of the phrenologists, and those who laugh at his maps of the mind and his so-called ethics, must both admit that much knowledge of the structure of the brain, much wise care of

---

1 In 1840 the "penny post" was established; this uniform mail service was considerably less expensive than the previous system, enabling the sender to purchase postage stamps per letter, and charging the same rate for all domestic letters.

human health and faculties, has issued from the pursuit, for the benefit of man.[1] This Mesmerism again: who believes that it could be revived, again and again at intervals of centuries, if there were not something in it? Who looks back upon the mass of strange but authenticated historical narratives, which might be explained by this agent, and looks, at the same time, into our dense ignorance of the structure and functions of the nervous system, and will dare to say that there is nothing in it? Whatever quackery and imposture may be connected with it, however its pretensions may be falsified, it seems impossible but that some new insight must be obtained by its means, into the powers of our mysterious frame — some fixing down under actual cognizance, of flying and floating notions, full of awe, which have exercised the belief and courage of many wise, for many centuries.

After smiling over old books all our lives, on meeting with quaint assumptions of Humoral pathology as true,[2] while we supposed it exploded — behold it arising again! One cannot open a newspaper, scarcely a letter, without seeing something about the Water-Cure;[3] and grave doctors, who will listen to nothing the laity can say of anything new, (any more than they would tolerate the mention of the circulation of the blood in Harvey's day,[4])now intimate that the profession are disposed to believe that there is more in the humoral pathology than was thought thirty years ago, though not so much as the water-curers presume. Is it not pretty certain, then, that something will come of this rage for the water-cure, (something more than ablution, temperance, and exercise,) though its professors must be embalmed as quacks in the literature of the time? Is there not still another operation of the same prin-

---

1   Coryphaeus was the leader of the Greek chorus. Martineau means the chief authority on phrenology, one who might speak for the whole field. Phrenology, quite popular in Martineau's day, refers to the study of the skull's shape and surface for an understanding of a person's mental faculties and character.

2   Theory that the key to health is the balance of four substances in the body, or humors — i.e., blood, yellow bile, black bile, and phlegm.

3   The "water cure" refers to hydropathy, a therapeutic system in vogue in early Victorian England that sought to cure disease and debility by capitalizing on the supposed medicinal benefits of bathing in and drinking water.

4   William Harvey (1578-1657), the British physician who discovered the circulation of blood through the body.

ciple involved in the case? Are we not growing sensibly more merciful, more wisely humane towards empirics themselves, when they cease to be our oracles? Are we not learning, from their jumbled discoveries and failures, that empiricism itself is a social function, indispensable, made so by God, however ready we may be to bestow our cheap laughter upon it? To us retired observers of life there is too much of this easy mockery for our taste, or for the morals of society. Ours seems to be an age when it is to the credit of others, besides statesmen, that they can live and learn; and there is no getting on in our learning without empiricism. It is less wise than easy to ridicule its connection with non-essential modes and appearances prescribed or suggested by the passions, needs, or follies of the time. It is most wise, and should be easy, to have faith that the determining conditions of all experimental discovery will be ascertained in due season. If, meanwhile, we can obtain from the magnetisers any light as to any function of the nervous system, we may excuse them from the performance of some promised feats.[1] If the Homœopathists can help us to any new principle of natural antagonism to disease, they may well abide the laugh which I am not aware that the serious of their number have ever provoked by any extreme and unsupported pretensions.[2]

But at this rate, occupying this scope, I shall never have done. I might write on for every day of my life, and be no nearer the end of our speculations. Let what I have said go for specimens of our observation of life in two or three particulars. When I think of what I have seen with my own eyes from one back window, in the few years of my illness; of how indescribably clear to me are many truths of life from my observation of the doings of the tenants of a single row of houses; it seems to me scarcely necessary to see more than the smallest sample, in order to analyze life in its

---

1   Martineau here refers to mesmerism, a form of hypnotism believed to involve animal magnetism. Mesmerism takes its name from an Austrian physician F.A. Mesmer (1733-1815). Martineau's *Letters on Mesmerism* (1845), written shortly after *Life in the Sick-Room*, testify to her belief in the powers of mesmerism to cure.

2   Homeopathy is a system of medical practice that treats disease using small doses of medicine that would produce the disease in a healthy person. It was one of several unorthodox medical responses to widespread over-drugging in the first half of the nineteenth century.

entireness. I could fill a volume—and an interesting one too—with a simple detail of what I have witnessed, as I said, from one back-window. But I must tell nothing. These two or three little courts and gardens ought to be as sacred as any interior. Nothing of the spy shall mix itself with my relation to neighbours who have ever been kind to me. Suffice it, that if I saw no further into the world with the mental than with the bodily eye, I should be kept in a state of perpetual wonder, (of pleasing wonder, on the whole,) at the operation of the human heart and mind, in its most ordinary circumstances. Nothing can be more ordinary than the modes of life which I overlook, yet am I kept wide awake in my watch by ever new instances of the fulness of pleasure derivable from the scantiest sources; of the vividness of emotion excitable by the most trifling incidents; of the wonderful power pride has of pampering itself upon the most meagre food; and, above all, of the infinite ingenuity of human love. Nothing, perhaps, has impressed me so deeply as the clear view I have of almost all, if not quite the whole, of the suffering I have witnessed being the consequence of vice or ignorance. But when my heart has sickened at the sight, and at the thought of so much gratuitous pain, it has grown strong again in the reflection that, if unnecessary, this misery is temporary,—that the true ground of mourning would be if the pain were not from causes which are remediable. Then I cannot but look forward to the time when the bad training of children,—the petulancies of neighbours—the errors of the ménage—the irksome superstitions, and the seductions of intemperance, shall all have been annihilated by the spread of intelligence, while the mirth at the minutest jokes—the proud plucking of nosegays—the little neighborly gifts, (less amusing hereafter, perhaps, in their taste)—the festal observances—the disinterested and refined acts of self-sacrifice and love, will remain as long as the human heart has mirth in it, or a humane complacency and self-respect,—as long as its essence is what it has ever been, "but a little lower than the angels."[1]

How is it possible to give an idea of what the gradual disclosure of the fates of individuals is to us? In reading chronicles, and

---

[1] Psalms 8:5.

the lighter kinds of history, we have all found ourselves eagerly watching the course of love and domestic life, and pausing over the winding up, at death, of the lot of personages whose mere names were all the interest we began with. To us, in the monotony of our lives, it seems as if other people's lives slipped away with the rapidity with which we read a book, while the interest we feel is that of personal knowledge. It is as if Time himself were present unseen, whispering to us of a new kindled love,— of marriage, with all its details of "pomp and circumstance;" and then comes the deeper social interest,— the opening of a glimpse into the vista of new generations, while all around the other interests of life are transacting, and the children we knew at their parents' knees are abroad in the world, acting for themselves, and putting a hand to the destinies of society.

Of all the announcements made in the silence of our solitude, none are so striking as those of deaths, familiar as the thought of death is to us, and natural as our own death would appear to ourselves, and to everybody. To present witnesses, and in the midst of the activity of life, the spectacle of death loses half its force. It is we who feel the awful beauty of it, when the great Recorder intimates to us that they who were strenuous in mutual conflict have lain down side by side; that to old age its infirmities matter no longer, as the body itself is surrendered; that the weary spirit of care is at rest, and that the most active affections and occupations of life have been brought to a sudden close. Many young and busy persons wish, as I used to wish, that Time would be prophet as well as watchman. On New Year's Eves, such long to divine how many, and who of those they know, will be smitten and withdrawn during the coming year. We, in our solitude, do not desire to forestal the unrolling of the scroll. To ponder the register of the year's deaths at its close, is enough for us, to whom our seclusion serves for all purposes of speculation. While we are waiting, every year conveys away before us the infant, (a new immortality created before our eyes); the busy citizen, or indispensable mother, (showing how much more important in the eye of God is it what we are than what we do;) the young maiden, full of sympathy, (perhaps for us,) and of hope; and the aged, full of years, but perhaps not less of life. Such is the register of every year at its close.

To us, whose whole life is sequestered,—who see nothing of the events of which we hear so much, or see them only as gleam or shadow passing along our prison-walls, there is something indescribably affecting in the act of regarding History, Life, and Speculation as one. All are enhanced to us by their melting into each other. History becomes like actual life; life becomes comprehensive as history, and abstract as speculation. Not only does human life, from the cradle to the grave, lie open to us, but the whole succession of generations, without the boundary line of the past being interposed: and with the very clouds of the future so thinned,—rendered so penetrable, as that we believe we discern the salient and bright points of the human destiny yet to be revealed.

It would be impossible to set down, within any moderate limits, notices of changes in the Modes of life,—modes arising from progressive civilisation, and deeply affecting morals;—but there is one branch of one great change, which I will mention, as it bears a relation to the morals of the sick-room.

We all know how the present action of our new civilization works to the impairing of Privacy. As new discoveries are causing all-penetrating physical lights so to abound as that, as has been said, we shall soon not know where in the world to get any darkness, so our new facilities for every sort of communication work to reduce privacy much within its former limits. There are some limits, however, which ought to be preserved with vigilance and care, as indispensable, not only to comfort, but to some of the finest virtues and graces of mind and life.

It is to be hoped that the privacy of *vivâ voce* conversation will ever remain sacred: but it is known that that which ought to be as holy, that of epistolary correspondence,—(the private conversation of distant friends,) is constantly and deliberately violated, where there are certain inducements to do so. The press works so diligently and beneficially for society at large, that there is a tendency to commit everything to it, on utilitarian considerations of a rather coarse kind: and the moment it can be made out that the publication of anything will and may do some ostensible good, the thing is published,—whatever considerations of a different or a higher sort may lie behind. If the people of note in society were inquired of, they would say that the privilege—the right—of privacy of epistolary correspondence now exists only for the obscure;—and for them, only till some person meets them whose zeal for the public good leads him to lay hold on all material by which anybody may be supposed likely to learn anything. As for people of note,—their letters are naturally preserved by the recipients: when the writer dies, these recipients are plied with entreaties and remonstrances,—placed in a position of cruel difficulty (as it is to many) between their delicacy of affection for the deceased, and the pain of being made responsible for intercepting his fame, and depriving society of the benefit of the disclosure of his living mind.

Under this state of things, what happens? Some destroy, through life, all the letters they receive, but those on business. Some, with an agonising heart, burn them after the writer's death, to escape the requisitions of executors. Many, alas! resign their privilege of freedom of epistolary speech, and write no letters which any one would care to preserve for an hour. Some call in their own letters;—a painful process, both to writer and receivers. Of such as do not care what becomes of their letters, there is no need to say anything. Their feelings require no consideration, for their letters cannot be of a private,—nor, therefore, of the most valuable kind. The misery of the liability is in regard to letters of affection and confidence,—letters which the writer could no more bear to see again than to have notes taken of the out-pourings of his heart in an hour of confidence. It is too certain that many such letters are now never written which crave to be so: and it is much to be feared that some letters, purporting to be private, are written with a view to ultimate publication; and thus the receiver is insulted, or there is a sacrifice of honesty all round.

I do not see any probability of a dearth of biographies. I believe that there will always be interest enough in human life and character to secure a sufficiency of records of individuals: — that there will always be enough of persons whose letters are not of a very private kind,—always enough of provided and exceptional cases to serve society with a sufficiency of biography, of a duly analytical kind. But if I did not believe this,—if I believed that the choice lay between a sacrifice of the completest order of biography and that of the inviolability of private epistolary correspondence, I could not hesitate for a moment. I would keep the old and precious privacy,—the inestimable right of every one who has a friend and can write to him;—I would keep our written confidence from being made biographical material, as anxiously as I would keep our spoken conversation from being noted down for the good of society. I would keep the power of free speech under all the influences of life and fate,—and leave Biography to exist or perish.

And pretty sure it is of existence. It has, for its material, the life and actions of all men and women of note;—their printed and otherwise public writings and sayings;—the recollections of those who knew them; and, in no small number of cases, material which, however we may wonder at, we have only to take and be thankful for. A Doddridge keeps a copy of every letter or note he ever wrote, labelled and put by for posthumous use.[1] A D'Arblay spends her last hours in elaborating her revelations of the transactions, private and public, of her day; and revises, for publication, the expressions of fondness and impulse, written to sisters and other intimates, long dead.[2] A Rousseau here and there gives more. One way and another, the resources of biography are secure enough, without encroachment on a sacred process of intercourse. Biography will never fail. Would that we were all equally secure of a higher matter,—our right of freedom of epistolary speech!

"But when all are dead,—and nobody concerned remains to be hurt?" remonstrates one. The reply is, that as long as people of note, who love their friends, remain, there are some left to be concerned and injured.

"But," says another, "would you object to do good, after your death, by your letters being published?" The reply is that, in the supposition, I see an enormous sacrifice of a higher and greater good to a lower and smaller. No letters, in any number and of any quality,—if they exhibited all the wisdom of Solomon, and all the graces of the Queen of Sheba, could do so much good as a single

---

1 Martineau probably refers here to Philip Doddridge (1702-51), a celebrated hymn writer. Her *Miscellanies* refer to *The Correspondence and Diary of Philip Doddridge, DD.*

2 Frances D'Arblay (1752-1840), married name of the novelist Fanny Burney.

clear and strong protest against the preservation of strictly private letters for biographical material.

"But," says another, "had you not better leave the matter to the discretion of survivors? Surely you can trust your executors;— surely you can trust the friends who will survive you." The reply is — when this critical state of our morals is past, no doubt executors may be trusted about letters, as about other matters. But the very point of the case is that its morality is not yet ascertained by those who do not suffer under the liability, and have not fellow-feeling with those who do. My executors may very sincerely think it their duty to publish my most private letters,—and even to be now laying them by in order for the purpose: while I feel that, once aroused to a view of the liability, I could more innocently leave to the discretion of survivors the disposition of lands and money than that of my private utterances to my friends. In a case of differing or opposing views of duty,—if my own is clear and stringent, I cannot innocently leave the matter to the chance of other persons' convictions. There cannot be a more strictly personal duty, and I must do it myself.

I have, therefore, done it. Having made the discovery of the preservation of my letters for purposes of publication hereafter, I have ascertained my own legal rights, and acted upon them. I have adopted legal precautions against the publication of my private letters;—I have made it a condition of my confidential correspondence that my letters shall not be preserved: and I have been indulged by my friends, generally, with an acquiescence in my request that my entire correspondence, except such as relates to business, shall be destroyed. Of course, I do as I would be done by. The privacy I claim for myself, I carefully guard for others. I keep no letters of a private and passing nature. I know that others are thinking and acting with me. We enjoy, by this provision, a freedom and fullness of epistolary correspondence which could not possibly exist if the press loomed in the distance, or executors' eyes were known to be in wait hereafter. Our correspondence has all the flow and lightness of the most secret talk. This is a present reward, and a rich one, for the effort and labor of making our views and intentions understood. But it is not our only reward. We perceive that we have fixed attention upon what is becoming an important point of Morals: and we feel, in our inmost hearts, that we have done what we could to guard from encroachment an important right, and from destruction a precious privilege. This may appear a strange statement to persons whose privacy is safe in their obscurity. Those who know in their own experience the liabilities of fame, will understand, and deeply feel, what I have said.

I have mentioned above, that, to us in seclusion, History, Life, and Speculation, assume a continuity such as would not have been believed possible by ourselves in former days, when they appeared to constitute departments of study as separate as moral studies can be. It would be curious and interesting to an observer of the human mind, to pass from retreat to retreat, and watch the progress of this fusion of objects; to see the formerly busy member of society — "the practical man," — growing speculative in his turn of thought; the speculative writer nourishing more and more of an antiquarian taste; and the antiquary finding seclusion serve as well as the passage of ages, and viewing the modes and instruments of the life of to-day with the eye and the gusto of the antiquary of ten centuries hence.

And not only in their studies would men of such differing tastes be found to be brought together under the influences of sequestration from the world. There are matters of moral perception and taste in which they would draw near no less remarkably. The one conspicuous, undying humanity, which is the soul of all the forms of life that they contemplate, must be, to all, the sun of their intellectual day, beneath whose penetrating light all adventitious distinctions melt into insignificance. Distinctions of rank, for instance, become attenuated to a previously inconceivable degree. To the antiquary, as well as to the most radical speculator, there would be little more in the sovereign entering the sick room than any other stranger whom kindness might bring. It requires that we should live in the midst of the arrangements of society, that our conventional ideas should be nourished by daily associations, in order to keep up even the remembrance of differences of hereditary rank, so overpowering in our view are the great interests of life which are common to all,— Duty, Thought, Love, Joy, Sorrow, and Death.

If the sovereign were to enter our rooms, there would be strong interests and affections connected with her, but interests relating to her responsibilities and her destinies, and scarcely at all to her rank—to the singularity, and not the exaltation, of her position.[1] It is a strong doubt to me, whether one of high degree, placed in our circumstances, could long retain aristocratic ideas and tendencies; whether to the proudest noble, shut up in his chamber for five years, the cottage child he sees from his window, the footboy who brings his fuel, must not necessarily become as imposing to his imagination and his heart as the young princes of the blood.

Something of the same process takes place, even with regard to the distinctions of intellectual nobility. As for the nothingness of literary fame, amidst the stress of personal trial (except in the collateral benefits it brings), an hour in the sick-room might convince the most superstitious worshipper of celebrity. As for the rest; in the presence of the general ignorance, on the brink of that black abyss, our best lights are really so ineffectual, that it is impossible to pride ourselves on our intellectual differences, ranging merely as from the torch to the farthing candle.

In truth, in our retreat, moral considerations are all in all. Moral distinctions are the chief; and moral interests, common to all, are supreme. They are so from their essential nature; and they are so to us especially, from the singular advantage of our position for seeing their beauty, and the abundance of it. We could make known—what is little suspected by busy stirrers in the world, and wholly disbelieved by despondent moralists who dwell amidst its apparent confusion—that there is a deep heaven lying inclosed in the very centre of society, and a genuine divinity residing in the heart of every member of it, which might, if we would but recognise it, check our longing to leave the present scene, to search for God and heaven elsewhere. All that is most frivolous and insignificant is ever most noisy and obtrusive; all that is most wicked is most boastful and audacious; all that is worst in men, and society, has a tendency to come uppermost; and thus the most superficial observers of life are the most despondent. Meantime, whatever is holy, pure, and peaceable, works silently and unremittingly; and while turbulent passions are exhausting themselves before the eyes of men, a calm and perpetual renovation is spreading outwards from the central heart of humanity. I have the image

---

1   Queen Victoria (1837-1901).

before my eyes at this moment—the awful type of the blessed reality—in the tossing sea, which the neighbors dare hardly look upon. It rages and rolls, it dashes the drift-wood on the shore, and heavy squalls come driving over it, like messengers of dismay. At this very instant, how calm are its depths! There light dwells, as long as there is light in heaven; and there is no end to the treasures of beauty on which it shines. If it be a fable that there are happy beings dwelling there, basking and singing, unconscious of the tempests overhead, it is certainly true that it is thus in the upper world, of which the ocean is a type. It is true, as a friend said to me, that "the dark is full of beautiful things." Without an image, speaking in the plainest and most absolute terms, the least known parts of human life are full of moral beauty. I am fully persuaded, that, if we wish to extend and confirm our ideas of heaven, we should not wander back and afar to the old Eden, or forward and upward to some bright star of the firmament, but we should look into the retired places of our own actual world, of our own country, of our own town and village. We should look into the faces to be met in the street every day; we should look round by the light of our common sun. However, my immediate business is to say that we, who are not abroad in the streets, and cannot go in bodily presence into the by-places of life, have more of this heaven disclosed to us than others, because we appear to need it more. If any one of us could and might tell what we know of the good of human hearts, the heavenly deeds of human hands, the desponding would hang their heads no longer with fear, but with shame for their fear. If I alone might make a record of the heavenly aspects which have been presented in this one room, such a record would extinguish all revilings of man and of life. And when I think that what has appeared to me must, in natural course, have appeared to all my companions in infirmity, when I gather into one all these revelations of the real moral life of society, I perceive that, till death satisfies us in regard to a local heaven, we may well be satisfied with that which lies all around about us—not mute, while tender and pitying voices speak to us; nor wholly unseen, while tearful or kindling eyes meet our own.

Thus, in some few of its leading aspects, does Life appear to the invalid.

CHAPTER FIVE

DEATH TO THE INVALID

"To smell a turf of fresh earth is wholesome for the body: no
less are the thoughts of mortality cordial to the soul."

Fuller.[1]

"And yet as angels, in some brighter dreams,
   Call to the soul when man doth sleep,
So some strange thoughts transcend our wonted themes,
   And into glory peep."

Henry Vaughan.[2]

WHAT subject is so interesting to the full of life as that of death?
What taste is so universal in childhood and youth as that for
learning all that can be known of the thoughts and feelings of the
dying? Did we not all, in our young days, turn to the death part in
all biographies; to the death articles in all cyclopædias; to the discourses on sickness and death in all sermon books; to the prayers
in the prospect of death in all books of devotion? Do not the
most common-place writers of fiction crowd their novels with
death scenes, and indifferent tragedy writers kill off almost all
their characters? Do not people crowd to executions; and do not
those who stay at home learn all they can of the last words and
demeanour of the sufferers? Are not the visions of heroic children, (and of many grown children), chiefly about pain and a
noble departure? Is there any curiosity more lively than that
which we all feel about the revelations of persons resuscitated
from drowning? Is it not their nearer position to death which
makes sick persons so awful to children who are not familiar with
them,—so interesting a subject of speculation to all? How is it
then with the invalids themselves?

Nothing need be said here of short, sharp, fatal illness. Most of

---

1   Thomas Fuller (1608-61), "The Virtuous Lady."
2   Henry Vaughan (1621-95), "They are All Gone Into the World of Light" (1650).

us know that short, sharp illnesses, not fatal, have not enlightened us much in regard to death and its appropriate feelings. Either pain or exhaustion usually causes, in such cases, an apathy which leaves nothing to be remembered or revealed. I was once told by a child, after some hours of exhausting pain, what she had over-heard below,—that if some contingency, which she specified, did not arise, I should die before night. I fully believed it; and I felt nothing, unless it were some wonder at feeling nothing. Almost every person has a similar anecdote to tell; and there remains only the short and pregnant moral, that all preparations for leaving this life, and entering on the next, should be made while the body is well and the spirit alive.

But how does death appear to those who rest half-way between it and life, or are very gradually passing over from one to the other?

Much depends, of course, on how far the vital forces are impaired—on whether the condition be such as to obscure or to purify the spiritual vision. If we want to know the effect of near-ness and realization, and not the pathology of the case, we must suppose the vital powers to remain faithful, however they may be weakened.

In such cases, I imagine the views of death remain much what they were before, though they must necessarily become more interesting, and the conception of them more clear. I know of no case of any one who before believed, or took for granted, a future life, who began to disbelieve or doubt it through sickness. I have known cases of those who disbelieved it in health, seeing no rea-son to change their opinion on the approach of death,—being content to have lived—satisfied to leave life when its usefulness and pleasantness are gone—not desiring a renewal of it, but ready to awake again at the word of their Creator, if indeed a further existence be in reserve for them. Such cases I have known: but none of a material change of views in the prospect of death.

To me, the presumption of the inextinguishable vitality of the spirit afforded by the experience of material decay, is the strongest I am acquainted with. No amount of evidence of any fact before the reason, no demonstration of any truth to the understanding, affords to me such a sense of certainty as the action of the spirit yields, with regard to its own immortality, at times when there can be no deception from animal spirits, or from immediate sympathy with other minds, or from what is called the natural desire for life. It is a mistake to say, as is frequently said, that, with regard to a future life, "the wish is father to the thought,"[1] always or generally. Long-suffering invalids can tell that there are seasons, neither few nor short, when the wishes are all the other way,— when life is so oppressive to the frame that the happiest news would be that we should soon be non-existent,— when, thankful as we are that our beloved friends, the departed and the remaining, are to live for evermore with God, and enjoy his universe and its intercourses, we should be glad to decline it for ourselves, and to lie down in an eternal, unbroken rest. At these seasons, when, though we *know* all that can be said of renewed powers and relish, and a more elevated and privileged life beyond the grave, we cannot *feel* it; and, while admitting all such consolations as truth, we cannot enjoy them, but, as a mere matter of inclination, had rather resign our privileges;—in these seasons, when the wish would be father to an opposite thought, the belief in our immortality is at the strongest; the truth of our inability to die becomes overwhelming, and the sleep of the grave appears too light to satisfy our need of rest. I believe it to be owing to this natural and unconquerable belief in our immortality, that suicide is not more common than it is among sufferers. I am persuaded that the almost intolerable weariness of long sicknesses, unrelieved by occasional fits of severe pain, would impel many to put out a hand to the laudanum-bottle, in hours when religious considerations and emotions cannot operate through the indisposition of the frame, if it were not for the intense conviction that life would not thus be extinguished, nor even suspended. I do not believe much in the "natural love of life,"[2] which is usually said to be the preventive in such cases. I do believe in the vast operation of religious affections in withholding from the act: but I also believe in frequent instances of abstinence from death, from a mere despair of getting rid of life—a sense of necessary immortality.

---

1 Aeschylus (525?-456 BC), *Prometheus Bound*.
2 Martineau may possibly refer here to *Gulliver's Travels* (1726) by Jonathan Swift (1667-1745).

I have spoken of the relief afforded by visitations of severe pain. These rally the vital forces, and dismiss the temptation, by substituting torture for weariness—at times a welcome change. The healthy are astonished at the good spirits of sufferers under tormenting complaints; and the most strait-laced preachers of fortitude and patience admit an occasional wonder that there is no suicide among that class of sufferers. The truth is, however, that the influence of acute pain, when only occasional, and not extremely protracted, is vivifying and cheering on the whole. The immediate anguish causes a temporary despair: but the reaction, when the pain departs, causes a relish of life such as the healthy and the gay hardly enjoy. Though a slow death by a torturing disease is a lot unspeakably awful to meet, and even to contemplate, there can be no question to the experience, that illness in which severe pain sometimes occurs is less trying than some in which a different kind of suffering is not relieved by such a stimulus and its consequent sensations.

Thus much it is useful to know,—useful to the student of human nature, to the nurse, and to a sufferer under sentence of lasting disease. But instances have been known, perplexing to those inexperienced in pain, of devout thankfulness for the suffering itself, under its immediate and agonizing pressure; and this in men far superior to the superstition of believing present pain the purchase-money of future ease,—the fine paid down here for admission to heavenly benefits hereafter.

Strange as this rejoicing in misery may appear, it is to some minds as natural and authorised by the laws of our being, as the joy which attends the acquisition of a great idea, or the verification of a potent truth. It is as verification that such pain is welcome. To men of the most spiritual tone of mind, every attestation of the reality of unseen objects is a boon of the highest order; and no such attestation can surpass in clearness that which is afforded by the sensible progress of decay in the material part of the sufferer's frame. All attempt at description is here vain. Nothing but experience can convey a conception of the intense reality in which God appears supreme, Christ and his gospel divine, and holiness the one worthy aim and chief good, when our frame is refusing its offices, and we can lay hold on no immediate outward support and solace. It is conceivable to the healthy and happy, that, if waked up from sleep by a tremendous earthquake, the first recoil of terror might be followed by an intense perception of the fixity and tranquillity of the spiritual world, in immediate contact with the turbulence of the outward and lower scene. It is conceivable to us all that the drowning man may, as is recorded, see his whole life, in all its minute details, presented to him, as in clear vision, in one instant of time, as he lapses into death. Well,—something like both these experiences is that of extreme and dissolving pain, to a certain order of minds. The vision and the attestation are present, without the horrors caused, amidst an earthquake, by the misery of a perishing multitude, though at the cost of more bodily anguish than in the case of the drowning man. Though there may be keen doubts in a modest sufferer how long such anguish can be decently endured,— whether the filial submission will hold out against torment,— there is through, above and beyond such doubts, so overpowering an impression of the vitality of the conscious part of us, and of the reality of the highest objects for which it was created and has lived,—so inexpressible a sense of the value of what we have prayed for, and of the evanescence of what we are losing,—that it is no wonder if the dying have been known to call for aid in their thanksgivings, and to struggle for sympathy even in their incommunicable convictions. If the shadows of the dark valley part, and disclose to such an one the regions that lie in the light of God's countenance, it is no wonder that he calls on those near him to look and see, though he is making the transit alone.

Those who speculate outside on the experience of the sick room, are eager to know whether this solitary transit is often gone over in imagination, and whether with more or less relish and success than by those at ease and in full vigour. In my childhood, I attended, as an observer, one fine morning, at the funeral of a person with whom I was well acquainted, without feeling any strong affection. I was somewhat moved by the solemnity, and by the tears of the family; but the most powerful feeling of the day was excited when the evening closed in, gusty and rainy, and I thought of the form I knew so well, left alone in the cold and the darkness, while everybody else was warm and sheltered. I felt that, if I had been one of the family, I could not have neglectfully and selfishly gone to bed that night, but must have passed the hours till daylight by the grave. Every child has felt this: and every child longs to know whether a sick friend contemplates that first night in the cold grave, and whether the prospect excites any emotions.

Surely;— we do contemplate it — frequently — eagerly. In the dark night, we picture the whole scene, under every condition the imagination can originate. By day, we hold up before our eyes that most wondrous piece of our worldly wealth — our own right-hand; examine its curious texture and mechanism, and call up the image of its sure deadness and decay. And with what emotions? Each must answer for himself. As for me, it is with mere curiosity, and without any concern about the lonely, cold grave. I doubt whether any one's imagination rests there,— whether there is ever any panic about the darkness and the worm of the narrow house.

As for our real future home,— the scene where our living selves are to be,— how is it possible that we should not be often resorting thither in imagination, when it is to be our next excursion from our little abode of sickness and helplessness,— when it is so certain that we cannot be disappointed of it, however wearily long it may be before we go,— when all that has been best in our lives, our sabbaths, all sunset evenings and starry nights, all our reverence and love that are sanctified by death,— when all these things have always pointed to our future life and been associated with it, how is it possible that we should not be ever looking forward to it, now when our days are low and weary, and our pleasures few? The liability is to too great familiarity with the subject. When our words make children look abashed, and call a constraint over the manners of those we are conversing with, and cause even the most familiar eyes to be averted, we find ourselves reminded that the subject of a person's death is one usually thought not easy to discuss with him. In our retirement, we are apt to forget, till expressly reminded, the importance of distinctions of rank and property in society, so nearly as they vanish in our survey of life, in comparison with moral differences; and, in like manner, we have to recal an almost lost idea, that death is an awkward topic, except in the abstract, when our casual mention of a will, or of some transaction to follow our death, introduces an awe and constraint into conversation.

Such familiarity may be, and often is, condemned as presumptuous. There may be cases in which it is so; but I think it would be hard to make the censure general. The confident reckoning on the joys of heaven for one's self, on any grounds, while others are supposed to be condemned to a contrary lot, is a superstition more offensive to my feelings than that which renders a trembling soul, clinging to life, aghast at the idea of meeting its Maker and Father. But a soul without any self-complacency, or ignorant confidence, may yet be easy and eager in the prospect of entering upon that awful new scene. Setting aside all the inducements from the hope of relief and rest, the humblest spirit may be conceived of as tranquil and aspiring in full view of the transition; and this under a full sense of its sins and failures, and without reliance on any imaginary security,— without need of other reliance than its Father in Heaven. There may be— there is — in some, so continual a regard to God in life, that there cannot seem anything very new and strange in going anywhere where He is. There may be—and there is—in some, so earnest a desire to be purified from sin, that they would undergo anything on earth to be freed from it, and therefore fear nothing, but rather welcome any discipline which may be reserved beyond. Knowing that the revelation of the evil of their sin must be most painful, but also most necessary to their progress, they are ready, even eager for it, pressing forward to the suffering through which they hope to be made perfect. If with such dispositions is joined that ardent, reverential, filial love which generates perfect trust, and rejects any interposition between itself and the benign countenance in whose light it lives, there may be nothing blameable or dangerous in the readiness for death, or in the happy familiarity with which the event may be spoken of. It is a case in which every man should be slow to judge his neighbour, while the natural verdict of thoughtful observers would seem to be that a sufferer under irremediable illness, who preserves a general patience, cares for others' happiness more than for his own, and has always lived in view of an eternal life, can hardly be wrong in anticipating that life with ease and cheerfulness, whatever analysis or judgment dogmatists may make of his state of mind.

Whether our imaginings of Death are more or less a true anticipation of it, can be proved only by experience. It may be found that they are no more just than my idea of the matter when I was a child, when my brother and I dug a grave, and then lay down in it, by turns, and shut our eyes, to try what dying was like. Practically, such failures of conception cannot matter much. A person who is setting out on foreign travel for the first time, takes no harm by expecting the voyage and the landing among foreigners to be something very unlike what they prove. His preconceptions answered their purpose, by rendering him ready and willing to go, and preventing his being taken by surprise by the summons. Still, those of us have greatly the advantage whose minds are enlarged by knowledge, and their imaginations animated and strengthened by exercise. Some of the most innocent and kind-hearted people I have known have been the most afraid of death,—not from consciousness of sin, but from dread of overpowering novelty—from a horror of feeling lost among scenes where there is nothing familiar; while, in opposite cases, a philosophic interest and wonder have been known to go far in reconciling a highly intellectual man to leaving the companions he loved best in life.

There can be no question as to the difference in the ease of departure (moral conditions being supposed the same) of the housewife, whose days and faculties have been occupied with the market, the shop, and the home where her whole life has been passed, and the philosopher, whose nerves thrill with delight, unmixed with terror, at the very first view of the new wonders revealed by Lord Rosse's speculum.[1] It is striking, that a man about to be thrust forth from life for a plot of murder on an enormous scale, should, while waiting for death the next moment, whisper to a fellow-sufferer, "Now we shall soon know the great secret;" while a pure and beneficent being, beloved by God and his neighbour, should pray to be loaded with any weight of years and sufferings rather than go from the familiar scene on which he has opened his eyes every day for sixty years. "Grand secrets" have

---

[1] William Parsons, Third Earl of Rosse (1800-67), was an Irish astronomer and builder of the largest reflecting telescope in the nineteenth century. Telescope mirrors originally were made from polished speculum metal.

no charms for him, but only horrors; and as for new scenes, even within our own corner of the earth, mountains and waterfalls overpower him, and he shuffles back to shops and streets.

Let persons so constitutionally different be shut into a sick room, knowing that they will issue from it only by death, and what will they do? By the habit of looking forward to this exit for relief, the timid may come to speak and think of it as tranquilly as the speculative; but then, when the sensation overtakes him, the difference is again apparent. It does seem as if there were in the seizure of death a sensation wholly peculiar, and which cannot be mistaken. Cases of unconsciousness are no evidence to the contrary; and there are so many instances of decisive declaration by the dying, as to make the fact pretty certain. Then finally appears (supposing both conscious) the distinction in the act of dying, between the enlarged and speculative mind and the contracted one which clings to details. Then the harassed sufferer, who has a hundred times exclaimed, in the struggles of disease, "O! this is dying many times over!" shudders out at last, in quite another tone, "O, God! this is death!" Then the exhausted debauchee, after every hollow show of preparation by decorous prayer, mutters, in the terror of the reality, "O God! this is death!" At such a time, the philosophic physician, seizing his sole opportunity of experience of the phenomena of death, keeps his finger on his pulse as his heart is coming to a stop, and notifies its last beat as a fact in useful science. At such a time, the diligent Christian—a judge, a rich man, without a crook in his lot—suddenly sentenced, struggles to breathe into his wife's bending ear his last words: "This is death! Our children ... tell them—I have had everything man could enjoy ... and all is nothing in comparison with holiness. Pure and holy—make them. Care for nothing else! O! all is well!" When he could no longer speak or move, his countenance was full of soul; not a trace of fear upon it, but a whole heaven of joyful expectation. Here are differences!

Of course, there is no waiting till the last moment for these differences to show themselves. Outside enquirers may be satisfied that invalids' anticipation of death varies with their habits of mind. Some merely anticipate; some contemplate. With some, the anticipation is merely of relief and rest; with others it is worthier of our human and Christian hope. In no case of permanent illness can I conceive the idea to be otherwise than familiar, under one aspect or another; so familiar, as that it is astonishing to us that we can obtain so little conversation upon it as a reality — a certainty in full view. To us this seems more extraordinary than it would be if the friends of Parry, and Franklin, or Back, were, as the season for a Polar expedition drew nigh, to talk to them about everything else, but be constrained and shy on that.[1] I say "more extraordinary," because it is not everybody that is bound, sooner or later, to the North Pole, but only a few crews; whereas, all have an interest in the passage of that other, that "narrow sea," and in the "better country" which is its further shore.

Perhaps the familiarity of the idea of death is by nothing so much enhanced to us as by the departure before us of those who have sympathised in our prospect. The close domestic interest thus imparted to that other life is such as I certainly never conceived of when in health, and such as I observe people in health do not conceive of now. It seems but the other day that I was receiving letters of sympathy and solace, and also of religious and philosophical investigation as to how life here and hereafter appeared to me; letters which told of activity, of labours, and journeyings, which humbled me by a sense of idleness and uselessness, while *they* spoke of humbling feelings in regarding the privileges of my seclusion. All this is as if it were yesterday: and now, these correspondents have been gone for years. For years we have thought of them as knowing "the grand secret," as familiarized with those scenes we are for ever prying into, while I lie no wiser (in such a comparison) than when they endeavoured to learn somewhat of these matters from me. And besides these close and dear companions, what departures are continually taking place! Every new year there are several — friends, acquaintance, or strangers — who shake their heads when I am mentioned, in friendly regret at another year opening before me without prospect of health — who send me comforts or luxuries, or words of sympathy, amidst the pauses of their busy lives; and before

---

1   Martineau refers to the Artic explorers Sir William Edward Parry (1790-1855), Sir John Franklin (1786-1847), and Sir George Back (1796-1878).

another year comes round, they have dropped out of our world—
have learned quickly far more than I can acquire by my leisure—
and from being merely outside my little spot of life, have passed to
above and beyond it. Little ones who speculated on me with
awe—youthful ones who ministered to me with pity—busy and
important persons, who gave a cordial but passing sigh to the lot
of the idle and helpless; some of all these have outstripped me, and
left me looking wistfully after them. Such incidents make the
future at least as real and familiar to me as the outside world; and
every permanent invalid will say the same: and we must not be
wondered at if we speak of that great interest of ours oftener, and
with more familiarity, than others use.

Neither should we be wondered at if we speak with a
confidence which some cannot share, of meeting these our
friends, and communing with them, when we ourselves depart.
We have no power to doubt of this, if we believe at all that we
shall live hereafter. I have said how intensely we feel that our spiritual part is indestructible. We feel no less vividly that of that spiritual part the affections are the true vitality; that they are the soul
within the soul—our inmost life. The affections cannot exist
without their objects; and our congenial friends—the brethren of
our soul—therefore survive as surely as God survives. If God is
recognisable by the worshipper, and Christ by the Christian, the
beloved are recognisable by those who love. To demur to this to
the sufferer who (all other life being weakened and embittered)
lives by the affections, divine and human, is, to him, much like
doubting whether the atmosphere bears any relation to music, or
the human understanding to truth.

If there are hours when, through pain and weakness, we would
fain decline existence altogether, as a sick and wearied child frets
at sunshine and music, and would rather sleep in darkness and
silence, there is no moment in which we do not believe, as if we
saw, that the departed righteous are in communion, full and
active, in exact proportion as the ardour and fidelity of their
mutual love deserves and necessitates. We believe this as if we saw
it, whatever be our own immediate mood, as, on every night of
winter, however cloudy, we are well assured that the constellations
are in the sky,—that Orion and the Wain have risen and are

circling, steady, clear and serene, whatever be the state of the elements below them.[1] As the life of the sick-room must necessarily be, whether its objects be high or low, one of faith and not of sight, those who visit it may easily perceive that it is not the appropriate field for demonstration. In its own province Demonstration is supreme. There let it dictate and pronounce. But we sufferers inhabit a separate region of human experience, where there is another and prophetic oracle; where the voice of Demonstration itself must be dumb before that of the steadfast, incommunicable assurance of the soul.

Here are some of the aspects of Death to the long-suffering Invalid.

---

1   Named after the hunter of Greek mythology, the Orion is one of the brightest constellations. The "Wain" refers to the constellation Ursa Major, the Great Bear or the Big Dipper Wain.

CHAPTER SIX

TEMPER

"We are not ourselves
When nature, being oppressed, commands the mind
To suffer with the body."

Shakspere.[1]

"Behold thy trophies within thee, not without thee. Lead
thine own captivity captive, and be Cæsar unto thyself."

Sir Thomas Brown.[2]

IT is very surprising, and rather amusing, to invalids whose constitution and disease dispose them to other kinds of ill-temper rather
than irritability, to perceive how this tendency, and no other, is set
up as a test of temper by persons inexperienced in sickness. There
are cases, and they are not few, where an invalid's freedom from
irritability of temper is a merit of a very high order indeed: but
there are many,—perhaps more,— where, to award praise on this
ground, is like extolling the sick person for being worthy of trust
with untold gold, or for his being never known to game or get
drunk. This last, indeed, may,—amidst the sinkings of illness, with
wine and laudanum in the closet,—often be actually the greater
merit. It is a case in which every thing depends on the existence
of temptation. Persons suffering under frequent fever, or certain
kinds of pain or nervous disturbance, or afflicted with ill-qualified
nurses, may be pardoned for almost any degree of irritability, or
may be unspeakably meritorious in resisting the tendency, with
more or less steadiness. But there are some of us who cannot but
smile at compliments on our freedom from irritability, when we
feel that we never have the slightest inclination to be cross, nor
have the least excuse for being so,— while we may be most abas-
ingly aware of other kinds of frailty of temper.

---

1   William Shakespeare (1564-1616), *King Lear*, Act II, Scene IV.
2   Sir Thomas Browne (1605-82), *Religio Medici* (1643).

To me it appears that we are, for the most part, in greater peril from other faults, because they are less looked for, less discussed and recognised, and we are, therefore, less put upon our guard against them: and also because their consequences are less immediately and obviously detrimental to our own comfort. Besides that all persons grow up on the look out for irritability of temper, and therefore are more or less on the watch against it when they come to be ill, it is clear to the idlest and most selfish mind, that the whole hope of comfort in the sick-room depends on the freedom and cheerfulness of the intercourse held in it,—a freedom and cheerfulness forfeited by irritability on the part of the sufferer,—necessarily forfeited, even if he were tended by the hands of angels. Children are the brightest, if not the tenderest, angels of the sick-room; and the alternative between their coming springing in, not only voluntarily but eagerly, and their being brought, for observance sake, with force and fear, is of itself inducement enough to self-control on the part of the most fretted patient, in the most feverish hour. Even in the middle of the night, when no one is by but the soundly sleeping nurse, the invalid feels admonished to suppress the slightest moan, when he sees in fancy his little friends the next morning either leaping from their beds at the joyful thought that they may visit him, or asking, with awe and gravity, whether they must go, and how soon they may come away. It is the sweetest of cordials to the heart of an invalid to learn, by chance, that children count the days and hours till they may come, and that all their gravity is about having to go away. It is the most refined flattery to let one know it: and the knowledge of it may well be almost a specific against ill-temper. And then again, the nurse. It is by no means sufficient for one's comfort that one's nurse should be well qualified,—ever so trust-worthy, and ever so kind it is necessary too that she should be free and happy. There must be no fear in her tread,—no reserve in her eye,—no management in her voice,—no choice in her tidings. There is no ill-temper in that jealousy of the invalid's spirit which requires assurance of being no burden, and no restraint. It is a righteous jealousy, and among the most effectual safeguards against the indulgence of ill-humour. That there are disorders, and seasons of illness, which almost compel the forfeiture of the mental and moral freedom and ease of the sick-room, is a painful truth; and those who suffer under such irresistible or unresisted irritation are supremely to be compassionated, whether their actual pain of body be more or less. But it is quite as certain that a large number of sufferers are exempt from temptation to this kind of failure, being subject, the while, to some other,— more tolerable, as affecting only, or chiefly, their own happiness.

The very opposite failure to that of irritability,— which shows itself in dissatisfaction with others,— is no less common,— unreasonable dissatisfaction with one's self. This lowering, depraving tendency to self-contempt requires for its establishment as a fault of temper, long protraction or permanence of illness: but when once established, it is as serious a fault of temper as can be entertained. Where religious faith and trust are insufficient for the need, this temper is almost a necessary consequence of any degree of mental and moral activity in a sick prisoner. The retrospect of one's own life, from the stillness of the sick room, is unendurable to any considerate person, except in the light of the deepest religious humility; and the strongest faith in the all-wise ordering of the moral world, is no more than sufficient to counteract that sickening which spreads from the distressed body to the anxious heart, when intervals of ease and lightness are few and brief. When to the pains and misgivings of such perpetual retrospect are added the burdens of a sense of present and permanent uselessness, and of overwhelming gratitude for services received from hour to hour,— there is no self-respect in the world that will, unaided, support cheerfulness and equanimity.

Without self-respect, there can be none of that healthy freedom of spirit which animates others to freedom, and exerts that influence which is ascribed to "a good temper," which removes hesitancy from the transaction of the daily business of life, and so permits life to appear in its natural aspect. Instead of this, where the spirit has lost its security of innocence, unconsciousness, or self-reliance, and become morbidly sensitive to failures and dangers,— where it has become cowardly in conscience, shrinking from all moral enterprise, and dreading moral injury from every occurrence, the temper of anxiety must spread from the sufferer to all about him, whether the causes of his trouble are intelligible to them or not. Moral progress, or even holding what he has gained, seems out of the question for one so shaken; for, constantly feeling, as he does, that he cannot afford to do the least questionable thing, and every act being questionable in one aspect or another, he can only preserve one incessant shrinking attitude before the fearful ghost of Conscience, instead of bestirring himself to prove and use his new opportunities of spiritual exertion and conquest. This abasement may co-exist with the most perfect sweetness and gentleness of speech and manners, and the sufferer may enjoy great credit for not being irritable, when he is in a far lower moral state than often co-exists with irritability.

One effect, deplorably mean and perilous, of such a tendency, is immediately opposed to the mood which prompts hasty words and complaints. The sufferer's spirits rise in proportion to the pain he experiences. He is never so happy as when he feels his paroxysms coming on,— not only because pain of body acts as relief from the gnawing misery of his mind, but because every tangible proof that he is under chastening and discipline, conveys to him a sense of his dignity — reassures him, as a child of Providence. From this may follow too naturally his learning to regard pain as a qualification for ease — as a purchase-money of future good — a superstition as low and depraving as almost any the mind can entertain.

To persons in health, and at ease, this detail of the tempers of a sick-room may well appear fanciful, irrational, and shocking enough. But the time may come when they may recognise it as true; and, meanwhile, it will be their wisest and kindest way to receive it with belief. It may possibly prove the key, even now, to a mystery which otherwise they can make nothing of, when they see one under tedious suffering, gentle but low when at ease — evidently borne down by speechless sadness — while, on the first return of pain, the spirits rise, and the more restless is the distressed body, the more at ease does the spirit appear. Such a state may be morbid and perilous; but, the more it is so, the more desirable it becomes that the attending friend should have an insight into the case, and a respectful and tender sympathy with it.

As to the remedy, it is easy to say that it is to be found in a cheerful trust in the Ordainer of our lot. While no one questions this, who can show how this trust is to be made available at every need, when the workings of the spirit are all confused, its vision impaired, and its powers distorted? The only advice that even experience can give in such an instance, is to revive healthy old associations, to occupy the morbid powers with objects from without, and to use the happiest rather than the lowest seasons for leading the mind to a consideration of its highest relations. As the case is opposite to that most commonly discoursed of in connexion with the sick-room, so must a wise ministration be also opposite to common notions; the appeal must be, in seasons of ease and enjoyment, to the sense of dependence on God; and, in times of mental distress, to the principles of endurance and self-mastery.

Other tempers of the sick-room are more easily understood by those without. The particularity about trifles is one. This, though often reaching a point of absurdity, should be scrupulously indulged, because no one but the sufferer can be fully aware of the annoyance of want of order in so confined a space and range of objects. A healthy person, who can go everywhere at pleasure, leaving litters to be put away by servants during absence, can have no idea of the oppression felt by a feeble invalid, when looking round upon the confusion left in one little room by careless visitors,—chairs standing in all directions, books thrown down here and there, and work or papers strewed on the floor. It is easy to laugh at such trifles—easy to the invalid himself at times; but if any healthy person will recal his feelings during convalescence from any former illness, he will remember the sort of painful sympathy with which he saw the servants going about their work—how his frame ached at hearing of a long walk, or even at seeing his friends sitting upright upon chairs. If he considers what it must be to have this set of feelings for life, he will think the particularity of the invalid not only worth indulging, but less absurd than in the eye of reason it appears; and if it be too much to expect of men, it may be hoped that women visiting the sick may be careful to leave the spaces of the room clear, not to shake the sofa or the table, to put up books upon their shelves, and leave all in such a state that the invalid may, immediately on being left alone, sink down to such rest as can be found.

No one challenges this particularity when it relates to hours.

The most careless observer must know that it is illness of itself to a sick person to have to wait for food or medicines, or to be put off from regular sleep. Meantime, the invalid cannot keep too careful a watch upon the increase of his own particularity—his refuge in custom. There is something shocking to us invalids, when we fix our meditation upon this, in our attachment to our own comforts, and cowardice about dispensing with them. I have myself observed, with inexpressible shame, that, with the newspaper in my hand, no details of the peril of empires, or of the starving miseries of thousands of my countrymen, could keep my eye from the watch before me, or detain my attention one second beyond the time when I might have my opiate. For two years, too, I wished and intended to dispense with my opiate for once, to try how much there was to bear, and how I should bear it: but I never did it, strong as was the shame of always yielding; and I have now long given up all thoughts of it. Moreover, though as fully convinced as ever of the moral evil and danger of being wedded to custom and habit, I have now a far too decided and satisfactory impression that the sick-room is not the place for a conquest of that kind, and that it is enough if the patient breaks through his trammels when he casts off his illness, and emerges again into the world, which is the same thing as acquiescing in the invalid for life being a life-long slave to custom and habit. Bad as this is, I do not see how it is to be helped; for the suffering and injury caused by irregularity of methods, and uncertainty of arrangements in the sick-room, seem to show that freedom of this kind does not belong to an invalid life: and perhaps the most that ought to be required or desired of the sick person is, rather to welcome than complain of any necessary interruption to his ways, by a change of nurse, or other accidental interference with ordinary comforts,—not to extend his particularity beyond the bounds of his own little domain, and no more to expect the healthy and active to be, in their own homes, as strict and punctual as himself, than to desire the servants to leave off rubbing tables and lighting fires, because it makes his frame ache to think of such work. If he can preserve sympathy enough in the impulses of the active abroad, he may hope for indulgence in his particularity at home.

There are other liabilities which may be clear to observers, or easily conceivable when mentioned. I hardly know whether we may allude, under the head of Tempers, to the despair which I believe to be universally felt (however discountenanced), by all, on the assault of very severe pain. The reason may speak, and even through the lips, of hope and courage; but the *sensation* of which I speak is peculiar, so peculiarly connected with bodily agony, that I cannot but believe it felt wherever bodily agony is felt. It has nothing to do with the courage of the soul; affords not the shadow of contradiction to patience, fortitude, religious trust. I mean simply that when extreme pain seizes on us, down go our spirits, fathoms deep; and, though the soul may yet be submissive and even willing, the sickening question rises,— "How *shall* I bear this for five minutes? What *will* become of me?" And if the imagination stretches on to an hour, or hours, there is no word but *despair* which expresses the feeling. The by-standers can never fully understand this suffering; no, though they may themselves have suffered to extremity. The patient himself, in any interval, when devoutly ready to endure again, cannot understand, nor believe in his late emotion, or fancy that he can feel it again. As it is thus peculiar and transient, there could be no use in mentioning it, except for two possibilities; that some sufferer may, in the moment of anguish, remember that the sensation has been recognised and recorded; and that attendants, on witnessing a sudden abasement of high courage, on seeing horror of countenance succeed a calm determination, may remember, at the right moment, that there is that passing within of which they can have no conception, and certainly no right to judge.

I might add, as a justification for allusion to so painful a subject, that it may teach us to honour, in some less faint degree, the strength of soul of those who, with any composure, die of sheer pain,—of the most torturing diseases. If, amidst successive shocks of this despairing sensation, their power of reaction, in the intervals, remains unimpaired, and they retain their spiritual dignities to the end, no degree of admiration can transcend their claims.

One strong peril to temper, in the case of a permanent invalid, I do not remember to have seen noticed, while, I am sure, none can be more worthy of being guarded against. By our being withdrawn from the disturbing bustles of life in the world; by our leisure for reading and contemplation of various sides of questions, and by our singular opportunities for quiet reflection, we must, almost necessarily, see further than we used to do, and further than many others do on subjects of interest, which involve general principles. Through the post, we hold the best kind of correspondence with the society from which we are withdrawn; we have the opinions of the wise, and the impressions of the active, transmitted to us, stripped of much of the passion and prejudice in which they would have been presented in conversation. Instead of one newspaper or pamphlet, we now have time to look over several, and can hear all sides. Far removed from the little triumphs or disappointments of the day, which warp the judgments of all men who have hearts to feel, whatever may be their abstract wisdom; endowed with long night hours of wakefulness, when our spirit of Humanity is all alive; permitted sequestered days, when our review of historical periods may be continuous, and when some great new idea, a stalactite of long formation, at length descends to our level, and touches our heads, or a diamond of thought, slowly distilled, drops into our hand as we penetrate and explore;— when some such gain— the guerdon of our condition— is frequently occurring, it cannot be but that— unless we are fools, our judgments of things must be worth something more than formerly. If formerly we associated with our equals, it cannot be but that we must now see further than they, on such questions of the time as interest us.

Such divergences of opinion as hence arise require care on the part both of sick and well, if a perfectly just and generous understanding is to be preserved between friends.

The liability of us sick is double. We are in danger of forgetting, amidst the inevitable consciousness of our own improved insight and foresight, that the activities of life have a corrective as well as a disturbing influence; and that transient incidents and emotions which do not reach us, may form real elements of a great question for the week or the year, though lost in our abstract view of it. In this way, our judgment may involve great imperfections, which it behooves us to remember all the more, the less we can supply them. A worse liability is that to our tempers, of impatience at others not seeing as far as we do. There is something strange, disappointing and irritating, in finding those whom we have always regarded as sensible and clear-headed, holding some expectation which we see to be unreasonable, and offering to our consideration some fallacy or misty notion, whose incorrectness is to us as distinct as a cloud in the sky. While religiously careful not to fret ourselves "because of evil doers," being so expressly desired, we are sadly prone to the far worse weakness of fretting ourselves because of mistaken thinkers. We long to send by a carrier-pigeon the answer or refutation which seems to us so clear: the post is too slow for us; and if we do not disburden our minds of their weight of wisdom, we are apt to spend the night in reiterating to ourselves our triumphant arguments, in the strongest and most condensed language we can find, till, exhausted by such efforts, at last the thought occurs to us whether truth cannot wait,—whether, supposing us ever so right intellectually, we are not morally wrong in our perturbation. This confession looks foolish and humbling enough in black and white; but I cannot escape making it, if, as I intend, I complain of some little injustice on the other hand, sustained by us.

Where such divergences of opinion arise, men of activity (and women, no less) are apt, whatever may be their abstract respect for closet speculators, and reverence for sequestered sufferers, to speak with regret, or at least with respectful compassion, of the warping influences of seclusion and illness, as particularly illustrated by the case in point. They attribute all differences to these causes, and never doubt that the old agreement would exist, by the invalid's views being the same as their own, but for the distorting medium through which the sick are compelled to regard events; or but for the influence which certain parties have obtained over his mind, by service or sympathy. This may be more or less true, in individual cases. Still, it is for the interests of truth and temper to remind the healthy and busy that the warp may possibly not be all on one side, and the enlightenment on the other; and that there may be influences in the life of the meditative invalid which may render his views more comprehensive, and his judgments more, rather than less, sound than heretofore. If there is any practicable test of this, it must be looked for in his habitual tone of mind and life. Unless this proves perversion of folly, his mind must, in justice, be held at least as worthy of consideration as at any former season of his life. If his fundamental opinions have undergone no change, but rather enlargement with special modifications, they are decidedly worthy of more respect than ever.

Thus does my experience moralize for both parties. If, in ordinary life, there is no peace of mind for those whose happiness depends on the good opinion of everybody, much less can there be tranquillity of mind in the sick-room for such. When we are in the world, our presence breaks down mistaken or slanderous allegations, and we are sure to be seen as we are, and to be rightly understood, by large numbers of persons,—by all, indeed, whose opinion is of value to us. But, while sequestered in the sick-room, we are, in point of reputation, wholly at the mercy of those who speak of us. It is true, most persons are so humane, and those about us are so touched by our affliction, as that the best construction is put on our manners and conduct by the greater number of reporters. But it is strange and fortunate if there be not, among our acquaintance, some intrusive person whom we have to keep at a distance,—some meddler whom we have to check, some well-meaning mischief-maker, of impenetrable complacency, who will most affectionately and compassionately report us as sadly changed, unable to value our best friends, or to estimate the most important services. Whether charges like these arise, or old misrepresentations reappear, while we are invisible and defenceless, we may be miserable enough if we let such things trouble us. Those least in danger, as to temper, are persons of note, who have had former experience of the diversities of the world's opinion. They can smile and wait. But it may be easily conceived that such incidents may be trying to invalids who are the subjects of notoriety for the first time,—of that sort of notoriety which affliction creates, through the universal sympathy of human hearts. Under so new an experience, the sufferer may feel more vexation by the accidental knowledge of one unjust representation of his state of temper, than cheered by a hundred evidences of the esteem and sympathy of those about him. For the evil there is no help; but there are abundant resources against the vexation,—the same resources which enable the humble and hoping Christian, whether strong or weak, rich or poor in outward blessings, to go through good or evil report with a heart tranquil in Divine Trust, and occupied with human love.

CHAPTER SEVEN

BECOMING INURED

"Sunt homines qui cum patientiâ moriuntur: sunt autem
quidam perfecti qui cum patientiâ vivunt."

St. Augustin.[1]

"No cruel guard of diligent cares, that keep
Crowned woes awake, as things too wise for sleep:
But reverend discipline, religious fear,
And soft obedience find sweet biding here!

The self-remembering soul sweetly recovers
Her kindred with the stars: not basely hovers
Below — but meditates the immortal way
Home to the source of light and intellectual day."

Crashaw.[2]

WE hear, every day, benevolent and compassionate persons, in discussing the woes of sufferers, dwelling on the thought of such
sufferers becoming inured; and we see them, if possible, reposing
on this as the closing and conclusive idea. How natural this is!
How often and how undoubtingly we did it ourselves, in our days
of ease! But how differently it sounds now! How quickly do we
detect in it the discharge and dismissal of uneasy sympathies!
How infallibly do we see how far it may be true; and what a tale
could we tell of what is included in the phrase, "becoming
inured," where it may be most truly applied! Of what experience
is involved in the process, where it is shortest and easiest!

I was lately speaking to a tender-hearted woman, who had
known suffering, but not torment, of more than one case of
persons who, dying slowly under a torturing disease, simply and

---

1   "There are men who die with patience; but there are some perfect men who live with
    patience." Saint Augustine (354-430), *Tractatus in Epistolam Iohannis ad Parthos* 9.2.
2   Richard Crashaw (1613-49), "Description of a Religious House and Condition of
    Life."

naturally declared, shortly before death, the season of their illness to have been the happiest part of their lives. There are different ways of explaining this fact, which, though I always believed it, I did not till lately understand. My friend, however, found no difficulty. She said, in a tone of pitying tenderness, but of perfect decision, "O! they become inured to it." I replied by some slight description of the suffering in the case which had impressed me most, and asked if she thought use and experience could soften pain like that. "O yes," she again said, "they become inured to it. That is certainly the thing."

Is it so? I am persuaded it is not. To the great majority of evils men may become inured; but not to all. To almost every kind, and to vast degrees of privation, moral and physical, they may become inured; and to chronic sufferings of mind and body: but I am convinced that there is no more possibility of becoming inured to acute agony of body than to paroxysms of remorse — the severest of moral pains. For the sake of both sufferers and sympathisers, it would be well that this should be thoroughly understood, that aid may not fall short, nor relief be looked for in the wrong direction.

The truth is, as all will declare who are subject to a frequently recurring pain, a familiar pain becomes more and more dreaded, instead of becoming lightly esteemed in proportion to its familiarity. The general sense of alarm which it probably occasioned when new, may have given way and disappeared before a knowledge of consequences, and a regular method of management or endurance; but the pain itself becomes more odious, more oppressive, more feared, in proportion to the accumulation of experience of weary hours, in proportion to the aggregate of painful associations which every visitation revives. When it is, moreover, considered that the suffering part of the body is, if not recovering, growing continually more diseased and susceptible of pain, it will appear how little truth there is in the supposition of tortured persons becoming inured to torture.

The inuring process which I hold to be impossible in the cases mentioned is, however, practicable and frequent in almost all cases of inferior suffering. But, while all join in thanking God for this, there is a wide difference in the view taken of the fact by those who feel and those who only observe it. To the last, it is a clear and satisfactory truth, shining on the rock of futurity, which they can sit and gaze at from the window of their ease, commenting on the blessing of such a beacon-light to those who need it. To those who need it, meanwhile, it is far far off—sometimes hidden and sometimes despaired of, as the waves and the billows go over them, and the point can be reached only through sinkings and struggles, and fears and anguish, with scanty breathing-times between. Why is this not admitted in the case of the invalid as it is in that of the person losing a sense? One who is becoming blind or deaf is sure to grow inured in time; but through what a series of keen mortifications, of bitter privations! Every one sees and understands this; while in the case of the invalid, many spring to the conclusion, overlooking the process of discipline which has, in that case, as in the other, to be undergone. It should never be forgotten how different a thing it is to read off this lesson from the clear print of assertion or observation, and to learn it experimentally, at a scarcely perceptible rate, "line upon line and precept upon precept;"[1] when every line is burnt in by pain, and the long series of precepts are registered by their degrees of anguish.

When the nature of the process has been sufficiently dwelt upon to be understood—that the hearts of the happy may be duly softened, and those of the suffering duly cheered by sympathy—then let all good be said of the inuring process; at least all the good that is true; and that is much. No wise man will declare that it is the best and healthiest condition for any one. No wise man will deny that the healthiest moral condition is found where there is the most abundant happiness. Happiness is clearly the native, heavenly atmosphere of the soul—that in which it is "to live and move and have its being"[2] hereafter, and in proportion to its share of which, now and here, it makes its heavenly growth. The divinest souls—the loftiest, most disinterested and devoted—all unite in one testimony, that they have been best when happiest; that they were then most energetic and spontaneously devoted—least self-conscious. This must and may joyfully be

---

1   Isaiah 28:10.
2   Acts of the Apostles 17:28.

granted. But, as the mystery of evil is all round about us, as we have no choice whether or not to suffer, we may be freely thankful next for the inuring process, as being the possible means, though inferior to happiness, of divine ends.

Far, indeed, does the sufferer feel from reaching those ends, when he contrasts his own state with that of the truly happy man. When he looks upon one so "little lower than the angels,"[1] on his frame, so nerved and graced by health, his eye emitting the glow of the soul, his voice uttering the music of the heart, his hand strong to effect his purposes, his head erect in the liberty of ease, his intellect and soul free from perplexities and cares, and not only at leisure for the service of others, but restless to impart to them of his own overflowing good; when the sufferer contemplates such a being, and contrasts him with himself, he may well feel how much he has to do, to approach this higher order of his race. Aware of his own internal tremblings at the touch of the familiar pain, sinking in weakness before the bare idea of enterprise, abashed by self-consciousness, smarting under tenderness of conscience, perplexed and bewildered by the intricacy and vastness of human woe, of which his own suffering gives him too keen a sense, well may he who is in the bonds of pain look up humbly to him who walks gloriously in joy; and the humility might sink into abjectness if the matter ended here, if the inuring process were not at work. But herein is ample ground for hope now, and greatness in the future; and if a secondary, still a sufficient greatness.

The sufferer may well be satisfied, and needs be abashed before no mortal, if he obtains, sooner or later, the power to achieve divine ends through the experience of his lot. If, beginning by encountering his familiar pain, and putting down the dread of it by looking merely to the comfort of the reaction when it ceases, he attains at length to conquering pain by the power of ideas; if, ease of body being out of the question, he makes activity of spirit suffice him; if, his own future in this life being a blank, he becomes absorbed in that of other men; if, imprisoned by disease, kingdoms and races are not wide enough for his sympathies; if, as

---

1 Hebrews 2:7.

this or that sense is extinguished, or this or that limb is laid fast, his spirit becomes more alive in every faculty; if familiarity with pain enables him so to deal with it, as resolutely to cut off every morbid spiritual growth to which he has been made liable by pain; if, instead of succumbing to unfavourable conditions, he has struggled against dwarfage and distortion, and diligently wrought at the renewal of the inward man, while the outward frame was decaying day by day, he may surmount his humiliations, whatever cause for humility may be left by so impaired an existence. For him the inuring process will have done its best.

For those who from constitutional irritability cannot become inured, there is, daily opening, and at a shorter distance, the grave, where "the weary are at rest."[1]

For those on whom the inuring process acts amiss,—petrifying instead of vivifying the soul, we may and must hope, on the ground that they are in the hands of one whose ways and thoughts are not ours, nor within our ken. They are a mystery to us, like the cankered buds and blighted blossoms of our gardens. Or it may be, that there is no corruption or decay, but only torpidity, induced by the protraction of their polar night of adversity. It may be, that their life is only hidden away for a season, and that when the breath of the eternal spring shall dissolve their icy bonds, they may start forth as new-born, and their preceding deadness be mercifully counted to them but as a long dream.

There is no danger, no false security to one's-self, in hoping thus much for them; for one must be as far from reconciling one's-self to their condition as from preferring dreams to contemplation, or the sleep of the frame to the life of the spirit.

---

1   Job 3:17.

CHAPTER EIGHT

POWER OF IDEAS IN THE SICK-ROOM

"Turn you to the strong hold, ye prisoners of hope."
Zechariah.[1]

"Wherefore, for virtue's sake,
I can be well content
The sweetest time in all my life
To deem in thinking spent."
Lord Vaux.[2]

IT is amusing (in a somewhat mournful way, however,) to sick people, to observe how children and other inexperienced persons believe, notwithstanding all explanation and assurance, that it must be a very pleasant thing to be ill—gently ill, so as not to be groaning with pain, or confined to bed. They derive an impression of comfort and luxury from what they see, which it is impossible to weaken by descriptions of suffering which they have never felt, and cannot conceive of. They see the warm room in winter, with its well-cushioned couch, and think how comfortable it must be never to have the toes frozen, or a shower of sleet driven in one's face. The fire in the chamber all night—the flowers and books that lie strewed about all day—the pictures on the walls—the dainty meals—the punctual and careful attendance—these are things which make illness look extremely pleasant to the healthiest people, who are those that have the keenest relish for pleasure. Few of such are there who have that insight of sympathy which drew from my little friend at my elbow the sighing exclamation—"Ah! but there is the unhealthiness! that spoils everything!"

Even if the ordinary run of inexperienced persons could see the whole of our day, I should not expect them to understand the

---

1   Zechariah 9:12.
2   Lord Thomas Vaux of Harrowden (1510-56), "On a Contented Mind."

matter much better. If they saw us turn from the dainty meal, and wear a look of distress and fear, in the midst of everything that to them indicates comfort and security, I imagine that they could only wonder, till they knew for themselves how bodily distress excludes pleasure from outward objects, and how the mental weaknesses which prevail amidst an unnatural and difficult mode of life convert the most innocent and ordinary occurrences into occasions of apprehension, or of self-distrust or self-disgust.

If they must witness the painful and humbling aspect of the mode of life, it is much to be wished that they might also see another fact belonging to it — to them, perhaps, no less mysterious than the misery; but not the less salutary for that, as it may teach them that there is much, both of good and evil, in our condition, which it will be wiser in them to observe than to judge of.

The benign mystery which I would have them witness is, the power of ideas over us. A child knows something of this in his own way. In war-time, little boys leave their pet plays to run about and tell everybody the news of a great battle. A child cannot eat the best dinner in the world on the day of first going to the play. The doll is thrown into a corner, when news comes of any acquaintance being burned out in the middle of the night; or when anecdotes are telling of any old martyr who suffered heroically. In their own way, children are conscious, when reminded, of the power of ideas; but they cannot conceive of our way of experiencing the same force — to us so renovating! If it is at times surprising to the most enlightened and sympathising of our companions, it may well be astonishing to those in the early stages of observation.

They see, with a sort of awe, how priceless are certain pictures to us, in comparison with all others. They hear us speak of the landscapes, the portraits, the graceful and beautiful images which adorn the walls; but they observe how, when restless and distressed, we steal a glance upwards at one picture, and find something there which seems to set us right — to rally us at once. If such a picture as the CHRISTUS CONSOLATOR of Scheffer be within view of the sick-couch—(that talisman, including the consolations of eighteen centuries! — that mysterious assemblage of the redeemed Captives and tranquilised Mourners of a whole

Christendom!—that inspired epitome of suffering and solace!"[1])—it may well be a cause or wonder, almost amounting to alarm, to those who, not having needed, have never felt its power. If there were now burnings or drownings for sorcery, that picture, and some who possess it, would soon be in the fire, or at the bottom of a pond. No mute operation of witchcraft, or its dread, could exceed the silent power of that picture over sufferers. Again—if the inexperienced chance to see us in an unfavorable hour, when our self-control cannot rise beyond constraint— when our words are fewest, however gentle the voice—when our posture is rigid, because we will not be restless, and our faces tell the distress we think we are concealing; if, at such a time, the post comes in, how miraculous must seem the change to one who does not know what we have just read in letters or newspapers— and, perhaps, could not understand its efficacy, if he had seen. He sees us start up on the couch, hears us become voluble, and talk in a free and joyous tone;—beholds us eat and drink, without thinking what is put before us;—perhaps is surprised at a flow of tears, which seems to dissolve the misery, whatever it was; and finds, to his amazement, that all this is caused by something to him so dry as the appointment of a committee in the House[2]—a speech on some hustings[3]—an improved quarter's revenue;—or, perhaps, something not dry, but merely curious, and to him anything but moving,—a new appearance attending an eclipse—an arrangement for embanking the Nile, or cutting through the Isthmus of Panama, or some vast discovery in science or the arts. He may, again, see the relaxation yet more complete—may perceive, without a word being spoken, that we are well for the hour,—the eye swimming in happiness, the voice full of gentle joy; so that he is convinced that illness does not "spoil everything." In this case, some comfort has come, too sacred to be told,—at least then;

---

1. Ary Scheffer (1795-1856) painted "Christus Consolator" in 1837. Inspired by Luke 4:18 ("He hath sent me to heal the brokenhearted, to preach deliverance to the captives"), it depicts Christ seated on a cloud and surrounded by the afflicted and downtrodden.
2. In Britain, the bicameral Houses of Parliament are comprised of the House of Commons, an elected legislative body, and the House of Lords.
3. A court held in London before the lord mayor, recorder, and sheriff or alderman.

some news or appeal from the primary christians and confessors of our day,—the American abolitionists,[1]—some opening to us for doing some little service,—or, as not seldom happens, some word of true sympathy which rouses our spirit, as the trumpet stirs the war-horse,—some sudden light showing our position on our pilgrim path,—some hint of our high calling,—some apt warning of a pregnant truth, administered by a wise and loving comforter.

If I were asked whether there is any one idea more potential than any other over every sort of suffering, in a mode of life like ours, most hearers of the question would make haste to answer for me that there is such a variety of potential ideas suited to such wide differences of mood of mind and body, that it must be impossible to measure the strength of any one. Nevertheless, I should reply that there is one, to me more powerful at present than I can now conceive any single idea to have been in any former state of my mind. It is this; that it matters infinitely less what we *do* than what we *are*. I can conceive the amazement of many at this announcement,—of many even who admit its truth, and feelingly admit it, as I myself did when it was first brought home to me from the printed page of one friend by the heart-breathing voice of another. I care not who wonders, and who only half understands, while there are some few to whom this thought may be what it is to me. No one will be so short-sighted as to apply it as an excuse for indolence in the active and healthy,—so clear is it that such cannot *be* what they ought to be, unless they *do* all they can. But perhaps it is only the practised in human sorrows who can see far enough into the boundless truth of this thought to appreciate its worth to us. Suffice it here that it *has* the power I ascribe to it, and that we whom it has consoled long to administer it when we see old age restless in its infirmity, activity disappointed of its scope or instruments, or the most useful agents of society, the most indispensable members of families paralysed by disease. We long to whisper it in the dungeons of Spielberg,[2] where it

---

1   Those who campaigned against slavery in the United States.
2   Spielberg Fortress, infamous for having been used as a political prison by the Hapsburgs in Austria. It was also an important prison during the French Revolution.

opens a career within the narrowest recess of those thick walls. We long to send a missive to every couch of the sick, to every arm-chair of the aged and the blind, reminding them that the great work of life is ours still,—through all modes of life but that of the madhouse,—the formation of a heavenly soul within us. If we cannot pursue a trade or a science, or keep house, or help the state, or write books, or earn our own bread or that of others, we can do the work to which all this is only subsidiary,—we can cherish a sweet and holy temper,—we can vindicate the supremacy of mind over body,—we can, in defiance of our liabilities, minister pleasure and hope to the gayest who come prepared to receive pain from the spectacle of our pain; we can, here as well as in heaven's courts hereafter, reveal the angel growing into its immortal aspect, which is the highest achievement we could propose to ourselves, or that grace from above could propose to us, if we had a free choice of all possible conditions of human life. If any doubt the worth of the thought, from the common habit of overlooking the importance of what is *done* in its character of index of what the agent *is*, let him resort at once to the fountainhead of spiritual exemplification, and say whether it matters most what Christ was or what he did.

The worth of this particular thought is a separate consideration from that of the worth of any sound abstract idea to sufferers liable to a besetting personal recollection, or doubt, or care. But, before I speak of this, I must allude to a subject which causes inexpressible pain whenever it occurs to us sick prisoners. I have said how unavailing is luxury when the body is distressed and the spirit faint. At such times, and at all times, we cannot but be deeply grieved at the conception of the converse of our own state, at the thought of the multitude of poor suffering under privation, without the support and solace of great ideas. It is sad enough to think of them on a winter's night, aching with cold in every limb, and sunk as low as we in nerve and spirits, from their want of sufficient food. But this thought is supportable in cases where we may fairly hope that the greatest ideas are cheering them as we are cheered: that there is a mere set-off of their cold and hunger against our disease; and that we are alike inspired by spiritual vigour in the belief that our Father is with us,—that we are only encountering the probations of our pilgrimage,— that we have a divine work given us to carry out, now in pain and now in joy. There is comfort in the midst of the sadness and shame when we are thinking of the poor who can reflect and pray,— the old woman who was once a punctual and eager attendant at church,— of the wasting child who was formerly a Sunday-scholar,— of the reduced gentleman or destitute student who retain the privilege of their humanity,— of "looking before and after."[1] But there is no mitigation of the horror when we think of the savage poor, who form so large a proportion of the hungerers,— when we conceive of them suffering the privation of all good things at once,— suffering under the aching cold, the sinking hunger, the shivering nakedness,— without the respite or solace afforded by one inspiring or beguiling idea.

I will not dwell on the reflection. A glimpse into this hell ought to suffice, (though we to whom imagery comes unbidden, and cannot be banished at will, have to bear much more than occasional glimpses;) a glimpse ought to suffice to set all to work to procure for every one of these sufferers, bread and warmth, if possible, and as soon as possible; but above everything, and without the loss of an hour, an entrance upon their spiritual birthright. Every man, and every woman, however wise and tender appearing and designing to be, who for an hour helps to keep closed the entrance to the region of ideas,— who stands between sufferers and great thoughts, (which are the angels of consolation sent by God to all to whom he has given souls,) are, in so far, ministers of hell,— not themselves inflicting torment, but intercepting the influences which would assuage or overpower it. Let the plea be heard of us sufferers who know well the power of ideas,— our plea for the poor,— that, while we are contriving for all to be fed and cherished by food and fire, we may meanwhile kindle the immortal vitality within them, and give them that ethereal solace and sustenance which was meant to be shared by all, "without money and without price."

It seems but just (if we may venture so to speak), that there should be the renovating power in ideas that I have described, for

---

1   Probably a reference to P.B. Shelley's 1820 poem "To a Skylark," ll. 86-87.

our worst sufferings arise from an unmitigated power of ideas in another sort. I am not qualified by experience to speak of severe continued bodily torment, but all testimony seems to concur with all our experience, that there is no such instrument of torture as a besetting thought. The mere description of the suffering, given by those who know it, seems to have wrought upon the general mind, for a kind of shudder goes round when it is mentioned, though it can no more be conceived of by the gay and occupied, than the continual dropping of water on the head can be imagined by him whose transactions with the element consist in a plunge bath every morning. It is known, however, that herculean men have shrunk to shadows under the infliction, that it has reduced heroes to tremble at the whispering wind, or the striking of the clock, that it turns the raven-hair gray, lets down genius into idiocy, and starves the most vigorous life into an atrophy. How then are the sick to meet this woe, which comes upon them with force exactly proportioned to their weakness!

If every sick prisoner in our land were questioned, and could and would answer truly, I believe all would reply (all who have minds) that their worst pangs are in the soul. For the moment,— for the hour,—no agony is, I know, to be compared with some pains of body; but when the question is of months and years (including the seasons of delicious reaction from bodily pains), I am confident that the peculiar misery of our condition—subjection to a besetting thought—will be owned to absorb all others. Whether the thought relate to any intellectual matter, or whether it be self-abasement and self-weariness at the perpetually-recurring apparition of sins, follies, trifling old misadventures and misbehaviour, or whether some more serious cause of remorse, the tormenting and weakening effects are much alike; the cold horror at waking up to the thought in the middle of the night, knowing that we shall sleep no more; the misery of opening our eyes upon a new day, with the spell of the thought full upon us; the dread of giving ourselves up to thinking, and yet the inability to read, while the enemy is hovering about the page; the faint resolution, broken almost as surely as formed, not to speak of this trouble to our nearest and closest friend, and the ending in speaking of it, in our agony, to many besides. O! there is no aching, no shooting or

throbbing pain of fibre or nerve that can (taken with its alterna-
tions) compare in misery with this! Even the anticipation
becomes in time the worst, though the bodily pain is known to
be real and unavoidable, while the ideal one is clearly seen to be
baseless, or enormously exaggerated. The close observer of a sick
sufferer may see the drops stand on the forehead, and the quiver
pass over the lip, at the bare thought of the certain return of a
periodical pain; but worse to endure is the sickening of the soul,
at the certainty that at such an hour we shall be under the spiritual dominion of a haunting demon, the foe, as foolish as cruel,
whom we defy now with our reason, but shall then succumb to in
every faculty. Here is an ordeal for the proud! yet it is not less
fearful to the humble; for the humble can no more dispense with
self-respect than the proud.

   Some may wonder at such a history of an unknown trouble,—
some who, when anything harasses them, mount a horse, and gal-
lop over the sea-sands or the race-course, or visit their friends or
the theatre, or resort to music, or romp with children. Let them
remember that we cannot do these things,—that the very weakness which subjects us to these troubles, forbids our escape from
them. We know, as well as they, that if once we could feel the
open air upon our brows, our feet on the grass, our bodies in
exercise and vigour, all would be well with us; but, as we cannot
use these remedies, the knowledge is of no immediate avail. If we
can get to the window and look abroad, that is well, as far as it
goes; but we are most subject to our tyrant in the night, and in
midwinter,—at times when we cannot look abroad; and it may
even happen, too, that the tyrant dims the sun at noon-day, and
blots out the landscape, or renders us blind to it. What then is to
be done? We evade the misery, when we can, by stirring books,
(the most objective that can be had),[1] or by seeing what we can of
the world by the telescope, or by resorting to some sweet familiar
spring of poetry; but this last expedient is impaired by the fear of
mixing painful associations with pleasures too sacred and dear to

---

1   Martineau's original footnote here reads: "Nothing can be better, in this view, than
    Macaulay's 'Lays of Ancient Rome,' which carried us out of ourselves at full speed, as if
    we had been one of the listening school-boys whose eyes grew larger as we read."

be endangered. Or we defy the foe in reckless anguish, or we endure in silent patience.

But there is something far better to be done,—not always; but still, not seldom. We can turn the forces of ideas against themselves—meet them with their own weapons. We can call in the power of an idea to overcome the tyranny of another idea; and then we come off conquerors, and with a soul-felt joy.

It is a joy to recur, in memory or imagination, to any moral conflict, past or possible, in which all our faculties are needed, and wherein that force is at least conceived to be employed which must otherwise corrode us. But if any such enterprise actually presents itself—confronts us at the moment—how great is the blessing! It may bring toil and difficulty to ourselves, and doubt and blame from others; but if it be clear to ourselves, how keen is the sense of life it gives at some seasons, though it may overpower our weakness at others! It seems hard, when we are feeble and suffering, to have irksome labour to do; to have to oppose the wishes and feelings of some whom we love, and to arouse argument when our longing is for unbroken and lasting rest: but, if our duty be but clear to ourselves, (or for the most part clear, with doubts only in our most sickly hours,) what a new position we find ourselves in, permitted once more to take the offensive side against evil, in alternation with the weary perpetual defensive posture! Happy they, who have been brought up in allegiance to Duty, more or less strict; and happiest they whose loyalty has been the strictest! In the hour of nature's feebleness, and apparent decay, they find themselves under the eye and hand of the Physician of souls, who has for them a cordial of heavenly virtue—of heavenly virtue for them, but of no virtue to such as have let their moral nature take its chance, and who, in their hour of extreme need, are no more capable of spiritual enterprise than of a bodily flight beyond the precincts of their pain. They must languish in self-corrosion; while they who happily find how Duty gives "power to the faint,"[1] "mount up with wings as eagles."[2] With every emergency of singular or unpopular moral action,

---

1   Isaiah 40:29.
2   Isaiah 40:31.

every occasion for saying with courage a true word, or advocating a neglected cause—with every opportunity, in short, of spiritual enterprise, they soar afresh, and their eyes kindle anew in the light of life.

But this kind of solace could not be,—nor any effectual kind,—but for the power of the master idea of our life. But for Him who "stirreth up the nest,"[1] and whose spirit "taketh and beareth them up"[2] sunwards on her wings, the flights of these eagle spirits would utterly fail. But for the ideas inspired by Faith, there could be no enterprise, no true solace, no endurance but of the low, merely submissive kind. Great is the power of all thought, congenial with our nature, over disease of body and morbid tendencies of the mind; but those which connect us with the Maker of our frame and the Ordainer of our lot are absolutely omnipotent. O! let the speculative observer of human nature consider well, and observe that human nature to its extremest limits, before he pronounces that our spirits are not created filial. Let him ponder well the universal aspiration towards a spiritually-discerned parent, before he declares the affection a mere venerable superstition. Let him feel in health and full action,—(or, if he feels it not, let him detect in others,) the pausing horror of a sense of orphanhood, beneath which the moral universe falls in pieces under the hands of its myriad builders. Let him see in the sick-chamber, where the outward and inward world seem alike to the sufferer to be crumbling asunder, how irresistible is the conviction of an upholding power, new-modelling all decaying things, and imbuing them with immortality. If he himself can but learn what protracted sickness is, let him ponder well whether a superstition, however early and solemnly conveyed and cherished, could stand the stress,—not merely of pain, but of the questionings prompted by pain. Let him say if it can be anything but truth,—absolute congeniality with our souls,—which can give such all-conquering power to the idea of our filial relation to the Ruler of all things.

No one will venture to say how this power is enhanced by the

---

1 Deuteronomy 32:11.
2 Deuteronomy 32:11.

earliest associations. No one will presume to declare precisely how happy above others are they, now sufferers, whose infant speech was practised in prayer at a mother's knee, and who can now forget the dreariness of the night and the weight of the day in listening for the echoes of old psalmody, and reviving snatches of youthful hymns and religious reverie. No one will dare to say how far the sweet call to "the weary and heavy laden" is endeared by the voice of the Shepherd having gone before us over all the hills and vales of our life. But the true philosopher must, as it seems to me, be assured that the power of these spiritual appeals would ooze away, in proportion as our faculties are weakened by disease, if they had not in them the divine force of truth to urge them home.

See what this force is, in comparison with others that are tendered for our solace! One and another, and another, of our friends comes to us with an earnest pressing upon us of the "hope of relief," — that talisman which looks so well till its virtues are tried! They tell us of renewed health and activity, — of what it will be to enjoy ease again, — to be useful again, — to shake off our troubles and be as we once were. We sigh, and say it may be so; but they see that we are neither roused nor soothed by it.

Then one speaks differently, — tells us we shall never be better, — that we shall continue for long years as we are, or shall sink into deeper disease and death; adding, that pain and disturbance and death are indissolubly linked with the indestructible life of the soul, and supposing that we are willing to be conducted on in this eternal course by Him whose thoughts and ways are not as ours, — but whose tenderness.... Then how we burst in, and take up the word! What have we not to say, from the abundance of our hearts, of that benignity, — that transcendent wisdom, — our willingness, — our eagerness, — our sweet security, — till we are silenced by our unutterable joy!

Whence this imbecility of the "hope of relief?"

Whence this power of the idea of God our Father?

Do we know of anything stronger and higher than ideas? In the strongest and highest, — (even an omnipotent and infinite) idea, — if we have not Truth, what *is* Truth?

CHAPTER NINE

SOME PERILS AND PAINS OF INVALIDISM

"But few that court retirement are aware
Of half the toils they must encounter there."
                                    Cowper.[1]

"We are not to repine, but we may lawfully struggle."
                                    Johnson.[1]

I DESIRE to notice, very briefly, some perils and pains of our condition,—briefly premising that, as only the initiated can fully sympathise, it will be sufficient, and therefore best, to indicate rather than expatiate.

We are in ever-growing danger of becoming too abstract,—of losing our sympathy with passing emotions,—and particularly with those shared by numbers. There was a time when we went to public worship with others,—to the theatre,—to public meetings; when we were present at pic-nic parties and other festivals, and heard general conversation every day of our lives. Now, we are too apt to forget those times. The danger is, lest we should get to despise them, and to fancy ourselves superior to our former selves, because now we feel no social transports.

A lesser danger is that of fearing to experience emotions. If a barrel-organ makes itself heard from the street,—or a salute, on anniversaries, from the castle,—or a crowd gathers on the ridge to enjoy a regatta,—what a strange thrill comes over us! What a shrinking from being moved! How we wonder when we recal some discourse, whereby the voice of the preacher roused the souls of a multitude at once,—or when we awake within us the echoes of some Easter anthem, or of the Hallelujah Chorus in Westminster Abbey,—or when we image to ourselves a crowded theatre, when one tragic fear or horror bound together all the

---

1   William Cowper (1731-1800), "Retirement" (1782).
1   Samuel Johnson (1709-84), *The Rambler*, 32 (7 July 1750).

spirits that came for pleasure! When we try to imagine a flow of talk in which minds uttered themselves without thought of individuals;—when we revive these scenes of our former lives, we gasp for breath,—we wonder what we could have been made of to endure the excitement;—we are certain that we should die on the spot if we encountered it now. It might be so: but we must remember that our present condition is the morbid one, and not the former. We must keep up our sympathies, as far as we may, by cherishing such festal feelings as may survive; and ever remembering that our grave, and solid, and abstract life is adapted to only a portion of our nature, and that our exclusion from spontaneous emotions,—from all experience of sympathetic transport,—is a heavy misfortune, under which it behooves us to humble ourselves.

Those of us are well off who have, like myself, the advantage of some outward symbol which serves as communication between them and the world. Flags are my resource of this kind. Little do those who hoist them imagine how a hidden invalid appropriates their signals! The Union Jack[1] on the flag-staff, in the castle-yard, marks Sunday to me in a way I would not miss. When I look abroad on Sabbath mornings, it tells of rest and church-going; and it is a matter of serious business with me to see it brought down at sunset,—a mute token in which there is more pathos than I could tell. And then the flags on the churches of the opposite shore on festal days tell me of a stirring holiday world,—make me hear again the Park and Tower guns,—show me fireworks and illuminations, and arouse something of the hum and buzz of a gay and moving crowd. Once more, the foreign flags hoisted by ships coming into port,—mere signals for pilots in intention,—speak, unknown to any one, a world of things to me. I learned them long ago, by heart, and with my heart. When I see a foreign vessel come bounding towards the harbor, and perceive, the moment she hoists her flag, whether she has cut across from a Norway fiord, or has contested her way from the Levant, or found a path from the far Indies, or brings greetings from some familiar American port,—what a boon is that flag to me! Sometimes I point my

---

1   National flag of the United Kingdom.

telescope, to see the sailors' lips move in the utterance of a foreign tongue: at all events, I see in a moment the peaks of Sulitelma or of the Andes, or the summits of the Ghauts, or tropical sands, or chilly pine forests spread before me, or palmy West Indian groves. It is morally good, and unspeakably refreshing, to have some such instrumentality of signals with the world without, as these flags are to me.

There is a corresponding danger, though a less serious one, in such sympathy as we have making us repine. Though we may go on from month to month without one momentary wish that things were otherwise with us than as they are, yet, on occasion — once, perhaps, in a year — some incident wakens a thrill of longing to be as we once were. Some notice of a concert, or a picture, brings up the associations of a London spring, with all its intellectual and social pleasures: — or the mere mention of a lane or hedge, at the moment the March sun is shining in, recalls the first hunting for violets in our days of long walks: — or a foreign postmark in Autumn transports us to Alpine passes or the shores of Italian lakes; and a sickly longing for scenes we shall see no more comes over us. But the reaction is so rapid and sure, that there is little moral peril in this — only the evanescent pain, which gives place to that act of acquiescence which has in it more joy than can be gathered from all the lanes, mountains, and shores of the globe.

The occasional sense of our being too weak for the ordinary incidents of life, is strangely distressing. The cry of an infant makes us wretched for hours after, in spite of every effort of reason. I saw, through my telescope, two big boys worrying a little one, and I could not look to see the end of it. They were so far off that there was nothing to be done. The distress to me was such — the picture of the lives of the three boys was so vivid — that I felt as if I had no reason nor courage left. The same sort of distress recurred, but in a more moderate degree, when I saw a gentleman do a thing which I wish could dwell on his mind as it does upon mine. I saw, through the same telescope, a gentleman pick up from the grass, where children had been playing the moment before, under the walls of the fort, a gay harlequin — one of those toy-figures whose limbs jerk with a string. He carried it to his party, a lady and another gentlemen, sitting on a bench at the top of the rocks, whose base the sea was washing. When he had shown off the jerkings of the toy sufficiently, he began to take aim with it, as if to see how far he could throw. "He never will," thought I, "throw that toy into the sea, while there are stones lying all about within reach!" He did it! Away whirled harlequin through the air far into the sea below: and there was no appearance of any remonstrance on the part of his companions! I could not look again towards the grass, to see the misery of the little owner of the toy, on finding it gone. There was no comfort in the air of genteel complacency with which the three gentry walked down from the rocks, after this magnanimous deed. How glad should I be if this page should ever meet the eye of any one of them, and strike a late remorse into them! To me the incident brought back the passions of my childhood—the shock I have never got over to this hour—on reading that too torturing story of Miss Edgeworth's, about the footman, who "broke off all the bobbins, and put them in his pocket, rolled the weaving-pillow down the dirt lane, jumped up behind his lady's carriage, and was out of sight in an instant."[1] I think these must be the words, for they burnt themselves in upon my childish brain, and have stirred me with passion many a time since; as this harlequin adventure will ever do.

Many will wonder at all this—will despise such sensitiveness to trifles, considering what deeds are done every day in the world. They do not know the pains and penalties of sickness—that is all: and it may do them no harm to learn what they are, while my fellow-sufferers may find some comfort in an honest recognition of them.

This sensitiveness takes worse directions, however, and inflicts more misery still. It subjects some of us to a scrupulosity, particularly about truth, which brings endless troubles. Every mistake of fact that we happen to know of afflicts us as if we were responsible for it,—and more than it ought if we were so responsible. We tend to an absurd restlessness to set everything right; and of course, above all, what concerns ourselves. If any kind friend

---

1   Maria Edgeworth (1767-1849), Irish novelist.

pities us too much, and praises us for our patience under sufferings which he supposes to be greater than we are actually enduring, we remonstrate, and explain, as if his sympathy were not good for him and us, at any rate; and as if, having told only truth ourselves, it could matter much how our troubles are rated—whether over or under. We call up images of all who suffer far more than ourselves, and implore him to go and pity them—to honor them and not us. If he smiles and answers, well, he will go and pity and honor them—but he must be sorry for us, too—we smile, also, at our own scrupulosity, though we see in it only a new system of disease.

There is yet a worse direction taken by this sensitiveness—both morally and in experience worse. Though our observation of life encourages hope, on the whole, to a boundless extent, both as to affairs and to human character, it teaches some truths about individual characters which are almost too much for our weakened condition. It may be absurd—it may be wrong—to be more afflicted about the faults and failings of the best and most beloved people, than about the vices and gross follies of a lower order of men; but such affliction is, to us, quite inevitable. It is not wholly irrational; for it is a melancholy sight to witness the encroachment of any bad habit of mind in those who should be outgrowing such bad habits, instead of being mastered by them. But we know it to be the common order of things that every man, even the best, carries about with him through life some fault or failing (the shadowy side of his brightest quality, if nothing worse), and that it is the rarest thing in the world to see any strong tendency overcome after the age of resolution, the youthful season of moral heroism, is past: yet, knowing this, it is not the less painful to witness it, with the clearness and strength with which the spectacle offers itself to us, on our post of observation. While working in the world, side by side with those whose doings we now contemplate, we were willing to be deceived in each particular instance; willing to expect that the judgment and action of those we loved and clung to would, in each case, be accordant with their best gifts and graces; and, however often disappointed, we made allowance for the known frailty, and inconsistently hoped it would be better next time. We now see too clearly to be deceived. With the discernment of love, and the power of leisure, we can accurately calculate the allowance to be made—we can precisely measure the obliquity beforehand—and save ourselves at least from disappointment. But there is no solace in this. There is more pain in the proof of the permanent character of faults (permanence including inevitable growth), than in perpetual new evidence of their existence; more sorrow in our prophetic power now than in our credulous weakness of old. The accurate readers of human character may be admired and envied for their infallible knowledge of how men will think and act; but, if they have a true heart-love for those whom they watch, they cannot much enjoy their power. If they have not love, neither can they be happy; so that it requires a penetrative knowledge indeed, into the ways of God as well as man, for such skill to be reconcilable with peace and with our human affections. It is a burdensome knowledge for us to wield, in our weakened condition, and one which it requires an ever-strengthening faith to convert into a nourisher of love.

The faults I have alluded to are such only as are compatible with general sincerity—such as to have a character of frailty. Those which include tendencies essentially low—untruth, double-dealing, and selfish policy—assume so disgusting an aspect, when tested by the trying light and amidst the solemn leisure of the sick-room, that it cannot be wrong to follow willingly the irresistible leadings of nature—to dismiss them with loathing, and invite to our arms the simple and heroic sincerity, and the cheerful devotedness to the honour of God and the interests of man, which here assume much of the radiance in which they come back in vision from beyond the grave. If it be true that our moral taste becomes more sensitive in our seclusion, I trust that such sensitiveness has not necessarily any fastidiousness in it, but that its relish of good grows in full proportion to its discipline. I trust that if its disgust deepens as the low and cowardly order of faults are stripped to nakedness, so does its appreciation become more expanded and generous in regard to qualities which befit our heroic and aspiring nature and destination. As for our best resource under the liabilities I have alluded to, a mere reference will suffice. "Whatsoever things are honest, pure, holy, lovely—to think on those things;"[1] to fill our souls with conceptions of the

---

1   Philippians 4:8.

god-like, so that our sensitiveness may turn in time to a keen apprehension of all that is in affinity with these; this is what we have to do—partly for present solace, and much more for the chance of converting our weakness into power—our mortal discipline into a heavenly habitude.

As for the ordinary and familiar sufferings and dangers of our state, the weariness of life which every one but the physician wonders at, often as it is witnessed; the longing for non-existence, which some pious people, who admit no bodily origin of any mental affection, are very much shocked at; the despair during protracted violent pain, which, however, being dumb, is seldom known at the moment—these cannot be illustrated, nor remedied, by anything that can be said on paper. One can only suggest to the sufferer, and to wise nurses, that in the power of ideas we are furnished with an implement of natural magic which may possibly operate at the most hopeless times. It was in a sort of despair that the father of the lame child, inconsiderately led out too far, gave the boy his stick to ride home on; whereupon the aching foot actually traversed the needful mile without being felt to ache. So the wise nurse may possibly find that a nobler idea than any hope of rest or relief may reanimate a spirit under a far severer pain. And assuredly there are some who could tell how, in the midst of anguish, the briefest suggestion of endurance, the slightest spiritual touch upon deep filial affections, has made a miraculous truce for them with torment and despair.

Observers of the sick think very seriously of their liability to become wedded to their own ways, and engrossed by their own occupations. The fact is as they see it; but it would be happy for us if we had no worst mistakes to apprehend. Those of the sequestered who may re-enter the world will be pretty sure to fall in love with new ways and employments, and to feel a quite sufficient disgust with their own. And if they are never to re-enter life, is it not well for them that they can spend some energies, which would otherwise be corrosive, upon outward things? If their souls are too narrow and purblind to live beyond the bounds of their abode, the best thing for them is to get through the rest of their time as easily as they can, in the way that suits them best. If they are of a higher order, their observers may be assured of two things—that their investment of energy on the ways and occupations of their singular and trying life, is no more than a needful absorption of a power which would otherwise destroy them; and also, that there is no fear of these things becoming indispensable to them or sufficient for them. There are hours, witnessed by no observers, when they find it wise to desist from their most esteemed employments, in condescension to their own weakness, and recognise in this discipline the lesson of the day. There are hours, witnessed by no observers, when the insufficiency of such objects is felt as keenly and pressingly as by the Missionary on his way to the heathen, or the Prime Minister with the interests of nations in the balance before his eyes—or by the drowning man before whose soul life lies pictured in the instant of time which remains to him. This liability, though real, is insignificant and transient, compared with many others.

There is a safeguard against it, too, in our own weakness. There is even, for some, a danger of growing absolutely idle, from a sense of the littleness of what they can do. Formerly they acted on the rule—"not a day without a line,"[1] and now, thrown out of their habit by the absolute incapacity of some days, and disheartened by the small show made by their utmost rational diligence, they give up, and do nothing,—or nothing with regularity. This is a fearful danger. Nowhere are habits of regular employment more necessary than in such a life as ours; and, if we cannot preserve the absolute erectness of rationality,—if we must lean to the error of particularity or of indifference—I have no doubt of the former being the safer of the two;—the least injurious, and the most curable under a change of influences.

One of our most humbling and trying liabilities I do not remember to have seen mentioned anywhere, though it is so common and so deeply felt, that I have no doubt of a response from every sick prisoner (of a considerate mind), whose eye will fall upon this page. I mean our unfitness for doubtful moral enterprise. For *doubtful* moral enterprise, let it be observed. Where the case is clear, where the right appears to our own eyes

---

1   Martineau may allude here to "The Golden Fleece" by William Vaughan (1577-1641) or to "An Epistle to a Friend Concerning Poetry" by Samuel Wesley (1662-1735).

to be all on one side, whatever may be on the other, moral enterprise becomes our best medicine; it becomes health and new life
to us, as I have elsewhere said, be the responsibility and the immediate consequences to ourselves what they may. But when the
case is not so clear, when we are pressed (as all conscientious people, sick or well, strong or feeble, are at times) by antagonist considerations of duty, we cannot, as in our vigorous days, take a part
in some clear hour, and strengthen ourselves to bear recurring
doubts, and to take cheerfully even conviction of mistake, if experience should prove our conscientious decision to have been
unsound. We are not in a condition to bear recurring doubts, or
to take cheerfully a conviction of moral mistake. Our duty, in our
depressed circumstances, is to avoid such moral disturbance as we
have not force to quell. We must, in submission and compassion
to our own weakness, evade a decision if we honestly can; and if
we cannot, we must accept of help — human help — and proceed
upon the opinion of the soundest and most enlightened mind we
can appeal to.

If there are any who lift the eyebrows, and shrug the shoulders
at the supposition of this case, and declare that there is infallible
direction to be found, in all particular cases, in the principles of
religion, in answer to prayer, in the guidance of clergy, or the general opinion of mankind, I warn such that they will discover,
sooner or later, that there is yet something for them to learn of
morals, of the human mind, and of God's discipline of humanity.

There is no point of which I am more sure than that it is
unwise in sick people to keep a diary. Some suppose this task to
be one of the duties of the sick-room; whereas I am confident
that it is one of the most dangerous of snares. The traveller, moving from scene to scene in high health and spirits, keeps a diary;
he looks at it a few years after, and can scarcely believe his own
eyes when he sees how many entries there are of his hunger,
thirst, and sleepiness. He searches anxiously for a record of some
fact, important to the determination of a truth in science — some
fact of which he has a vague impression; he cannot find it, but
finds in its stead that he was chilly on that morning, or went to
bed hungry that night. If it be so in his case, how should the journal of a sick-room avoid becoming a register of the changes of a

morbid state? Not only this; but it can scarcely contain anything better. The experiencing and recording instruments themselves, the mind and body, are in a morbid condition, and cannot be trusted to perceive and record faithfully. Moreover, our tendency is, at the best, to an intense and growing self-consciousness, and our efforts should, therefore, be directed to having our minds called out of themselves — to causing our days to pass away as little marked as possible. A diary of public events, a register of books read, or of the opinions of those whose opinions are valuable on the great questions of the time, may be more or less amusing and profitable to keep; but then the rule should be absolute to exclude all mention of ourselves: and my own belief is, that it is wisest to avoid the temptation altogether — to keep clear of all bondage to ourselves and to habit that can be declined.

I was unutterably moved, lately, by the reading of a diary, preserved in MS., of one of the most innocent, holy, and devoted of God's human children; a creature who entered upon life endowed with good gifts, spiritual, intellectual, and external, and who wasted away in body, dwindled away in mind, and sank early to the grave, clearly through the force given by superstition to a corroding self-consciousness, to which she was by constitution liable. Her diary yields clear lessons which might profitably be made known, but that they are not apparently recognised by those who had the charge of herself in life, and hold her papers now. Among these lessons, one is to our present purpose. Her diary became more and more a register of frames and feelings, each mood of which was fearfully important to herself as a token of God's dispositions towards her. To an eye which now reads the whole at once, side by side with the dates and incidents of her life, nothing can be clearer than that the risings and fallings of her spiritual state exactly corresponded with the condition of her health. In one portion, the record becomes almost too painful to be borne. While her days were passed in heavenly deeds, and her solitude in prayer, she sinks daily lower and lower in hope and cheer: and at last, after a record of most mournful humiliation, we find a notice which explains all — of the breaking of a blood-vessel. To us it is nothing strange to experience fluctuations of more than spirits — of heart and soul, and to ascertain, after a time, that they were owing to physical causes. We even anticipate these changes, and know that when we awake in the morning, we shall be harassed by such and such a thought; that at such an hour of the day we shall suffer under remorse for such and such an old act and word, or under fear of the consequences of conduct which, at other seasons, we know to be right. We have that to tell of ourselves, which seems as a key to the mournful diary I have mentioned. This experience, and such warnings as that which has so deeply moved me, should teach us the wisdom and duty of not cherishing—by recording—our personal cares, but rather of "casting them upon Him who careth for us."[1] The most fitting sick-room aspiration is to attain to a trusting carelessness as to what becomes of our poor dear selves, while we become more and more engrossed by the vast interests which our Father is conducting within our view, from the birdie which builds under our eaves, to the gradual gathering of the nations towards the fold of Christ, on the everlasting hills.

---

1   1 Peter 5:7.

CHAPTER TEN

SOME GAINS AND SWEETS OF INVALIDISM.

> "God Almighty!
> There is a soul of goodness in things evil,
> Would men observingly distil it out!"
>
> Shakspere.[1]

> "Yet have they special pleasures, even mirth,
> By those undreamt of who have only trod
> Life's valley smooth; and if the rolling earth
> To their nice ear have many a painful tone,
> They know man does not live by joy alone,
> But by the presence of the power of God."
>
> Milnes.[2]

> "But here we are;— that is a great fact; and, if we tarry a
> little, we may come to learn that here is best. See to it only
> that thyself is here; and art and nature, hope and dread,
> friends, angels, and the Supreme Being, shall not be absent
> from the chamber where thou sittest."
>
> Emerson.[3]

IT is harder to be brief about our gains and privileges than about
our peculiar troubles: but I must try to be so; for the discoveries
we make, though to us all glowing with freshness and beauty, are,
to those who merely receive them, as trite as any old moralities
whatever.

One great and strange blessing to us is, the abolition of the
future—of our own future in this life.

It is commonly thought a chief privilege of childhood, that it is
passed without thought of the future—that the present is all in

---

1   William Shakespeare (1564-1616), *King Henry V*, Act IV, Sc. 1, ll. 3-5.
2   Richard Monckton Milnes, Lord Houghton, (1809-85), "Happiness."
3   Ralph Waldo Emerson (1803-82), "Heroism."

all. I doubt the truth of this. My own experience in childhood was of a painful and incessant longing for the future—a longing which enhanced all its innumerable pains, and embittered many of its pleasures—a longing for strength of body and of mind, for independence of action—for an escape, in short, from the conditions of childhood. The privilege which I then missed I have found now. Let it be a comfort to all sorrowing friends of those who are under any sort of doom without an assigned period, to know, that in such cases the sense of doom vanishes. When the future becomes a blank to us, it becomes presently invisible. And when we sustain this change we do not contract in our desires and interests, but, I humbly hope, the contrary. The thoughts which stretched forwards, with eagerness and anxiety, now spread themselves abroad, more calmly and with more disinterestedness. There is danger of our losing sympathy with the young, the healthy, the ambitious; for we soon require to be reminded of those states of mind, and those classes of interests which involve ambition, or any kind of personal regard for the future: but, if we can preserve these sympathies, it does appear to me that the change is, to ourselves, pure gain. The image of five, ten, twenty years of our present life, or decline into deeper suffering, ending in death, makes absolutely no impression upon us. We have not the slightest movement of a wish that it were otherwise;— we do not turn our heads half round to see if there be no way of escape: and this is because our interests are all occupied with immediate and pressing objects, in which we have ascertained our true life to consist. Of these objects we would not surrender one for the permission to go back to the most brilliant point of our lives. Wealth would be a trouble to us—a responsibility we would rather decline; and it is astonishing to us that any man can wish for more than is needed to furnish his children well for the probation of life. Ambition and its objects (or course, not including usefulness) appear to us so much voluntarily incurred bondage and fatigue. Subjection to the opinions of men—a dependence on their suffrages for any heartfelt object—seems a slavery so humbling and so unnecessary, that we could hardly wonder sufficiently at it, but for the recollection that all human desires and passions are the instruments by which the work of the race is done, and that ambition is far from being among the lowest of these instruments. Those of us who had known formerly, for a sufficient length of time, what it was to have fame, did not need to be laid by to discover how soon and how thoroughly it becomes disregarded (except for its collateral privileges), and left behind among our forgotten objects of desire: but our present position is the best for following out its true history — for tracing that path a reach beyond the point where moralists commonly leave it. The young aspirant is warned betimes, without practical effect, that the privileges of obscurity are irrecoverable: that, when he has become famous, he may long in vain for the quiet shelter of privacy that he has left. He feels this, with a sense of panic, when he has gained the celebrity he longs for, and is undergoing his first agonies from adverse opinion. If he would but believe us, we watchers could tell him that, though he can never retreat into his original privacy, there is a yet more complete shelter before him, if he does not linger, or take up his rest short of his journey's end. This shelter is not to be found in indifference, in contempt for human opinion — that ugly mask behind which some strive to hide the workings of an agonised countenance, while the scorchings of scorn beat fiercely on their brains, and the jeerings of ridicule torture their ears. There is no rest, no shelter, in contempt: and human opinion can never be naturally despised, though it has no claim to any man's allegiance. The true and welcome ultimate shelter of the celebrated is in great interests — great objects. If they use the power their fame puts into their hands for the furtherance of any of the great ends for which Providence is operating, they find themselves by degrees in possession once more of the external freedom, the internal quiet, the genuine privacy of soul, which they believed forfeited for ever, while the consciousness of the gaze of the world was upon them. They read what is said of themselves in print just as if it was said of any other person, if it be laudatory; and with a quieter feeling still if it be adverse, as I shall presently describe.

It is sometimes said, that it is a pity when great men do not happen to die on the completion of the one grand achievement of their lives, instead of taming down the effect by living on afterwards like common men; — that Clarkson[1] should have died on

---

1 Thomas Clarkson (1760-1846) was a well-known abolitionist and author of *An Essay on the Slavery and Commerce of the Human Species* (1786).

the abolition of the slave-trade,—Howard[1] after his first or second journey,—Scott on the publication of his best romance,—and so on. But there is a melo-dramatic air about such a wish, which appears childish to moral speculators. We are glad to have Clarkson still, to honor freshly in his old age. We see more glory about the head of John Quincy Adams contending, as a Representative in Congress, for popular rights, than he ever wore as President of the United States.[2] We should be glad that Rowland Hill[3] should live and work as a common man for a quarter of a century after the complete realisation of his magnificent boon to society. In truth, we behold great men entering early upon their heaven, when we see them tranquilly retired, or engaged in common labors, after their most memorable task is accomplished. The worthiest of celebrated men would, I believe, be found, if their meditations could be read, anticipating with the highest satisfaction, as the happiest part of their prospect beyond the grave, their finding a level condition once more—being encompassed by equals—or, as the popular preacher puts it, starting fair from the new post. Such being the natural desire of simple hearts, there is a pleasure to spectators in seeing them, while still here, encompassed with fellowship—not set above, nor apart, though enjoying the natural recompenses of their deeds.

The words "natural recompenses" remind me of another gain conferred on us by our condition—scarcely separable, perhaps, from those I have mentioned—from the extinction of all concern about our future in this world, and the ordinary objects of pursuit; but yet to us so conspicuous, so heartfelt, as to demand record as a blessing by itself. I mean the conviction of the hollowness of all talk of *reward* for conduct;—the conviction of the essential blessedness of goodness. What can appear more trite? Where is the church or chapel in which it is not preached every Sunday? Yet we, who heard and believed through all the Sundays and week-days of many years, seem but now to have *known* this

---

1   John Howard (1726-90) was a philanthropist and reformer in public health.
2   John Quincy Adams (1767-1848) was the sixth president of the United States, serving between 1825 and 1829.
3   Rowland Hill (1795-1879), originator of penny postage and various other postal reforms.

truth. Our knowledge is now tested by the indifference with which we behold men struggling for other objects, under a sort of insanity, as it appears to us, while the interests which animate us to sympathy are those of the pure in heart, seeing God before they die; and the dread which chills our souls is for the multitude who live in passion and die in moral insensibility. To us it appears so obviously the supreme good to have a healthy soul serenely reposing in innocence, and spontaneously working for God and man, that all divergence of aims from this end seems madness, and all imagery of rewards for moral desert the most profane of mockeries. It is a matter of wonder to us, that we ever conceived of royalty otherwise than as a title to compassion; of hereditary honors, as desirable; of fame, as an end; and we are apt to wonder at others, in their turn, that they do not perceive the most blessed of our race to be the moral reformers of each age, passing "from strength to strength,"[1] although wearing out in their enterprise, and the placid well-doers, whether high or lowly in their service. The appendages themselves of such a state—the esteem, honor, and love which wait upon moral desert—almost vanish from our notice when we are contemplating the infinite blessedness of the peace of a holy heart.

Then we have (not to dwell on a matter already spoken of) a peculiar privilege in the peculiar loveliness which the image of Death assumes to us. In our long leisure, all sweet and soothing associations of rest,—of relief from anxiety and wearing thought,—of re-entrance upon society,—(a society now sanctified!)—of the realisation of our best conceptions of what is holy, noble, and perfect,—all affections, all aspirations gather round the idea of Death, till it recurs at all our best moments, and becomes an abiding thought of peace and joy. When we hear or read of the departure of any one we knew,—of the death even of the youngest or the most active,—a throb of congratulatory feeling is our first emotion, rather than the shock which we used to experience, and which we now see sustained by those around us. Reflection, or tidings of survivors may change our view; but so does the image of Death become naturally endeared to us, that

---

1 Psalms 84:7.

our first spontaneous thought is of favour to those who are selected for it. I am not recommending this impression as rational, but
intimating it as characteristic of a peculiar condition. It is no
slight privilege, however, to have that great idea which necessarily
confronts every one of us all clothed with loveliness instead of
horror, or mere mystery. Till now, we never knew how any anticipation may be incessantly filling with sweetness.

It may be doubted whether there is a more heartfelt peace
experienced at any point of our moral progress than in the right
reception of calumnious injury. In the immediate return from the
first recoil into the mood of forgiveness, there is something heavenly even to the novice. In the compassion for one's calumniator
there is pain; and it is a pain which increases with experience of
life, and with our insight into the peril and misery of an unjust
and malicious habit of mind; but in the act of pitying forgiveness,
there is a solace so sweet as to make one wonder how long men
will be in adopting this remedy for their injuries. Any one who
has been ambitious, and with success, will, if he be wise, be ready
to declare that not the first breath of fame was to him so sweet as
the first emotions of forgiveness, the first stirrings of the love of
enemies, after his earliest experience of the calumny by which all
public effort is sure to be assailed. I am not supposing cowardly
acquiescence in insult and injury. I am supposing the due self-
assertion made, or defence found not to be practicable. This is all
that others have to do with. A man's self-communion on the
matter is his own private affair: and little know the systematic
calumniators, who for party's or prejudice's sake, assail those who
can only return silence, how they really work in some hearts they
seek to wound. In some they may excite rage or bitter anguish;
but there are others,—probably many,—in which they cause no
severer pain than a pitying sorrow for themselves, while they kindle a glow of courage, patience, and benignity,—they cause a
more exquisite mingling of sweet emotions,—than were ever
aroused by praise. The more defenceless the injured, the more
private and the more heavenly are these passages of his soul; and
none are more defenceless than sick prisoners. If subject to such
injuries in the world, where they could by their presence perpetually live down false aspersions, (aspersions on their opinions as

well as on their conduct,) helpless indeed are they when living out of sight, dumb in regard to society and through the press. Then, if their party foes take the opportunity to assail and misrepresent their opinions and their acts, those foes can have all their own way abroad in the world; but the very air of our sick-room turns them from foes into best friends. After one moment's sickening at the poor malice and cowardice, our thoughts fix on the high and holy truths to which they direct us,— on the transience of error,— the nothingness of fame, in the serious passages of life,— the powerlessness of assaults from without while we possess ourselves,— till we end in a calm and sweet mood of contentedness for ourselves and affectionate intercession for the victims of angry passion or of sordid interests. It does not move us painfully to think of our helplessness,— to contemplate leaving life without explaining our opinions, or justifying our views and enterprises. What is just and true will abide and prevail; and as for our claims to a share in the reputation, they seem in the sick-room worthy of only a smile. If we wrought for reputation, we must suffer, sooner or later, for the lowness of the aim; and now may be our time for taking a new growth through pain. But if we wrought for truth and good, we are not susceptible of the venom of the party slanderer. His sting proves no sting, but a beneficial touch rousing in us many tender, and resolute, and benignant feelings. These may be awakened wherever such a touch reaches us; but nowhere perhaps so sensibly as in the privacy and lowliness of the sick-room. I need say nothing of the benefit brought to us, by the same act, in the sympathy of generous minds. Of the blessing of sympathy I have already said so much that I dare scarcely approach the subject again. And never, as all know, does ministering affection so abound as towards the injured. When injury and helplessness unite their claims, there is no end to the multitude of hearts that throng to defend and aid. They are far more than are needed; for few — extremely few — are those who venture or who like to send the enmity of public life into the retreats of privacy. Very rare, I believe, is the species of men who insult when all the world knows there can be no reply. Still, such cases are witnessed; and of their operation I have spoken.

The greater number of invalids are under no such liability; but all may be subject to some injustice,—some misrepresentation which may reach their knowledge; and their emotions, both of recoil and of renovation, may be like in kind, and even equal in degree, to those I have intimated. If occasions for forgiveness should arise,—(and to whom do they not?)—may its relish be as sweet to them as it assuredly is to some more extensively tried!

An inestimable gain from the longest sickness is the outgrowth of the scruples and other conflicts which constitute the chief evil of merely long sickness. Of some perils and pains of our condition I have spoken, and I must therefore declare that there is a remedial influence in the very infirmity which appeared to create them. If it be but continued long enough,—if the struggle be not broken off before it is fairly exhausted,—victory will declare itself on the side of peace. We may be long in passing through the experience of weakness, humiliation and submission; but up, through acquiescence, we must rise, sooner or later,—true things separating themselves infallibly from the transient, and all that is important revealing itself in its due proportions, till our vision is cleared and our hearts are at rest. If the invalid of five years can smile at some of the anxieties and scrupulosities of his first season of retreat, much more clear-sighted must the ten years' thinker be in regard to the snares and troubles of his early or midway term. If, amidst the gain, as little as possible be lost, the privileges of our state may be such,—not as, indeed, to compare with those of health and a natural mode of life,—but as may satisfy a humble and rational hope that our season of probation is not lost, nor materially wasted.

The sick-room is a sanctuary of confidence. It is a natural confessional, where the spontaneous revelations are perhaps as ample as any enforced disclosures from disciple to priest, and without any of the mischiefs of enforcement. We may be excluded from much observation of the outer life of men; but of the inner life, which originates and interprets the outer, it is scarcely possible that in any other circumstances we could have known so much. Into what depths of opinion are we not let down! To what soaring heights of speculation are we not borne up! What is there of joy or sorrow, of mystery and marvel, in human experience that is not communicated to us! And all this not as if read in print,—not half-revealed, in the form of hints to such as can understand,—not in general terms, as addressed to the general,—but spoken fully and freely, with that particularity which fastens words upon the soul forever,—with those living tones of emotion which make the hearer a partner in all that is and has been felt. Here, we learn that the whole experience of humanity may be contained in one bosom, through such participation as we ourselves entertain; and even that all opinions, the most various and the most incompatible, may be deposited in one intellect, for gradual review, without inducing scepticism, and possibly to the strengthening of the power and privileges of Faith.

Göthe,[1] the seer of humanity, formed in himself the habit of agreeing with all the opinions uttered to him, alleging as his ground that there is always a sense in which everything is true, and that it is a good to encourage, and an evil to discourage, any belief arrived at in natural course. There are men with minds of a far lower order, but still somewhat superior to the average, who do precisely the reverse,—they see far enough to be aware that there is always something to be said to the contrary of what they hear uttered; and they cannot help saying it. They fall into a habit of invariable opposition, justifying the practice to themselves by the plea of impartiality,—of resistance to dogmatism,—of love of truth, and the like. I disapprove of both habits. Both practically injure belief, and damage the interests of truth. The natural operation of Göthe's method was to encourage in many indolence in the pursuit of truth and carelessness about opinions;—in some, doubts of the very existence of truth; and in all reflective persons, a keen sense of the insult conveyed, however unintentionally, by such treatment. Far worse, however, is the influence of the antagonist order of minds,—not only from their comparative numbers,—for there is not a Göthe in five hundred years,—but from the direct operation of their method and their example. A man who forms a habit of intellectual antagonism destroys more than can ever be repaired, both in his own mind and in those which he influences. He allows no rest in any supposition even to those

---

1 Johann Wolfgang von Goethe (1749-1832), German poet, novelist, and philosopher.

who have not power or leisure to follow out the research. He cuts their own ground from under them, and does not establish them on any other, for he himself appears to be established on none. Men of this order are, above all others, fickle in their opinions. Complacently supposing themselves impartial investigators into truth, they are, in fact, the sport of any one who, discerning and playing with their weakness, can put them up to the assertion and defence of any opinions whatever, and lead them into daily self-contradiction. What ensues is seen at a glance: — they tamper with truth till the structure of their own intellect becomes fatally impaired: — they denounce, as bigots, all men of every order of mind who remain steady in any opinions, and especially such as continue to hold opinions which they have themselves quitted: — they never doubt of their own fluctuations being progression, and that they are leaving all stable believers behind: — they learn no caution in the publication of their so-called opinions from their own incessant changes, but rather pique themselves on their eagerness to exhibit and insist upon each new view, and enjoy the occasion it affords for complacent amazement at all who hold the positions which they have themselves abandoned.

It may be said, that such men lose their influence, and with it their power for mischief. It is true that, by degrees, more and more decline argument with them, and they cease to have any convincing power, because it is seen that they themselves do not rest in permanent convictions; but their disturbing power remains. They can destroy, though they cannot build up. They can unsettle minds which yet they cannot lead. They can distress and perplex the humble and narrowly-informed; — they can startle, not only the slothful, (who will turn to sleep again, on the plea of the foible of the awakener) but the nervous and feeble who need repose; and, worse than all, they can irreparably injure the young, by spreading before them wide fields of inquiry, and then hunting them out of every corner in which they would be disposed to stay, and rest, and think. Men of this kind of mind have a certain power of sympathy with every species of opinion; and this good and attractive quality it is which mainly causes their self-decep-tion, and aggravates their power of injury. They mistake it for candour, at the very moment that they overflow with intolerance towards holders of opinions which they have relinquished. The result in such cases is always the same,—intellectual ruin, throughout the department of the understanding, however eminent the dialectical powers may appear, through the constant practice which has increased their original strength; and with the intellectual damage must be combined great moral injury. Göthe's method appears to be dangerous; but the opposite one is fatal.

To us, the depositories of vast confidences on these matters, it appears that there is no manner of necessity for either practice. We can avouch, from what we witness, that there may be sympathy with every order of understanding and every phase of opinion, without either hypocrisy, or tendency to disputation, or a surrender of differing views. We see how there may be an intrepid and continuous avowal of opinions, without disturbance to the unlearned and the feeble. We can fully agree with Göthe as to the unequalled mischief of endangering belief in that vast majority of minds which have other work to do than to investigate matters of opinion, without seeing it to be at all necessary to countenance what we know or believe to be error. We can fully agree with his practical antagonists as to the nobleness of candour, and the evils which ensue from dogmatism; while, at the same time, we would sooner die than dare to tempt one intellect to follow us, after one self-conviction of such an instability as theirs. Where there is a habit of mutability, there is intellectual infirmity, as is shown, with indescribable clearness, to us gazers into the mirror of events. It is a singular privilege granted to us, to witness the workings of the best method,—of that "simplicity and godly sincerity"[1] which is unconsciously adopted by the wise to whom Truth is neither the spirit of rashness, nor "of fear, but of power and of love, and of a sound mind."[2]

It has occurred to me, at times, that a second volume,—"On the Formation and Publication of Opinions,"—less popularly useful perhaps than the existing one, but deeper and more comprehensive, might be an invaluable gift from the hands of some one in a retreat, (in a sick retreat, as illness invites confidence,)—

---

1   2 Corinthians 1:12.
2   2 Timothy 1:7.

from the hands of some one who would know how to use with equal discretion and intrepidity his singular opportunities.

One of our most valuable discoveries is often made elsewhere, but is not sufficiently acknowledged and acted upon. We find, after a trial of many methods, that we learn to endure and achieve less by direct effort than by putting ourselves under influences favourable to the state of mind we seek. We have discovered the same thing before, in regard to mending our faults. We have found that childhood and youth were the seasons of resolution, and that, perhaps, we have not since cured ourselves of a single fault by direct effort. I am persuaded that instances are extremely rare of rectification by such means. I have myself amended only one bad habit—and that a very trifling one—by express effort, since I was twenty; and I could point out only two or three, of all my acquaintance, that I know to be capable of self-improvement in that direct manner; and I cannot but honour them in proportion to my sense of the difficulty and rarity of this exercise of moral power. Yet, how people go on expecting reformation in sinners from a mere conviction of the reason actuating the will, as they suppose, infallibly! The consequence of which foolish expectation is, that the true appliances are neglected. Wordsworth has it—

> "'Resolve!' the haughty moralist would say:
> 'This single act is all that we demand.'
> Alas! Such wisdom bids a creature fly,
> Whose very sorrow is that Time hath shorn
> His natural wings!"[1]

Instead of losing time, and practically invoking despair, by exhorting to impossible flights, wise guardians will rather remove the sufferer into an element of new enterprise, or one which may gradually exhaust and destroy his parasitical foes of habit. We sufferers experimentally ascertain this very soon. We find how little reason we have to trust to efforts of resolution under circumstances which tend to enfeeble resolution. We might be capable,

---

1 William Wordsworth (1770-1850), *The Excursion*, Fourth Book (1814).

as so many others are, of any amount of effort on a single emergency; but when we have to deal with a permanent infliction—to make the best of a difficult mode of life—we find that we must put our trust in abiding influences, and not in a succession of efforts. We therefore lay aside defiance; we submit ourselves—not to our troubles—but to every kind of natural preventive, remedy, and solace. We arrange our personal habits so as to husband our ease, and to conceal our pain; and we place our minds under such influences, intellectual and spiritual, as may best nourish our higher powers, and occupy our energies, to the alleviation, if it may not be to the exclusion, of the suffering, whose challenge we will neither entertain nor defy.

Among other merits of this method, may be reckoned this—that it helps to introduce us to a privilege which may be disregarded by many, but which to us is inestimable—that of causing pleasure, rather than pain, to those connected with us. It is the prerogative of the healthy and happy to give pleasure wherever they go; it is the worst humiliation and grievance of the suffering, that they cause suffering. To the far-seeing invalid, who is aware not only of this immediate effect, but of its remote consequences, this is the most afflicting feature of his condition. If we can, by any management, evade this liability, we have cause to be grateful indeed. If, by submitting ourselves to all softening and ennobling influences, we can so nourish and educe the immortal part of ourselves as to subdue our own conflicts, and present our active and enjoying aspect to those who visit us, we are absolved from the worst penalties of our state. If, as years pass on, we find ourselves sought from the impulse of inclination, as well as from the stringency of duty—if we are permitted to see faces light up from ours, and hear the music of mirth succeed to the low serious tones of sympathetic greeting—we may let our hearts bound with the assurance that all is well with us. When we cannot refuse to see that children come to us eagerly, and that our riper companions stay late by our sofa, and come again and again, till nothing short of duty calls them away, any one might envy us the feelings with which we lie down again in our solitude. We are not proud, like the young beauty with her conquest over hearts, or like the political or literary hero with his sway over the passions

or the reason; but we are elate — and not without cause — elate in
our privilege of annihilating the constraint and distaste inspired by
our condition, and of finding ourselves restored to something like
an equality of intercourse with the healthy in soul. The best and
highest must ever be selected from among the healthy and the
happy — from among those whose conditions of being are the
most perfectly fulfilled; but, without aspiring to their consummate
privileges, we feel ourselves abundantly blessed in such a partial
emancipation as permits us, on occasion, and without shame, to
join their "glorious company."

Appendix A: Introduction to the American Edition of Life in the Sick-Room[1]

Although this work, which cannot fail to be a blessing to humanity, had no name attached to it, yet every line of it so proclaimed its author, that the effort to be lost in her subject was vain. All those in England who read it, found their thoughts and their hearts visiting, with grateful love, the sick-room of her to whom MILNES[2] addressed these beautiful lines in the "Liberty Bell"[3] for 1843:

TO HARRIET MARTINEAU.

CHRISTIAN ENDURANCE.

BY RICHARD MONCKTON MILNES, M.P. FOR PONTEFRACT.

Mortal! That standest on a point of time,
    With an eternity on either hand,
Thou hast one duty above all sublime,
    Where thou art placed, serenely there to stand.

To stand, undaunted, by the threatening death,
    Or harder circumstance of living doom;
Nor less untempted by the odorous breath
    Of hope, that issues even from the tomb.

For hope will never dull the present pain,
    Nor fear will ever keep thee safe from fall,
Unless thou hast in thee a mind, to reign
    Over thyself, as God is over all.

'Tis well in deeds of good, though small, to thrive;
    'Tis well some part of ill, though small, to cure;
'Tis well with onward, upward hope, to strive;
    Yet better and diviner to endure.

---

1   Life in the Sick-Room was published by Leonard C. Bowles and William Crosby in Boston in 1844.
2   Richard Monckton Milnes, Lord Houghton (1809-85).
3   The Liberty Bell was annually published between 1839 and 1859.

What but this virtue's solitary power,
    Through all the lusts and dreams of Greece and Rome,
Bore the selected spirits of the hour
    Safe to a distant, immaterial home?

But in that patience was the seed of scorn—
    Scorn of the world, and brotherhood of man;
Not patience, such as in the manger born,
    Up to the cross endured its earthly span.

Thou must endure, yet loving all the while;
    Above, yet never separate from thy kind;
Meet every frailty with a tender smile,
    Though to no possible depth of evil blind.

This is the riddle, thou hast life to solve;
    And in the task thou shalt not work alone;
For while the worlds about the sun revolve
    God's heart and mind are ever with his own.

These lines furnish the key-note to the tone that pervades this whole work. Such was Harriet Martineau's earnest desire to do what she could for her fellow-sufferers, by giving them the results of her painful but precious experience through a hopeless illness of five years, that she was irresistibly impelled to utter herself to the world once more; but her reluctance to the self-exposure, was so great, that she threw what veil she could over her words by withholding her name: not even her nearest and dearest friends knew that she had written such a book, 'till the grateful public declared that no one but her, could have written "Life in the Sick Room." I cannot but think that it will form a new era in the history of every invalid that reads it and enters into its wise counsels, its inspiring views.

As it is no longer a secret who is its author, some of her friends in this country have consented that her name should be attached to the book, trusting that she will forgive them for the liberty they take. She will doubtless be astonished to find it so soon republished here; but I feel assured that when she hears of it, she will be rejoiced. The wider and farther her words of "lofty cheer" to the sick can be heard, so much the happier will she be: therefore, without consulting her, yet with entire trust in her joyful acquiescence, I dedicate, in her name, this reprint of "Life in the Sick Room," to all the prisoners to disease in America,—the land that she truly loves.

The publisher, Mr. Bowles, has set a worthy example to his brethren of the profession, by proposing to set apart for the author a certain proportion of the sales of this republication. Of course no other publisher will do anything to interfere with his just and generous purpose.

E. L. Follen.[1]
April, 1844.

---

1 Eliza Lee Follen (1787-1860), author of *Poems* (1839).

Appendix B: Contemporary Reviews of Life in the Sick-Room

1. From *The Christian Examiner* 38 (March 1845): 158-69.

Some may, possibly, have been misled by the title of Miss Martineau's volume to expect in it a manual of the common sort, for the use of invalids. But it is found to be far other, and vastly more, than this. Not deficient in whatever pertains to its special purpose, it is rich in thoughts and suggestions of high value, relating to topics of a wide and general interest. It supplies the results of much and profound reflection on the science of human nature. It is occasionally eloquent on themes which connect themselves with the higher spiritual philosophy. It combines the discussion of great principles with the noblest persuasives to great virtues.

The variety of tone and manner, as well as of topics, in these Essays is remarkable. We are far from being confined to the same wailing chord. One may even detect a sportive fancy at work among the graver faculties, pleasantly doing the bidding of a kind heart. We might cite in proof the Essay styled "Nature to the Invalid." How exhilarating, and how beautiful it is! So too, that entitled "Life to the Invalid," in which we almost forget we are reading any other than a very lively discussion by a fine mind in high health and spirits. Nothing morbid occurs in the whole book. The evils which it brings to view are those we recognize, as found in all sick-rooms, not heightened, sometimes softened in the description, and always spoken of with a calm, uncomplaining spirit. The author is quick to acknowledge every mitigating circumstance which blends with painful scenes, every remnant of good in any, however unhappy condition. Her affectionate gratitude may exaggerate, but never undervalues. In giving moral counsel, or enumerating moral dangers, her humility prompts to the phrase, "the liabilities of *us* sick." And we know not what disparager of human merit would not be reenforced from her lowly depreciation of all solace borrowed from the conscience, to which she refuses the office of consoler altogether. We mark on every page some new proof how calamity has been overborne by spiritual power: how the mind that "by disuse had forgotten its sense of enjoyment," has yet kept its lights undimmed, its aspirations still ascending, its love disinterested and fervent, and its piety, like the wave-worn rock, immovable amidst the storm. Indeed, it is for its rational yet elevated and spiritual views of religion, its clear and simple, yet sublime and ennobling inculcations of duty, that this production will make most interest for itself in the general mind.

The charm of the book to those in whose behoof it was written, will be the thorough apprehension of their case which it manifests, and that true and deep sympathy with them which pervades it throughout. The sick sometimes need the spiritual aid and comfort, which can be found only in the presence with them of one who enters into their condition, understands and feels it. They languish, not seldom we fear, as hopelessly in want of a perfect sympathy, as for the adequate relief to their outward malady. Here they have, reproduced from another's experience, whatever in their own has most perplexed and disheartened them. They are taught by one who has known all they know of the condition of which she speaks, and are encouraged and strengthened by sympathy and affection in a fellow-sufferer. That she has tasted their griefs and felt their trials they are painfully sure, but the pain is removed by the triumph over all these which is revealed in her work, and of which she shows them how they may partake. There is no indulgence to their faults indeed, and no attempt to screen them from the truths which search the wounded heart unsparingly. But there is a merciful tenderness intermingling with this fidelity, all the more soothing and dear for its coming from so true a spirit. Those who suffer with us cannot easily offend by admonitions which their better wisdom prepares them to give, and which are explained and enforced in the evident fruits of their own experience. Never was there a more cordial welcome to friend in the sick-room, than, we are confident, will reward the author of this excellent volume. She will give a new life to minds which were almost paralysed by the blow, that severed them from the influences on which they were too dependent for health and vigor. We can conceive no higher beneficence than that which has thus converted the very wreck of personal happiness to uses of charity, and made the severest personal endurance tributary to others' good.

...

But we must forbear, and commit this gift of Christian wisdom, piety, and love to the thoughtful and, we are sure, thankful use of those whose highest welfare it was intended to subserve. For the principles which it inculcates, for the exalted ideal it presents, for the renovating spirit with which it is filled, the book cannot fail to be "a blessing to humanity."

Recent inquiry has brought to light many startling facts, in relation to permanent unhealthiness, with its occasions. From these, one would almost infer that perfect, continued health had come to be the exception, instead of the rule, with the human race. What small community cannot array a host of invalids? What family is without one or more? Upon examination, there must needs be discovered, among the immediate causes of the loss of health, much ignorance respecting the conditions on which that great blessing of God is conferred and prolonged, and much neglect or wanton violation of the laws which determine the state of the human constitution. The blame which is called forth in these cases is sometimes extended to others, which properly fall under a different category. Hence some even talk, as if it were morally wrong to be sick. And the victim to even unmerited suffering is flouted, if he say, "There is a Providence in it."

Unquestionably, there is large room for the severe but kindly meant animadversions, to which we here allude. Men and women, who might and ought to know better, do disregard the conditions and laws upon which health is dependent, expose and squander good constitutions, and bring on themselves and their children irreparable evils in the various forms of disease. In compliance with the merest follies and extravagances, which happen to be called "fashions," thousands rush on their own death. The facts should be promulgated. The doctrine which reaches them should be solemnly, rigorously, we had almost said inexorably, enforced. Such infatuated solicitation of physical ruin ought to be repressed and rebuked with all reasonable severity. But still there is a limit to be respected. There are distinctions, important to be drawn, which may be neglected in our sweeping censures. Some things are more precious than health, or than life. The human heart is among them.

It were idle, to go about to prove that many other causes, besides the censurable ones which benevolent moralists concern themselves with, may induce an invalid's condition. Health may have never been possessed in soundness; hereditary disease may have prevented its enjoyment; it may be lost through innocent error, or sacrificed to benevolent impulses. One loathes the sensual view which would make man's best estate a healthful condition of his frame merely, irrespectively of the great purposes for which life and all our powers were bestowed. It is for the sake of those purposes chiefly, that we may covet permanent health, and be at great cost and pains to secure, or recover the boon. Apart from these, wherein lies its value to a noble mind? To a duty one might sacrifice his life, much more his health.

However induced, in spite of every care, diseases will come upon men. They come, *under* a Divine Providence, if not *by* it,—permitted, if not sent. Life in the sick-room is a common phase of human existence everywhere. While we direct to its removal all the power which better knowledge and increasing virtue yield, it becomes a proper and interesting question, how disease is to be considered with regard to the soul's life and progress? To what spiritual uses may the discipline of this form of suffering be conducive?

...

To this position, taken as it is designed to be, we assent of course, although we might prefer it stated with its implied qualifications. Who doubts, that a vast many of our race would have been better, if they had been happier? Who,— that has seen, what too often occurs, youth become apt to evil, when the morning of life has been shorn of "its natural blessedness," and the man grow reckless of duty, after he has despaired of reaching the good for which he has panted and struggled long years in vain? It is clear, that the moral nature is likely to fare best where the whole being is in its proper, normal condition. Yet, the human soul has energies enough to burst all the bonds of untoward circumstance. It has shown that it *can* "make its spiritual growth" in spite of the limitations which tend to dwarf its powers, and the sufferings which threaten to blight them. The heroic virtues, which have honored and blessed our common humanity, are the trophies of such a victory. Some sublimer redeeming influence has superseded the inferior agencies of good, in such instances, but not demonstrated their inutility. If, however, according to the test above cited, abundant happiness be the soul's more genial atmosphere, without which it may pine, in which flourish, what shall we say to the invalid's lot? Small is the portion of this propitious element which gathers around life in the sick room.

It would be worth our while to trace, amidst the desolations which permanent disease creates, the footsteps of that Mercy which descends to repair them. We do not admit to our minds freely enough the lights which might gild, if they could not dissipate, the clouds which brood over them. God forbid we should represent as less than they are the sorrows of the sick. They can hardly be spoken of unreservedly to the healthy and happy, without the semblance of exaggeration. But they who will enter the dark retreats which cover them, may know for themselves what those sorrows are. Others cannot know by being told. Yet sternly, terribly, as the evils in the prison-house of the victim to disease may frown upon us, there are good angels among them, whom having seen we remember forever with inexpressible tenderness and joy.

One element among those most obvious in this sad condition, is the deep, entire, often dreary seclusion it implies. In health we range far and wide, unrestrained. Our track is on the morning dews "o'er every pleasant hill and dale;" we linger at nightfall by the murmuring brook, or the shore which echoes the moan of the sea. Nature opens for us all her springs of delight. Society awaits our coming, with other pleasures and gifts of instruction to bestow. And there are yet other resources for mind and for body, wholesome and not without their charms, in the scenes where business traffics. This free contact with a thousand varieties of outward objects and interests is replete with spiritual uses. We lose and forget ourselves in the open world. Collision brings out thoughts and feelings which had else slept within us, and the soul may be thus enriched, and is always quickened and animated. The intellectual activity receives here direction as well as impulse, and when tending to excess is conducted off through many safe channels. But with health this liberty passes away. The invalid must dwell apart where the world will not follow him. He has few severer pangs than the one which accompanies the conviction, that he is henceforth cut off from free intercourse with nature and society, and has no longer a part in the common business and amusements of life. Long will images of objects once cherished, but abandoned now, continue to haunt his waking and his sleeping hours. In his feverish dreams he resumes suspended tasks, stands at the wonted desk and writes, makes sales, calculates accounts; or he revisits favorite places, sits beneath the tree on the rock which he rested by when a child, joins the merry ring on the green sward, kneels on the hassock with his parents to pray. But he wakes to find it only a dream. He is alone in a retirement from which he can seldom, perhaps never, be withdrawn. Not his, the solitude which the scholar knows well to enliven. Happy were it so. With his aching frame and unstrung nerves few studies could be made compatible, supposing he had the disposition and the means to pursue them. Not his, the solitude of the artist; those are brighter and happier hours than his, which are spent with pallet, pen, or chisel in hand, however spent alone. Intelligence with him has put off its dignities, and genius has done with her creations. The hands which hang down and the feeble knees are no more unsuitable to their wonted uses, than the higher faculties to their former employments, in their present drooping and spiritless condition. He sits, alike in pain or quietness, idle, or with varied expedients, all poor enough, to keep from seeming idle. What exertions of mind or body he puts forth are so different from those he once made, that he can find nothing in them to raise self-esteem, though they help to beguile the sorrows he must still endure. Other and yet darker incidents overshadow the picture, but we will not name them. Enough, if we have indicated what is implied in sequestration from the common paths and interests of men.

And have we any offset to all this? There is one, arising from the very circumstances that produce the evils we have adverted to. In exclusion and banishment, amidst dreariness and despondence, when heart and flesh are failing, the soul obtains a new, and a more profound conviction than it ever had before, of the highest truths. How does it then begin to apprehend as a reality the great presence of God! He was near in happier scenes and hours, as He is in these. But many other objects were interposed, which turned the thoughts from Him, or attracted to themselves what should have been his alone. In the captivity which has torn it away from them, it is restored to Him. God becomes to the soul then a refuge and solace, when the idols it had suffered to supplant him have been all destroyed.

There are few situations in which man feels his relation to God and his dependence on the Divine mercy more sensibly, than in the solitude created by a hopeless disease. The stillness necessary to the shattered frame is propitious to the holiest thoughts and emotions. The humiliations which are attendant upon infirmity and pain bring low, even into the dust before him, whatever exalteth itself against God. The helplessness, that knows not what to do nor where to look for relief, carries us to him who is able to supply all our need. Ah! with what emphasis might a sick and dying man reiterate the exclamation, "I have heard of Thee with the hearing of the ear, but *now* mine eye seeth Thee!"

With its new sense of God, the afflicted and humbled spirit attains also a better knowledge of itself. The essential worth of a human soul is effectually taught by the process which takes all its dross away. Life in the sick room is existence stripped of its factitious adornments, from which all pomp and pride and festal shows, the glory of man, have departed. Whatever had been fuel to vanity is consumed in that furnace; all that was beautiful to the eye of a fond self-esteem is marred there; but beneath these is disclosed what outvies them by an infinite value. It is when man has seen all distinctions but moral ones reduced to nothing, and has learned how unavailing are riches and titles and pleasures to meet life's sorest exigence, and prepare for death's severing blow, that he begins to know in what his own worth consists. And in the penitent endeavor to repair what by the frailty of his nature and his own sinfulness has been lost of that true worth, he has a consolation which beguiles him of all that is bitter in the thought of other losses, which he wants power to make good again.

To the better knowledge of himself, and more intimate communion with God, the discipline of his peculiar lot will add, for the invalid's solace, a more adequate appreciation of his fellow-beings. They who minister to his wants, give him the daily blessing of their sympathy, and lavish their affection upon him, are understood now and valued as they deserve. His dependence upon their assistance and care for the alleviations which his suffering state admits, makes him feel how little he deserves in comparison with the much which he receives. Their sacrifices of rest and ease and enjoyment for his sake, teach him the disinterestedness which he requires to have constantly in exercise, if he would not sink from wretchedness to self-contempt and despair. How the voices penetrate us, which "whisper of peace" to our sick hearts! What a beauty is there in the smile that beams within our close apartment! How we welcome the kind ones, who come to break the long stillness of our solitary room with their pleasant words! Then are love's divinest offices made known to the soul. And to the help of our purer purposes and humbler efforts to improve the fruit of the sharp teachings of pain, comes the strong impulse which is imparted by the virtues in others which have so redounded to our good.

Yet another element in the spiritual process which is going on amidst the sorrows of sickness, is the deeper conviction obtained through them of the value of our Christian faith and hope. It is when the night of life's direst experiences has fallen upon us, when the true light pours down upon a mind bewildered and fainting in an untried, unimagined way, that the Gospel proves itself divine. "He that believeth hath," then "the witness in himself."[1] The conviction produced in life's best and happiest hours, cherished amidst every vicissitude, having borne the soul onward in peace "through all time of its prosperity and all time of its tribulation," remains to cheer and strengthen it in the season of desolation, decay, and death. In the methods which God employs to deepen and secure such a faith in himself, in the Redeemer, and in immortality, the lingering agony which belongs to an invalid's experience has its place. The endurance is more than compensated by the unutterable feeling of the preciousness of those promises and hopes, which is obtained by the fiery trial.

E.Q.S.[2]

2. The Dublin University Magazine 23 (May 1844): 573-82.

ESSAYS. BY AN INVALID.

This is a wise and thoughtful book—the offspring of a lofty mind—and, coming to us with its pleading motto,

"For they breathe truth that breathe their words in pain," cannot fail in finding a welcome. Its tone is healthy; and the subjects with which it deals are of the highest kind. We have seldom opened a volume more pregnant in noble thought; and throughout are the traces of a disciplined spirit—a spirit raised and exalted by suffering, which finds "good in everything" it encounters by the way to its rest.

The writer is evidently a woman. Were we without the half acknowledgment that it is so, we should have surmised the fact from the tone and temper of the work. There is the characteristic fortitude of the sex under great privation and trial manifest; the silent endurance; the patient hope; the weakness where man would be strong, and the power where man would be weak; and, above all, the deep religion of the heart, and its inner devotion, which we find so difficult—and sometime impossible—to attain to. Moreover, the style betrays the practiced hand; it is simple, yet eloquent, never deficient in power, and always unaffected and chaste; its beauty is not marred by false ornament. We were constantly reminded by it of what the old Spectator quaintly termed "thinking aloud"—the highest praise that can be given to the essay form of composition.

---

1   1 John 5:10.
2   Possibly Elizabeth Sewall.

But we hear some of our own readers turning impatiently from the title of our review. "'Essays; by an Invalid!'—pooh, pooh! what does the sick man, or woman—whichever it be—mean by chronicling his, or her, pains and griefs?—cataloguing, I suppose, the physician's visits, and copying out the apothecary's bills. I'll none of it, and pass on." Be not so hasty, good friend, for we know you are not in general so thoughtless. Have you never looked upon sickness in its true light, as a course of moral probation, which it is a blessed thing to pass through, albeit the journey itself be wearisome? Have you never experimentally felt the new ideas it gives one—beheld the new light it floods this world in—and found in your own breast such revealings of present and future good as more than atoned for whatever of trial it brought you? We know well that health and sickness are two states so different, that there can exist—naturally—but little sympathy between them; and now we are not going to bring you into the gloom of a sick chamber, but into bright light. In examining the work before us, we shall show you trains of thought which the healthful are too giddy to seek after, and which perhaps they are not constituted to experience, even were their search most diligently conducted.

In truth, the daily life of the mind is a thing too generally neglected. No doubt metaphysical studies are more followed now than at any previous time, and the progress we have made in them is as pleasing as it has been unexpected; but in these we have more the mind's history than the record of its daily experiences. They rather lay before us the development of its marvelous powers, than reach and touch us by a sense of personal engagement. Thus they want *individuality*; and relate to the common possessions of the species, chiefly if not altogether. It is far different to know these things ourselves, to learn them from our own inner thoughts, and form our philosophy less on books than on the γνωθι σεαυτον.[1] When laid aside from the busier scenes of life, we are in a manner constrained to this wise self-searching. The period of invalidism, which unfits us for the turmoil of active existence, seems peculiarly adapted for the acquirement of this hallowing wisdom. We breathe a purer air. When worldly hope dies, a better hope is born; and in a few days or hours of sickness, we acquire experiences which the long years of previous health had failed to impart.

The measure of time is not the years we live, but the feeling we have present with us during their progress. Thus, some hours are longer with us than as many days; and some days seem as though they would never end. We speak of seasons of agony, whether of mind or body. Byron says to the purpose—

---

1   The Delphic wisdom, "Know Thyself."

"A slumbering thought is capable of years,
And curdles a long life into one hour."[1]

Pain or joy become, in their several ways, the gauges of duration—the former lengthening it out into an apparently interminable existence—the
latter causing even years to pass away in rapid and unmarked flight. The
experience of every one will confirm our statement. But these antagonistic
principles (and not less so in their nature, than in their present effects) leave
behind them, with the heart that receives them aright, one abiding
influence of good. Pain passes away, and is forgotten; good subsists, and
immortally survives...

We trust that there are hundreds whose experiences are of a like nature;
but clearly it is not every sufferer who possesses equal strength of mind. To
recognize in pain a chastisement whose tendency is unmixed good—"a
mere disguise of blessings otherwise unattainable"—a holy medium
through which the soul must pass to a higher life—one must feel that it is
sent us from a divine hand. Imperfectly as we frame our ideas now, calling
very often evil good, and good evil, when we acknowledge that we are at
present in a state of moral discipline, we come of necessity to this happy
conclusion. We look not so much on the narrow present, as "before and
after" with the eyes of memory and hope, and see light gradually evolving
from the darkness, and heavenly intentions of good wrought out by means
apparently the most adverse. And so our invalid is enabled to speak, at the
twelvemonth's end of all...

We have next the subject, sympathy to the invalid, discussed. How
difficult to sympathize aright! Good-nature will not do this; it is too often
as repulsive as it is kindly-intentioned. Friendship itself here at times fails; it
has no plummet for the depths of hidden sorrow. But when this nearness of
identification is reached, what boon on earth beside could compensate for
it?...

Yes; the fitting habitant of the sick room is truth, simple truth; yet, in no
other place is deception, in all its hollowness, so often found; and false
hopes are excited by well-meaning friends, who with cruel mocking
promises bid the sufferer look forward to reviving health, even when it has
wholly departed. The true friend is he who tells the truth...

Of the false kinds of consolation, that which sends us back to our former lives to meditate on what we have done, and draw comfort from it, is
the very vainest; and we truly agree with our author, that the function of
conscience is not that of a comforter. The stern rebuker of all that we do

---

1   George Gordon Byron (1788-1824), *The Dream*.

amiss, how can it rejoice beings whose lives are so many multiplied wanderings? Oh, little at any time can it do other than chasten; but, when crowding in its images upon the heart weakened by sickness, what can it else do than irrevocably condemn? And yet men speak of the "happiness of an approving conscience!"...

There are next some touching allusions to those "marked days" — anniversaries — so joyous with us in early youth, so mournful when time's finger inscribes them upon tombs. These commemorative seasons, and, above all, that day of olden merriment, Christmas, our invalid recommends should be passed alone. With her sprigs of holly over the fire-place, she can flit away, fancy-plumed, to a thousand hearths, enter "rooms full of young eyes," or gaze for a moment on "the cozy little party of elderly folk round the fire or tea-table," and make her memories her companions during the livelong day. But these subjects are lightly touched on, as though the heart within her failed in giving them utterance; and the sorrowful Now was, we fear, victorious in the end. A birth-day spent — we can hardly say kept — in a sick room is sufficient to make the most heedless think; but she draws her comfort from the reflection — "If with every year of contemplation the world appears a more astonishing fact, and life a more noble mystery, we cannot but be re-animated by the recurrence of every birth-day, which draws us up higher into the regions of contemplation, and nearer to the gate within which lies the disclosure of all mysteries which worthily occupy us now, and doubtless a new series of others, adapted to our then ennobled powers." A sublime imagining, and no less true than solemn; yet declaring too well that mere human help was insufficient on such occasions.

The subject of the third Essay is nature to the invalid; it is admirably considered. We need not dilate on the theme, in introducing it, for its power and beauty are sufficient recommendation. All who have seen the look of rapture with which the eyes of the dying are lighted up on beholding fresh and living flowers, remember that sight for ever. It is wonderful, that power of nature over sick and wasted forms, acting upon them like an enchanter's spell, and calling back life to beat strongly about the heart, as in better days! The sights and sounds about us, at such a time should be well-chosen; they will vary with different dispositions — some are satisfied if they can lie all day long, with eyes beholding heaven — others look lower to the green earth or the sea expanse...

We are less inclined to agree with the writer's speculations on Life, than with any other portion of the volume. The world's amelioration, and the consequent increase of human happiness, are her fond dreams; and she grounds their now probable nearness upon the growing influence of the popular classes. We are old-fashioned enough to regard the movements of the present day with fear, rather than hope. We do not think we have strengthened our political building by knocking away the buttresses and carefully picking out the corner-stones; nor do we see that we have wisely legislated for the masses, by giving them, through our new enactments, fifty masters where they had formerly one. We are stupid enough also to discredit the people's advancement in virtue, since the era of reforms began. Neither increased power, nor increased knowledge, imply of necessity augmented goodness. A sword in a child's hand is most dangerous to the weak wielder of it; perhaps it had better for ever rested in its sheath. We want faith, moreover, in the world's improving itself; and we shall continue to hold such a thing as of impossible occurrence so long as we perceive man deficient alike in the power and in the will to effect the change. We are sure that when such an advancement comes, it will not be from the operations of the human mind, but from a change in the human heart.

The essay "Death to the Invalid," though eminently beautiful, appears to us over full of shadowy mysticism. There is too much of philosophy in it — too little of religion. Here, if any where, on account of our utter ignorance, speculation should have little place. None but they who tasted of it, can tell what it really is; yet the living love to colour it with their own fancyings, and according to different dispositions or different emotions, to invest it at one time with terrors, at another time with surpassing beauty. To the invalid, and chiefly to the one who is so permanently, it is of course a constant thought; he turns to it without alarm as the natural exodus from captivity; and as the star brightens on which the eye fastens for a while, he sees in it hour by hour an added glory...

In the inquiry on temper, the writer searchingly examines the causes and modifications of the irritability produced by sickness, whether in relation to oneself, or to others; in the former case, as conducting to self-contempt, if not self-despair, and in the latter, as debarring one especially from the visits of children, "the brightest, if not the tenderest, angels of the sickroom." She shows well, how widely friends in health may err in the estimation of the sufferer's fortitude — at one time imagining that all power of endurance has passed away, because, through intense agony the soul is made to "cleave to the dust;" and at another time giving him credit for sublime patience, when he had really no cause or temptation to feel otherwise. She denies, from deep experience, the possibility of becoming inured to pain, so as to disregard it; but she would have it encountered by antagonistic forces, and thus subdued by the power of ideas. An omnipotent host of these she can call up at will, by her books and pictures, and their associations. From her couch she has but to turn her eyes to the wall above, and behold "the consolations of eighteen centuries" in one portrait—the CHRISTUS CONSOLATOR of Scheffer;[1] and the fullness of her varied emotions she gives us in this, our last, extract:

... Our failing space constrains us to pass over the two remaining essays, with but a brief allusion. They relate to the perils and pains of invalidism, and its gains and privileges, respectively; and are fully equal to any of the preceding papers. Our readers will gather from our quotations the character of the work, which is of the purest kind. It is not a volume to be read through hastily, and then laid aside; but one at once requiring, and repaying, the severest study. The mind of the writer is plainly of that stamp, which Bacon[2] calls "full;" and her sentences are weighty in thoughts—thoughts which create thoughts. It was a notion of Shelley's,[3] that feeling so lengthens out life, that the man of talent who dies at thirty is immeasurably older than the dullard who drags on his unmarked existence to threescore. He has, emphatically, lived more. If we might reason similarly, the writer of these essays has lived centuries. Each hour has brought its thought-life with it, and emotions sufficient for years; and hours upon hours have gone over thus with her in her solitary chamber, and she has lived them all. In the present volume we have the records of a few. She possesses, almost in intensity, that lovely, yet how fearful, gift, the capability of suffering; and she has largely used it. Yet her experiences have ever brought some good with them, vivifying the heart, not hardening it; and when they depart, she invariably discovers that they have left a blessing behind them.

We have thought for many a day—and the book before us revives the impression—that more true heroism is needed for a severe sickness, than for mingling in the terrors of a battlefield. With life beating strong in his pulses, and health careering in his veins, and now half-maddened by the braying of pibroch[4] or clarion, the soldier rushes again his foeman—determined to "do or die." If he possess a minute to think, his memories are thronged with the *vivas* of his countrymen, and the undying remembrances of generations to come; and danger, and wounds, and death are disregarded, when he feels that his name shall yet be a household word. But oh, how changed is every thing, when with nerves unstrung, and health—that life of life—departed, we have to encounter the enemy amidst the heart-depressing silence of the sick-room! The trial to be undergone is not a whit the less fiery, while the power and stimulant to endure it are wanting.

---

1 The Dutch painter Ary Scheffer (1795-1856) painted "Christus Consolator" in 1837.
2 Francis Bacon (1561-1626), English philosopher and statesman.
3 Percy Bysshe Shelley (1792-1822), Romantic poet.
4 A series of variations for the bagpipe; this reviewer uses the term as if to mean bagpipe.

Blessed be God for it, a new series of helps then comes in; and when the sun of this world has gone down, it is not darkness rules omnipotent, but the moon and stars arise in heaven to guide the wanderer.

We reluctantly close this beautiful volume, only to make it the frequent companion of our own leisure hours. It needs no further exposition, and what we have extracted will sufficiently plead its cause. We have only to add that the gifted writer is, we understand, Harriet Martineau.

3. From *Tait's Edinburgh Magazine* (January 1844): 131-35.

We have rarely perused a volume more calculated to impress sympathetic and reflective minds than these Essays of an Invalid. They are the wise teachings, the hallowed breathings of a tried and purified spirit, which comes forth of the furnace, firm as the Faith and Truth on which it rests. They are the lessons of one who can truly say, "It is good for me that I have been afflicted;" and who sees a Father's hand, a dispensation of Mercy, in the heaviest bodily ills with which frail humanity is disciplined. And the beauty and occasional profundity of the thoughts and sentiments, lack nothing of the lighter graces of felicity and elegance of expression. Some of the sketches are, indeed, eminently beautiful in the description of familiar scenes and things; or of matters "fond and trivial," and almost marvellous; as the production of a mind struggling with, and overmastering severe physical suffering. In this light the Essays will be viewed by the most indifferent reader; the most healthy and robust individual: but how much more closely must their "divine philosophy" come home to those sufferers in the sick-chamber, who require to be fortified by the strength which they impart, or soothed by their consolations. They intimate the long experiences of dreadful and racking bodily agonies, and of consequent prostration of mind; but they also tell whence comes the chastisement, for what good purpose it is sent, and how it may best be endured, surmounted, and improved;—how a sick-room may become the post of the loftiest human speculation, and the portal of Heaven. When we have said this, we are still aware that we convey but a vague idea of a work of which we think very highly. It sets out with the sublime idea of the transitory nature of all evil, and the permanent character of all good; an idea which is never so emphatically brought home to the soul as in the sick-room. This great truth is thus happily illustrated...

The Invalid, profiting by her experience, brings forward another important truth: she asserts, what must be quite just in her own experience, that no true sympathy can be shown to the victim of hopeless disease, save what is displayed by plain-dealing, strict, and simple truth. This, and this alone, has power to reach the heart of the sufferer. Praise of past services done to society, or for the patience and fortitude with which suffering is endured, is felt idle, if not hollow, and, therefore, irritating. And this may be true of invalids of strong intellect and cultivated minds; though individual character, and even the nature of the malady, must make some distinction, and management necessary in the manner of offering consolation, or displaying sympathy with the diseased. The hopeless victim of incurable organic disease may be in a state of mind to hear, with calmness, those abrupt truths with which his thoughts already have grown familiar during many a weary, languid hour, and torturing vigil, which would completely overset the nervous or consumptive patient...

The Invalid carries her faith in frank-speaking so far as to doubt if there ever was any weak and faltering spirit that required to be soothed by fallacious hope. If any exist, she has never known them. Yet they undoubtedly exist. That no Invalids, save a few of the most vain, deluded, or self-complacent of human creatures, can find solace, or receive consolation from reflecting upon, or being reminded of the good they have accomplished, and of what ought to be their satisfactory, self-rewarding consciousness of the active fulfillment of duty before they were rendered inactive and sequestered by ill-health,—is much more probable. The office of an enlightened conscience is ever more that of a vigilant watcher and uncompromising accuser, than of a consoler. The author of these Essays imagines this common and foolish sort of consolation more likely to conjure up the ghosts of past sins, follies, and errors; to raise a long train of regrets and shames, than to soothe and tranquillize the mind of the sufferer, whose mental orb is cleared by pain and solitude. The peace which, if rightly sought, is sure to come at last, springs from a very different source than the whisperings of conscience, however void of offence it may be, can supply. How, then, is the invalid to be consoled? It is by speaking to him "the truth in love."...

One of the permanent and chief pleasures or soothe of the sequestered invalid is described as the free contemplation of Nature at all times and seasons. This leads to charming descriptions of scenes and sights which are able to soother "all sadness but despair;" and which inexpressibly relieve the invalid, who knows that he is condemned for years or for a life-time to the chamber of his solitary suffering...

Why should we not say that the locality here traced is Tynemouth, the Invalid Miss Martineau! Since this notice was written, we perceive, that what could be a secret to no one acquainted with her writings, has been freely revealed by the London press....

The description of many of those familiar and yet neglected sights which Nature lavishly furnishes to every observant eye, but which are doubly enjoyed by the imprisoned invalid, concludes thus...

Next to the daily and hourly contemplation of the varied face of

Nature, the possession, and the training of plants is held as a pleasure; and the perusal of books of travels and voyages; "objective books."

It is, it would seem, in the loneliness and seclusion of the sick-chamber that people first learn to look upon life with the calm, dispassionate eye of philosophy; and, with enlarging views and opinions, become rational and moderate in their expectations, and indulgent in their judgments; indifferent to fame, steeled against censure and calumny; and, however mortifying it may be, remarkably oblivious of the judgments of the press...

The Invalid exercises, and appears to enjoy one of the best privileges of Invalidism, in speculating upon the endless events that are offered to her observation by the strife of passion and party, and by the progress of society in all its departments. She expatiates on opinions and theories, and illustrates the use of this privilege of the sick, by reference to many of those things which are shadowed by the Magic Lantern of the daily life that is busy around her, and of which she judges as a spectator deeply interested by strong sympathies, if no longer by direct interests.

From their nature and plan, these Essays on Invalidism are discursive, though generally made to bear, either upon the personal condition or the relative position of Invalids. One subject discussed is, the prevalent and increasing practice of rifling the repositories of the dead, — or ransacking old trunks, to gratify vanity, or make money by the publication of private letters — of things written in the entire faith of the most confidential correspondence. The Invalid, from particular circumstances, perhaps, views the subject in a more serious light than we think it deserves. We must look to the question mainly as it affects the living; for dead people can no more have power over their old letters than over anything else that once was theirs...

A strong protest, though the grounds of it are not clear, is taken against the publication of private letters, even where, as in the case of the late memoirs of Romilly, Wilberforce, Horner, Scott, and others,[1] they are most essential to the purposes of biography. That the Invalid is sincere in her opinions, though they are pushed to the extreme, is proved by the course which she has adopted about her own correspondence. And if she have numerous American correspondents, there may be some reason for alarm. That the publication of private letters had occasionally been pushed too far, and, in some instances, grossly abused, there is no denying; yet we can hardly imagine any great injury in the publication of almost any letters that are worth preserving, nor yet how the blank is to be filled up, were all strictly private letters swept from French and English literature. Can we regret that

---

1   Sir Samuel Romilly (1757-1818); William Wilberforce (1759-1833); Leonard Horner (1785-1864); Sir Walter Scott (1771-1832).

the most confidential of familiar letters, those, for example, of Madame de Sevigné[1] to her daughter, or, to take an extreme case, Swift's Journal to Stella,[2] which certainly were never intended to meet the public eye, should exist for the entertainment and instruction of posterity? In writing really confidential and familiar letters to the friends one trusts, we cannot imagine that the idea of their being one day subjected to public scrutiny, ever enters into any minds save those of individuals morbidly occupied about themselves and their doings. The distant, or phantom-fear of publication, can prove no restraint to the free expression of the sentiments of a frank and ingenuous mind, and an affectionate disposition, if such cowardly fear should ever once assail it. After all, our objection is merely to what is either a matter of taste and discretion, or an occasional subject, of some abuse being made a weighty and urgent question of morals. Upon the principle, that philosophers have, for the benefit of science, bequeathed their bellies for dissection, men of note might be impelled to bequeath their most private correspondence to the world; or their surviving friends might be justified in thus acting by them: thus honouring their memories, by preserving their best thoughts, the expression of their finest feelings.

The various aspects under which dissolution may be supposed to appear to one who lives in constant fellowship with death, forms the subject of a fine essay; and the management and control of his temper by the invalid, the theme of another. One frequent trial of temper to the confirmed invalid, is the tacit understanding of his friends of his mental incapacity. It is understood that disease must have affected and weakened his mind, along with his body; and that he can no longer see or judge of actions, but through a dim or perverted medium. This absurd notion sustained by the ignorant pride of strength, and which then leads to what, if addressed to persons in health, would be considered and insult, is thus rebuked.

Certain forms of hypochondria, or nervous disease—for it is not quite monomania, though that way madness lies—are powerfully depicted in the following passage. Happily, comparatively few are, by personal experience, qualified to comprehend, in its fearful extent this most baleful attendant, in imaginative minds, of the severer forms of bodily prostration, this might have of the spirit...

The work closes with a view of the gains and privileges of ill health. The compensation amounts to this: That the reflecting invalid sees surrounding life, and its varied passions, aims, and ends, in the steady light of reason and truth, and looks placidly and hopefully through the dim veil which shrouds from all, Death and the Mystery of the Future.

---

1   Marie de Rabutin-Chantal, or Madame Sévigné (1626-96), a French writer.
2   Jonathan Swift (1667-1714), Anglo-Irish clergyman and satirical writer.

We now recommend our readers to study these Essays for themselves. If found so instructive and attractive to the healthy and happy, what power must they possess in the chamber of the solitary invalid? It is among the peculiar gains and privileges of the invalid endowed with intellect and talent, thus efficiently to minister to the numerous sons and daughters of affliction....

4. From *British and Foreign Medical Review* 18 (1844): 472–81.

...We gather from the internal evidence of the book itself that the writer is a confirmed invalid, confined to her room, and convinced that she is "under sentence of disease for life." She is a constant sufferer from pain, sometimes of the acutest kind, and the habitual use of opium has become an invariable habit. Debility of body, languor, malaise, incapacity for continuous exertion, with loss of all gaiety of mind and sense of enjoyment; and, with the exception of a few hours twice in a year of light-heartedness, over all the rest a cloud of care—apparently causeless, but not the less real;—are the bodily and mental symptoms which in her case, as in so many of her sex, indicate an exhausted nervous system.

But a very few lines in her book, scattered here and there, are devoted to a description of her bodily ailments; the object of the writer is to unfold the effects of sickness upon the mind, and its manifold helps and hinderances, perils and pains, advantages and compensations, injury and profit: a comprehensive theme, well worthy of deep study, and one which can be treated of satisfactorily alone by one who has had a long apprenticeship to suffering. This book differs materially from the majority which fall under our notice as critics. Where every word tells it is impossible to condense, and where each sentence is full of matter, and all closely connected into a whole, it is difficult to abridge. It is not our province to go into the whole subject: we shall therefore confine ourselves to those parts only which have some practical bearing, either illustrating morbid states of mind, the existence of which or their connexion with disease of body in invalids it is our province to recognize and to study, or affording hints for the better management of such patients. Those who are further interested in the subject, and who are desirous to know the uses to be made of adversity, we must refer to the book itself.

To man, with his stronger self-reliance, the deep need which women have of sympathy is a matter of observation rather than experience, and he cannot fully enter into the want. It has been said that man lives in his understanding, woman in her affections; and if so, the fellow feeling which a cultivated man needs is more with his intellect than his feelings. But as the feelings are much more connected with bodily states, the sympathies with feeling which women seem absolutely to require, must necessarily be very considerably influenced by the disorders of the body; and no part of this volume is more strikingly morbid than its revelation of sympathies. There is a separate chapter on sympathy; but the intense craving after this, which is called "a hunger of the heart," "a heavenly solace," and the delight which those afford who have the "true genius for sympathy," who are "archangels of consolation," and the uneasiness, irritability, and vexation which awkward consolers give, are disclosed throughout the book. The following hint to "awkward sympathizers" may be remembered when dealing with this class of patients:

… It is difficult for men in health to realize the evident annoyance which such invalids feel at any hope being held out of recovery, but the physician often meets with such. Is it not from the deeper sympathy which is seemingly given, if the cases are considered hopeless? The "genius for consolation" does this…

A man of the highest intellectual power, who was himself an invalid, a severe sufferer from pain, to ease which he habitually took opium, said "that the best physician in nervous diseases was the best inspirer of hope." This was a man's feeling. He resents pity; but how different with a woman; with her "pity is akin to love;" give her no hope and she blesses you…

The whole chapter will repay perusal. The genial healthy reader will become acquainted with states of feeling which are new to him; the more sickly mind will find some of his own feelings embodied in words, and both will learn something as to the best way of dealing with such patients.

What should be the arrangements of a permanent invalid, with regard to companionship is an important consideration…

This unsentimental, but very practical truth, our invalid accounts for metaphysically, and dresses up her reasons becomingly and sentimentally. But many of the reasons with which the work abounds are evidently à posteriori arguments. The matter is first settled, not by any argumentative process whatever, but by the will, and then the decision is accounted for in the most "interesting" way. But, although "sic volo, si jubeo"[1] is the feminine way of settling such matters, she is not disposed to add "stet pro ratione voluntas,"[2] but rather to puzzle herself afterwards, with trying to frame reasons; a mistake; as she often arrives at the truth in such practical matters by a shorter and surer process than ratiocination…

Our invalid has chosen a sea view, for its variety, and from the wide expanse of sky it affords. But not too much sea, which would tire; between

---

1 "thus I will, if I command."
2 "let the will stand in the place of reason."

her house and the sea is a green down, a river, ponds, the ruins of a priory, and beyond a busy harbour; a sandy beach, and a rocky shore. A windmill, a railroad, a colliery, farm-yards and paddocks give a living interest to the whole, and here a telescope is a great additional source of pleasure. This whole chapter, entitled "nature to the invalid," is genial and beautiful. To such invalids, flowers are the most acceptable presents; and "fern-houses" (that is, ferns growing in close glass-cases, devised by a member of our profession) are in a town "a compensation for rural pleasures," and in the country an addition to them.

The good effects of books of travels are alluded to. Such are advisable from carrying the invalid out of himself for a time; they are objective, whilst his mental malady is "subjectivity." The effect of seclusion, in rendering the mind speculative rather than practical, is discussed. The writer thinks that large and more distant views are taken, and that many doubts and difficulties which beset the mind immersed in actual life, are cleared away: that "moral considerations are all in all," and that seclusion is peculiarly fitted for seeing their beauty and abundance, and recognizing the "deep heaven lying inclosed in the very centre of society, and a genuine divinity residing in the heart of every member of it."

… A chapter full of matter worth reflecting on is devoted to "temper."

It was John Hunter, we think, who used to define organic irritability as action with weakness.[1] And all forms of "temper," or mental irritability may be included in the same definition. Two forms are mentioned,—dissatisfaction with others, and dissatisfaction with one's self; they are opposite poles of the same mental disease, but they alike render their possessor miserable to himself, and an object either of pity, annoyance, or dislike to those who come in contact with him…

This masterly dissection of one form of morbid mind, gives to the reader that vivid impression of truth which no writer on such subjects can produce, unless he writes out of his own heart. What is the remedy? We believe that this condition is much connected with an exhausted state of the nervous system; it is one of those forms of disease which result from the over-excitement of the nervous system continued so long as to be followed by permanent depression. Our neighbours alone, (notwithstanding, or perhaps owing to their natural gaiety,) have words expressive of other shades of this unhappy condition, *ennui*, *blasé*, or still more exquisitely discriminative the epithet which Madame Maintenon[2] applied to Louis XIV, when she complained that she had to amuse a king who was no longer "*amusable*." To ascertain the cause when it is a physical one, as it often is, is the first step

---

1   John Hunter (1728-93).
2   Francoise d'Aubigne (1635-1719).

towards a cure. But in a case like the one here supposed, of incurable (or rather we would hope uncured) indisposition, in which the patient is confined to her room, and indebted to opium alone, for physical ease, a moral remedy can alone be offered, and the following advice is the result of our invalid's personal experience:

... We have said that we believe the physical cause of this condition may be an exhausted nervous system. The causes of this may be physical or mental, or more often both. It may be the result of the early and long-continued indulgence in sensual excitements; or of the wear and tear of mind by its intense application to business or to study, with great neglect of the health. Disappointment in women of a very sensitive temperament is a frequent cause. But looking at it psychologically, is it not a form of pride, or rather of morbid vanity? Extremes meet. There is a pride which apes humility, and this too unconsciously. Dissatisfaction implies that the mind is annoyed at and resents its own low condition. True humility would acknowledge that there was too much reason for this, and would wisely submit. And if the root of this defect is pride and vanity, then unconditional submission is the cure. What are "appeals to endurance and self-mastery," but deceitful and injurious flattery, which, like opium, relieves pain for the time, at the expense of aggravating and fixing the disease. The hardest lesson in the world to learn is that of humility, more difficult than the endurance and self-mastery of the hardest and coldest stoicism. Christianity alone teaches its importance and the sole means of its attainment...

We are all, when in health, apt enough to "dismiss our uneasy sympathies" by assuming that invalids become inured to suffering, and to moralize on this wise provision. But how few of us take into consideration the meaning of this cheap phrase, "becoming inured," and reflect "on the series of keen mortifications, of bitter privations" which it includes — even in those cases in which the inuring process at last brings relief! But there are sufferings to which this slow relief never comes. Those who have watched the progress of tic douloureux, stone, carcinomatous tumours involving nerves, or cancer of the uterus, will assent to the individual experience of this writer...

We have thus given the Invalid's own description of some states of mind and feeling produced by permanent and long-continued disease of body. We must refer to the volume itself for the consolations offered, and for the writer's own views on the compensations afforded to such withdrawal from active life, by increasing the power of that prerogative of a thinking being, "looking before and after." But there is another side from which this book may be studied: not merely the writer's own conscious conception of her state of mind, but the display of her own actual condition which every such writer makes, to a great extent unconsciously.

That the writer is a woman would, we think, have been evident from the work itself, had it not been attributed, without contradiction, to one of the best known authoresses of the day. The confession of such faults and failings as create "interest," the hunger after sympathy, the undisguised love of praise, the annoyance at "not being understood," are unmistakable characteristics. Admitting, as we do most fully, the writer's intellectual powers, her lofty and deep thoughts conveyed in a style of consummate clearness, a true feeling for the beautiful and the good, and the power of embodying the poetry of her mind in graceful, captivating prose, aspirations after a high state of moral purity, and a deep conviction that man's moral being should be his prime care—yet we cannot help feeling—and all the stronger, perhaps, for our favorable impressions—to quote the saying of a child to herself, which she repeats more than once: "But there is unhealthiness, and that spoils all."

The head desires ardently to strike the stars; but the poor unwholesome body pulls it down very low, and contradicts its right to any such elevation. The contradiction between the idealism of the abstracted mind, and the actual feelings of that mind when brought into contact with realities, affords the strangest and strongest contrasts. The world and its great parties are seen in a new and clearer light: they are looked at by the invalid with stoical philosophy, as part of history: what before was dark in the ways of Providence, becomes clear: the common distinctions of rank are "attenuated to a previously inconceivable degree," so that "there would be little more in the sovereign entering the sick-room than any other stranger whom kindness might bring"—"so overpowering in our view are the great interests of life which are common to all—duty, thought, love, joy, sorrow, and death." And yet—alas for poor human nature—if a kind visitor, who has not the organ of order well developed, leaves the chairs awry, and the books unreturned to their shelves, all this lofty philosophy is overthrown, and its possessor cast into a state of miserable irritability. With the clearest supposed insight into the most difficult problems that politicians are working out, there is an incapacity to appreciate correctly the individual's own condition, producing unreasonable dissatisfaction with self, self-distrust, even self-disgust. With the conviction of the paramount importance of being, rather than seeming, there is the painful wincing at a suspicion of being misinterpreted, and not understood—at being thought to be more comfortable, or more miserable as an invalid than in health; at any outward circumstances, in fact, which contradicts at the moment the peculiar feeling of the mind. We do not bring this forward as mere criticism, but as truth in which we are deeply interested as pathologists, as elucidating the effects of disease of body on the mind; and the conclusions we would draw from it are:

1. That the feelings which are certainly most closely connected with the body are the most affected by this disease in which the nervous system is exhausted and depressed, and that they are the most morbid; whereas the intellect remains little disturbed, and, when able to act at all, capable of clear thought.

2. That the advice offered to the individual by his own intellect is very incapable of correcting these disordered states of the feelings.

3. That the mere intellectual powers may be cultivated and improved to a very high extent, and yet, if there is depressing disease of the nervous system, the feelings and what are called the active powers which put us in relation with our fellows, may be in a much lower state than in the healthy whose intellects are comparatively uncultivated—simple-hearted, good people, who are engaged in the active and humblest duties of life.

Self-consciousness has been said to be the disease of the present day; and assuredly a morbid self-consciousness which defeats its object, and becomes blind and puzzled, and bewildered by dwelling too incessantly on the individual's emotions and feelings is one of the morbidities of mind portrayed here. A celebrated thinker of the present day goes so far as to assert that all self-consciousness is disease, that the mind should no more be conscious of its operations than the stomach, and that in either case the consciousness of the work going on, is disease. We cannot go this length. The power by which the mind observes its own acts and judges them as if there were two beings within a man, one the passive spectator of the other's thoughts, feelings, and actions, is the prerogative of the highest class of minds. Much of what we call genius consists in the power of embodying these observations which the soul makes on herself, in words, "giving to airy nothings a local habitation and a name,"[1] so that others less highly gifted with expression, on reading them embodied in words exclaim, "I have thought and felt the same thing." "This comes home to me." "This meets me." And although all have not this genius, yet the power of looking inwards is common to all who think at all. It cannot then be called a disease, and be put in the same class with gastrodynia, hypochondriasis, or palpitations of the heart, without a very false and hasty generalization. But, like all other natural powers, it may become diseased when too exclusively cultivated. It becomes a lamentable disease, especially when the feelings and emotions are too constantly self-contemplated, and one to which cultivated minds are peculiarly liable. Its corrective is action; and when invalidism prevents this wholesome counterbalance, a sensitive and thoughtful mind is very apt to become engrossed in its own thoughts and feelings, and to get into a condition of helpless and egotistical selfishness; just in the same degree as a mere hypochondriac

---

1   A reference to Shakespeare, *A Midsummer Night's Dream*, Act V, Sc. 1, ll. 16–17.

becomes engrossed in his own bodily sensations. As we can know our own powers by action only, this condition of self-consciousness is (although seemingly a contradiction) one of great self-ignorance. Whatever becomes the object of constant thought or attention becomes unduly magnified. The individual's own importance is thus greatly increased in his own estimation, and when called into action or into collision with others, the consciousness of his weakness, (often true from want of practice,) combined with his own sense of self-importance makes him irritable to others, or dissatisfied with himself, or both. This unreasonable dissatisfaction with one's self, this "mental weakness which converts the most innocent and ordinary occurrences into occasions of apprehension, or of self-distrust, or self disgust," is one to which the weaker sex are especially liable, and particularly those who, though compelled to inaction by disease, have active intellects, and quick and strong feelings.

Appendix C: Harriet Martineau and the Medical Profession

1. "Medical Report of The Case of Miss H—— M———."[1]

MEDICAL REPORT

OF
THE CASE OF MISS H— M——.

BY T.M. GREENHOW,

FELLOW OF THE ROYAL COLLEGE OF SURGEONS OF ENGLAND; SENIOR
SURGEON TO THE NEWCASTLE-UPON-TYNE INFIRMARY,
AND EYE INFIRMARY.

LONDON: SAMUEL HIGHLEY, 32, FLEET STREET.
E.CHARNLEY, NEWCASTLE. 1845.

PREFACE

The publication of the following case is forced upon me, in some degree, by the general interest which it has excited, but, especially by the misapprehensions which have arisen and been extensively circulated through the medical and other journals, respecting the correctness of the opinion I had entertained of its nature, and the treatment pursued for its relief.

In laying a full, but concise history of it before the profession, I need scarcely declare that I have the entire concurrence of the patient; whose high sense of duty both to other sufferers from similar disease, and to myself, as her medical attendant, during the long period of her confinement as an invalid, enables her to lay aside those feelings of false delicacy which

---

1   As noted in the introduction, Harriet Martineau was highly distressed when this report was published, and she discontinued contact with Greenhow, who was her brother-in-law. Her reaction, coupled with the graphic nature of the gynecological detail that Greenhow includes, made me quite reluctant to reprint the report. After lengthy consideration, I decided that Martineau's reaction—so often referred to in biographies—cannot be fully appreciated without access to the report itself. As importantly, Greenhow's Report provides a fine example of the "case study" model of medical diagnosis and of the medical profession's response to the pecularities of Martineau's case.

might have led many, of less firmness of purpose, to shrink from the explanation of the precise causes of such continued suffering, although, scarcely any one was ignorant of their general character.

How far the relief from the sympathetic nervous distress, attendant on this case, is to be attributed to the direct agency of mesmerism — whether it has acted by a power *sui generis*,[1] or by supplying a powerful and well-timed stimulus to the mind, and thus acting through the imagination and the will, is a question which every one must be left to answer for himself, after a careful consideration of the facts related in the following pages and in the communications to the *Athenaeum*, lately supplied by the patient herself.

The numerous and striking claims in favour of mesmerism, emanating from so many sources, have, at length, rendered it a subject of serious and philosophical inquiry, which can no longer be resisted by the members of the medical profession. It is by them only that its pretensions can be properly weighed — and it certainly behoves them to enter on the inquiry with candid and unprejudiced minds.

If there be such a power, careful investigation will, doubtless, enable them to detect it beyond dispute; and they will presently be prepared by the accumulation of facts, if not to determine its precise nature, at any rate, to ascertain its modes of operation and to define its capabilities and proper limits.

It is in this spirit of calm and dispassionate inquiry, that I have myself entered on the investigation, though I must admit that my efforts have not yet been attended with any results confirmatory of the powers of mesmerism; but I shall proceed circumspectly in my experiments, till repeated failures shall either confirm my doubts, or positive practical results remove them; in which case, I shall not fail to make such results known to the profession.

T.M. Greenhow.
Newcastle-upon-Tyne,
Dec. 14, 1844.

CASE.

In a letter from Venice, dated June 14th, 1839, Miss H.M., aet. 37, first communicated to me her early feelings of indisposition. During the preceding year she had been sensible of a "great failure of nerve and spirits, and of strength." Frequently she experienced sharp pain in the uterine region. The

---

1 of its own kind.

Catamenia became more frequent, occurring every two or three weeks; and a very irritating discharge, of a brown or yellowish colour, took place in the intervals.

The irregular uterine discharges continued, occasionally mixed with clotted blood, and she suffered from many distressing nervous symptoms, evidently arising from uterine irritation; "inability to stand or walk, aching and weariness of the back, extending down the legs to the heels;" "tenderness and pain, on pressure, in the left groin, extending by the hip to the back. The spirits became much depressed, and the power of enjoyment was gone." At the same time, "a *membranous substance*, like the end of a little finger," was discovered projecting from the os uteri.

This substance is described in the following terms, in a letter to Dr. Nardo, of Venice, who was consulted on the occasion, by a friend who accompanied Miss H.M. on her journey. "Twice there has been a discharge similar in colour and substance to the blood. Two days ago it was found, that from the same passage (vagina) was protruding the extremity of a solid substance, totally insensible, of a reddish-brown colour, in form resembling the end of a bullock's tongue, with a decided edge or point—it can be pushed back without difficulty or pain, but it falls again." Dr. Nardo, who had no opportunity of actual examination, conjectured either Prolapsus Uteri or a Polypus tumour, of a fibrous nature, to be the occasion of these appearances; and recommended the careful avoidance of violent motion, and all that was found to increase indisposition.

The following extract from a letter, dated Lucerne, July 6, 1839, seems to fix the period when one character of the complaint, which will be presently noticed more particularly (*Retroversion of the Uterus*), took place: — "I cannot walk without injury, as I said, and keep my feet laid up, and my knees somewhat raised, as the easiest posture. I began to use the syringe, as you and Dr. Nardo recommended: it was a great relief, but in *three days* there was *no room for it*, and on this account I have never been able to use it since. I discontinued the sponge, finding it irritating, as you say, and it is not now *necessary*."

The use of the sponge as a pessary, and the syringe for injecting tepid water, or other fluid, into the vagina, is referred to in this passage, and needs no comment; it is the occupation of the cavity of the vagina by the enlarged and retroverted uterus, which I wish to be held in view, as throwing some light on the subsequent history of the case.

In the end of July, 1839, Miss H.M. arrived in Newcastle, and placed herself under my care. She was then suffering from the various morbid nervous sensations already described; and though she continued to take moderate walking exercise, it was attended with great discomfort and inconvenience. There was no difficulty in referring the whole train of symptoms to some organic or functional derangement of the uterus; and an examination was soon instituted to ascertain its proper character.

The uterus was found large, retroverted, and fixed low down in the vagina, the os, and cervix uteri occupying the anterior part of the cavity, and the body and fundus of the organ passing horizontally backwards, till the latter approached the sacrum. The enlarged uterus thus occupying the antero-posterior diameter of the pelvis, pressed, respectively, against the urethra and neck of the bladder and the lower part of the rectum; and the embarrassment occasioned by this pressure produced corresponding symptoms, which were often the occasion of great uneasiness and inconvenience. While the fundus uteri extended backwards towards the sacrum, the cervix was bent downwards behind the pubes, nearly at a right angle, and hanging from the lip was a small polypus, which was soon removed; but without any alleviation of symptoms. I was assured by my patient that the projecting body, which showed itself at Venice, was different from, and much larger than, this small polypus; and though the os uteri was not dilatable with the finger, and, from its preternatural position, was in a very unfavourable condition for the exclusion of any body contained within the uterus, I was for some time led to hope that another and larger polypus might again make its appearance. Notwithstanding the use of suitable measures — warm baths and ergot of rye — to promote this object, my expectations were disappointed; and the treatment of the case soon resolved itself into the employment of appropriate palliatives.

The tenderness in the left groin was somewhat relieved by leeches. The increasing difficulty of bearing exercise, however moderate, soon rendered rest absolutely necessary; and the feelings of nervous discomfort indicated recourse to opiates, from which, though always used in great moderation, much relief was obtained. One of the most distressing symptoms which subsequently supervened, was an oppressive sickness, frequently amounting to retching; and much difficulty in micturition and in emptying the bowels was occasioned by the pressure of the uterine tumour. From the same cause arose the distressing pains down the lower extremities, frequently extending to the heels. The abdomen became considerably distended during the progress of these symptoms; but this arose more from a general distension and fullness of the bowels, from flatus and other contents, than the enlargement of the uterus, which could never be felt rising above the brim of the pelvis: though its increased size, doubtless, by pushing the abdominal viscera upwards, tended in some measure to produce a general enlargement of the figure.

It not unfrequently happened, although, by the use of gentle aperients or emollient injections, a pretty regular action of the bowels was secured, that a gradual accumulation of their contents took place, giving rise to increased distress; which required the use of more active purgatives for its relief. An occasional attack of more acute disease from accidental causes — for example, a large abscess in the throat, or severe gastrodynia (from which Miss M. suffered long and acutely many years ago), was superadded to the ordinary symptoms arising from the local disease, aggravating their intensity, and leaving for a time the feeling of increased debility and inaptitude for physical exertion. The constant and distressing aching in the back rendered it painful to rest upon the sacrum in reclining on the sofa; and some relief was obtained by resting in a prone position. A couch, contrived for this purpose, was found a source of much comfort to the patient.

So little variation took place in the character of the symptoms, or the pathological condition of the affected organ, as to render needless minute details of continued morbid feelings, or of the treatment suggested for their relief.

In 1840 I made a statement of the case in writing to Sir Charles M. Clarke,[1] who concurred with me in thinking that rest and palliative treatment, the general health being carefully maintained, could alone be depended upon.

In September, 1841, Sir Charles M. Clarke having occasion to visit this part of the country, I had an opportunity of availing myself more directly of his opinion.

After a very careful investigation of the case, Sir Charles gave an opinion verbally, which I was induced afterwards to request him to express in writing. In a note dated September 30th, 1841, he says, — "It was my intention to say that I perfectly agreed with you as to the nature of the complaint, that the Disease was an enlargement of the BODY of the Uterus; that the NECK of that organ was perfectly healthy; that although the majority of these cases of enlargement of the BODY of the uterus did not yield to external applications or to internal remedies, that, nevertheless, the disorder produced mechanical symptoms only, and *did not lead to any fatal result*, to which termination Disease of the *Neck* of the Uterus did lead.

"Farther, I mentioned that in an instance or two I had known such complaints as Miss M.'s subside, and that I would suggest the employment of certain means for this desirable purpose." The means proposed by Sir Charles M. Clarke was the continued external use of Iodine Ointment.

To this measure my patient had so decided an objection, that she could not be prevailed upon to carry it into effect. It was on this account that I was induced to propose a course of Iodide of Iron, which, with few and short intervals, was persevered in till July or August of the present year.

---

1   Sir Charles Mansfield Clarke (1782-1857), a leading practitioner in midwifery and author of "Observations on those Disease of Females which are attended by Discharges."

Under the use of this medicine the distressing sickness was greatly mitigated, the appetite improved, some morbid feelings were alleviated, and an increased tone of general bodily health, as well as of mental energy, showed itself. The following extract from a note written in September, 1843, will show her own opinion of its effects at that time: — "I suppose I owe my much improved comfort mainly to them (the pills of iodide of iron); indeed, it is very great. The pulling and sinking — the mechanical troubles as one may call them — of course continue, but the almost total absence of sickness, and the striking lessening of the 'distress' are such a comfort to me!" Occasional, but not very frequent examinations took place into the pathological condition of the affected organ but no appreciable change could be discovered, except the appearance of a membranous substance at the os uteri, which, generally, scarcely protruded beyond its lips, though occasionally it was described as of larger extent. This was said to resemble the appearance observed at Venice, though of smaller dimensions. This substance evidently proceeded from the interior of the uterus, and had no attachment to the neck, the point of the finger passing round it on all sides. Its appearance naturally gave rise to the renewed supposition that the uterus might contain a preternatural growth of a polypus character, the separation and discharge of which might be effected by time.

On the 2nd of April, 1844, I was first enabled to detect a slight change in the condition of the uterus. The attachment of the fundus was less fixed, and it could be slightly raised from its position. The membranous pendicle described above, and the general position of the organ, remained as on former examinations.

In the beginning of June, Miss M. suffered much from an attack of indigestion, with disordered and loaded bowels. The symptoms proper to the organic affection, especially the distressing pain in the back, were for a time increased; and while proper means were resorted to for the correction of visceral derangement, a Plaster with Belladonna was applied to the sacral region, from which but slight relief was obtained. The unwonted symptoms of indisposition had subsided, when, on June 22nd, the Mesmeric treatment was commenced, of which a full account has been published in the Athenaeum by Miss M. From this time she ceased to be properly under my care, though her accustomed remedies were not yet laid aside. I shall therefore pass over the interval till September 4th, on which day I carefully repeated my examination, and found, as on April 2nd, that the posterior connections of the uterus were less fixed than formerly. The retroversion continues, but the fundus, which rests against the rectum and sacrum, feels looser, and admits of being raised to some extent with the finger in vaginam.

The uterus feels altogether less firm, and more yielding in its substance, and the os uteri is to a certain extent dilatable, yielding to the finger in a slight degree more than formerly. Within, and slightly projecting from the os uteri, can be felt *two* substances, which convey to the finger a sensation as if two lumbrici, of moderate size, hung through the mouth of the uterus. These membranous projecting bodies are said, on pressure, occasionally to exude a reddish discharge. In addition to the knowledge obtained by this examination, Miss M. supplied me with the following reports of herself, at this and several succeeding visits which I made her, previous to the next and final examination into the pathological condition of the uterus, on December 6th. On this day, (September 4th,) she informed me that the Catamenia which for many years had taken place at shorter intervals than natural, (every two or three weeks) have resumed their natural course. That the breasts have increased in bulk. The Pills of Iodide of Iron, and all aperients, have been discontinued, the bowels having lately acted with ease and regularity. The use of opiates has been greatly diminished by Enema, and internally, altogether omitted. The sickness and other gastric inconveniences have eased; the irritation in the rectum and neck of the bladder are no longer complained of;—quietude and repose have succeeded to restlessness and irritability; and the nervous system has acquired a greatly improved tone.

11th. —Miss M. continues comfortable, with greatly diminished doses of the opiate; other medicines unnecessary. Has this day been in the garden for some time laid on a sofa cushion.

21st. —Miss M. reports favourably in all respects of herself. Opiate reduced to a very small dose. Yesterday walked round the Castle yard; today, the same, with the addition of a walk to the Haven—feels somewhat tired, but no other uneasy effects.

October 8th. —Miss M. informed me that she can now take long walks—to-day, two miles and a half. Has discontinued opiates for five days. At first the nights were bad. Last night she slept well, having taken a small quantity of warm brandy and water. No irritation is now felt at the neck of the bladder. Some pressure still on the rectum, but otherwise feels well. Bowels regular without medicine.

December 6. —Again I made a careful examination into the state of Miss M. The fundus uteri is more disengaged than at the last examination, and admits of being raised somewhat higher. It is certainly *less fixed*, and in this respect has improved at each time of examination since April 2nd, when the first degree of improvement was observed. The retroversion continues, the fundus still extending towards the sacrum, while the os uteri approaches the pubes—the organ remains large and firm, and is yet turned back nearly at a right angle from the cervix uteri. The two membranous pendicles remain hanging out of the os uteri, as at the last examination. The health is represented as quite good, and the catamenia as regular—the nervous pains and irritations having all subsided. The person is less but, as abdominal distension depended principally upon the gaseous and other contents of the intestines, and in a sight degree only, on the uterine tumour, it is probably that renewed habits of activity have greatly contributed to restore the symmetry of the person in this respect.

I have purposely avoided interrupting the narrative of the case by details of the medicines prescribed. But I shall here append the prescriptions employed, except on particular emergencies, during the last three years. A glance at them will suffice to show how erroneous is the supposition entertained by many persons that Miss M. was in the habit of seeking relief in large and unmeasured doses of opium.

1. Anodyne Lotion.
Rx Misturae Camphorae
Mis. G. Acaciae, aa 5 viii.
Tincturae Opii. 3 viii. M.
One ounce to be injected into the rectum every alternate day.

2. Anodyne Pils.
Rx Pilulae Rhei. co.gr.xviii.
Mur. Morphiae, gr.iii. M. et divide in Pilul. xii.
One anodyne pill to be taken every alternate day, and occasionally when suffering more than ordinary distress.

3. Aperient Pills.
Rx. Ext. Colocynth. co.
Ext. Hyoscyami, aa 3i. M. et divide in Pilul. xxiv.
Two aperient pills to be taken every alternate night, between the use of the anodyne injection.

4. Tonic Pills.
Rx Ferri. Iodidi.
Pulv. Zingib.aa gr.xxx. Cons.q.s.ut ft. Pilul.xxx.
One tonic pill to be taken three times a day.

Before the use of the anodyne lotion, it was occasionally found necessary to empty the rectum, by means of a common domestic injection.

I have endeavoured to render the preceding sketch comprehensive and concise, avoiding equally unnecessary details, and omitting nothing essential to the full comprehension of the true character of the case. Knowing well that no symptoms of malignant disease of the affected organ existed, I always believed that a time would arrive when my patient would be relieved from most of her distressing symptoms, and released from her long continued confinement. The catamenial crisis appeared the most probable period, but I did not despair of this happening sooner; though she never willingly listened to my suggestions of the probability of such prospective events, and seemed always best satisfied with anything approaching to an admission that she must ever remain a secluded invalid. This state of mind, perhaps, may be considered as an additional symptom of the morbid influence over the nervous system of the class of diseases in which this case must be included.

During the last year or two, in common with many of the friends of Miss M., I had frequent opportunities of observing the increased ease and freedom with which she moved about her sitting-room; and my conviction became confirmed, that the time was approaching when she would resume her habits of exercise in the open air. Oftener than once I have made use of the somewhat strong expression, that some day, probably before long, Miss M. *would take up her bed and walk.*

In the history of this case it is probable that the advocates of mesmerism will find reasons and arguments in support of their opinions. But the experienced practitioner, carefully distinguishing the *post hoc* from the *propter hoc*,[1] will have little difficulty in bringing the whole into harmony with the well-established laws of human physiology.

As regards the pathology of the case, he will conclude that the condition of the uterus in December is but the natural sequel of progressive improvement begun in, or antecedent to, the month of April; and as regards the relief from the distressing nervous symptoms connected therewith, that the time had arrived when a new and powerful stimulus only was required, to enable the enthusiastic mind of my patient to shake them off.

After bestowing my best consideration on the subject, this is the conclusion which most strongly forces itself on my own mind.

2. "Termination of the Case of Miss Harriet Martineau." By Thomas M. Greenhow, M.D. *British Medical Journal* (14 April 1877): 449-50.

Since the publication of the autobiography of Miss Harriet Martineau, it has become incumbent on me to say a few words to the profession on the termination of her case, which, thirty-two years before her death, excited so much interest and attention.

First of all I may observe, what will be obvious to all readers, that section

---

1 "after this" and "on account of this," respectively.

III, vol. ii, page 191, contains *little fact* and *much imagination*; and that, as was shown by the *post mortem* examination, instead of her being cured by mesmerism or any other agency, although the distressing symptoms were greatly relieved by the palliative treatment exclusive of mesmerism pursued while she was at Tynemouth, *no cure* was effected, but temporary suspension of suffering took place from natural causes connected with local disease. But, before giving a report of the proofs ascertained after death of what she had suffered so much discomfort from during life, I may refer to her constantly expressed conviction that her disease was of a fatal malignant nature, and could only terminate in early death, and to the fact that, in 1855, eleven years after I had seen her, she consulted two eminent physicians in London, Dr. Latham and Sir Thos. Watson,[1] by whom she was assured that she was free from heart-disease; she nevertheless maintained and asserted her conviction that she would soon die from that cause. In proof of this circumstance, I need only refer to the letter from Sir Thomas Watson,[2] which appeared in the BRITISH MEDICAL JOURNAL for July 8th, 1876, and in many newspapers.

With these preliminary remarks, I shall now relate the substance of the report of the *post mortem* examination made by Mr. King, by whom Miss Harriet Martineau was attended during the later years of her life, and furnished to me by my friend Mr. Higginson of Liverpool. She died on June 27th, 1876, at the age of seventy-four, twenty-one years after Dr. Latham and Sir Thomas Watson had declared her free from disease of the heart. Of the history of her health since she ceased to be under my observation, thirty-two years before her death, I know nothing except from occasional imperfect reports.

POST MORTEM EXAMINATION. — Forty-two hours after death a *post mortem* examination was made by Mr. King. He says: "On opening the abdomen, the muscular tissue I cut through showed decided signs of fatty degeneration, and a vast tumour became apparent at once. I could pass my hand round it and turn it completely out of the cavity, where it hung by

---

1   Dr Peter Mere Latham and Sir Thomas Watson were both considered specialists in diseases of the heart. Sir Thomas Watson was author of *Lectures on the Principles and Practices of Physic* (1843). Peter Mere Latham, M.D. (1789-1875) was appointed physician extraordinary to the queen in 1837 and in 1845 published *Lectures on Clinical Medicine, comprising Diseases of the Heart*.

2   The original footnote to this reference reads: "Sir Thomas Watson says: 'I have been in the habit of illustrating my caution by likening the heart so affected to a china jar slightly cracked, which, if carefully handled, may remain long unbroken, but which heedlessness or accident might ruin much more easily than if it were sound: but in Miss Martineau's case there was no such obvious rift, and I therefore affirmed to her that her life was in no immediate danger.'"

one pedicle, which was found to be attached to the broad ligament close to the corna uteri. The broad ligament and the Fallopian tube were spread over the surface of the tumour, to which they were adherent, and the tube admitted a wire to be passed through to the extent of three inches or more till it reached the pedicle. The tumour was pear-shaped, with the narrow end within the pelvis. In the longer diameter, from the upper to the lower extremity, it measured twelve; in the lateral direction, ten inches. On cutting into the tumour, about half a pint of brown fluid escaped; the remainder of the contents consisted entirely of a mass of greyish-brown soft stuff. I can only compare it to bread soaked in tea, dotted here and there with white hardish pieces, exactly like half of apple-pips, generally two halves being together. I have had the sac preserved in spirits. On sewing up the incision, Mr. Higginson found that it would contain 110 ounces—10½ imperial pints. The larger circumferences measured 30 inches, the smaller 28 inches. The pedicle had the appearance of having been cut pretty close to the uterus. The interior was still lined with abundant flakes of white and rather glistening substance, which did not grease the paper nor melt under heat, but gave off a slightly grizzled smell. Under the microscope, crystals of cholesterine were sparingly found, and granular matter. The disease was in the left ovary. The uterus was small and unaffected. The right ovary was normal. The liver was elevated into the chest by pressure from below, but otherwise appeared normal. The kidneys showed nothing remarkable. The intestines nearly entirely occupied the upper cavity of the abdomen, the stomach being much pushed up, and to the right overlapping the liver a good deal. The diaphragm was much arched, by which the cavity of the chest was much diminished. There must of necessity have been considerable interference with the action both of the lungs and heart from pressure." Mr. King says that circumstances did not admit of his examining the chest, but "I conclude that the heart sympathised in the general fatty degeneration of muscular tissue, and during life I was convinced that fatty degeneration existed." "As to the mode of death, this was unquestionably due to failure of the heart's action, which had for some time (about eighteen months) been gradually weakening; and, during the last few weeks of Miss Martineau's life, that organ had failed very markedly."

I have carefully examined, with my friend Mr. Higginson, this very large cyst, which undoubtedly had its origin in the left ovarium. The surface was traversed by blood-vessels, and to it was adherent the broad ligament of the uterus with its fimbriated extremity, and the Fallopian tube, this remained pervious, and admitted a wire to be passed through to the extent of three inches, when it came into contact with the pedicle, which was attached to the fundus, or perhaps more properly to the left cornu uteri.

From these data I shall endeavour to deduce a pathological history of the case, which will reconcile the symptoms experienced by the patient with the progress of organic disease.

The first question that presents itself for solution is, How did the displaced ovarium arrive at its situation near the uterine extremity of the Fallopian tube just before it entered the cornu uteri?

In answer, may it not be inferred that it had passed through the tube itself, which remains pervious? And, we know, as in cases of extra-uterine pregnancy or the formation of tuberculous matter, the Fallopian tube will admit of almost any degree of dilatation, it might easily enough admit the passage of the compressed ovarium, and in process of time regain its original calibre.[1]

If this inference be correct, the passage of the ovarium through the Fallopian tube must have been a slow process, and attended with much suffering, experienced in the early stages of disease. In this respect, it would bear some analogy to the passing of gall-stones or of calculi through the male urethra.

The dislocated ovarium in the first stage of its morbid growth, by its weight and connection with the fundus uteri, dragged the uterus down into the lower part of the pelvis, and so produced the retroversion observed when Miss Martineau was at Tynemouth, and by its fixed position between the rectum and the bladder occasioned the distressing symptoms then experienced. But as the displaced ovarium gained greater dimensions, it would gradually raise the uterus from its imprisonment in the lower part of the pelvis, and in this way the patient was relieved for a considerable time from the pain and discomfort it had caused. It was this temporary relief which led to the conclusion, not unnaturally, that she was cured. At this time, it is probable, that the growth of the ovarian tumour was not rapid; but, as time went on, its size became so great as to reproduce symptoms of oppression, the history of which is imperfectly known to me, and death has at length revealed the pathological condition which has been described.

---

1   The footnote reads: "My friend Mr. Higginson does not quite perceive the probability of the passage of the displaced ovarium through the Fallopian tube; but pathology discloses many unlooked-for facts; and the situation of the pedicle, which appears to have grown from the Fallopian tube just before its terminations in the cornu uteri—the tube being pervious to that point and no further—and the division of the pedicle having taken place at the same point, so as to leave the uterus on the one side and the tumour with the remainder of the Fallopian tube and broad ligament on the other, seems to render it highly probable that the ovarium of its normal size forced its way through the Fallopian tube to its ultimate position. I can find no record of a similar process, but it may have happened in other cases without observation. But whether correct or mistaken in this conjecture, the general history of the case remains untouched in its three stages: first, of suffering; secondly, of temporary relief (supposed cure); thirdly, of renewed illness, associated with collateral symptoms and so ending in death."

In 1841, when Sir Charles Clarke saw Miss Harriet Martineau, careful examination led us to conclude that the retroverted uterus was itself enlarged, and that it would eventually gain such dimensions as to raise it from its fixed position and so afford relief to the patient. But we were convinced that no malignant disease existed in the uterus. The displaced ovarium was at that time behind the fundus uteri, and probably gave the impression of abnormal enlargement of the uterus itself. Or, it is possible, that such enlargement actually existed, and that in the subsequent progress of disease the ovarium might gain nourishment at the expense of the uterus, thus inducing the small size of that organ at the time of death. It is not easy to define the changes produced during the lapse of thirty-two years. Whether some years ago, while the constitution retained some vigour, and the tumour had not yet attained its great size, it might have been successfully removed by operation, so as to effect a *real cure* of the disease, I had no opportunity of judging.

Such is a brief sketch of the conclusions at which I have arrived after careful reflection on this interesting case: interesting, not only in reference to the eminent lady who was the subject of it, but, perhaps, as affording a contribution of some value to the class of diseases of which it is a remarkable example. Perhaps, too, it may serve in some degree to explain some of the peculiarities of character which were apparent during her remarkable career.

3. Selected Correspondence with Dr. Peter Mere Latham.[1] From *The Papers of Harriet Martineau 1802-1876.* **[Reproduced with the permission of the University of Birmingham Library.]**

i. ALS from Peter Mere Latham, HM 539

36 Grosvenor Street
Jan. 12 1855
Dear Madam

I do not see through your case so clearly as I could wish. Nevertheless I see enough to serve as a guide to treatment; and if what I order you does you good, I shall begin to understand the better the nature of the ailment I have to do with. You can easily conceive that the effect of the remedy often serves to interpret the disease. Whatever "the creak the stop and the thump" may mean, they can hardly *in you* mean organic disease of the heart. To walk 7 or 8 miles without inconvenience; to drink port wine

---

1   Peter Mere Latham, M.D. (1789-1875) was appointed physician extraordinary to the queen in 1837 and in 1845 published *Lectures on Clinical Medicine, comprising Diseases of the Heart.*

with *very good* effect, and to obtain" a *most comfortable* day from 12 drops of Battley's Laudanum[1] are enough almost to abolish any evil suspicion I might have from symptoms immediately referable to the heart itself—what I prescribe for you is a very mild opiate (⅛ of a grain) in combination with ammonia. Of this compound I wish you to take a Teaspoonful in half a wineglass of water as nearly every six hours as possible and to continue so taking it for a week—In the mean time you must give special care to the Bowels, that they be not constipated—Drink a little wine and take moderate exercise—Avoid all that you know to disagree with you—tea especially, if it be in that predicament. And after the lapse of a week let me hear from you and know how you have prospered—Pray do me the favor of being the bearer of my very kind regards to Mrs. WE Forster.

I remain, dear Madam,

Yrs faithfully,

P. M. Latham

ii. ALS from Peter Mere Latham, HM 540

36 Grosvenor St.

Jan. 18. 1855

Dear Madam,

I think it won't do for me to strike any hard blows in the dark—From what your letter of today tells me of your present condition it will not be safe for me to venture further upon your treatment without seeing you—Do not however undertake a journey to London in *this cruel* weather without the sanction of Mr. Shepherd—He knows you and what you will bear—I shall be glad to hear from him about you; if he thinks you had better not come to Town at present—Give up altogether what I have prescribed—See Mr. Shepherd daily. Though I cannot tell you *positively* what to do, yet I might offer him suggestions which he might make use of. Observe I do not forbid your coming to Town; far from it—I am only afraid just now of your taking harm from the extreme cold by the way.

I remain, dear Madam,

Truly yours,

P.M. Latham

---

1 A proprietary preparation widely used to relieve mild pain, Battley's sedative drops were made of opium dissolved in alcohol.

iii. ALS from Peter Mere Latham, HM 541

36 Grosvenor Street
Feb. 20 1855
Dear Mrs. H. Martineau,

Is it possible that the opiates may be guilty of producing the pain in the head? I hope not. But unhappily some of our best remedies, those which produce the most good and even while they are producing it, carry along with them some contingent evil. This is especially the case with opium. I must not tell you not to take it—For I know no substitute for it, and the evils, which without its restraint would be let loose upon you, would be less endurable than the pain in the head—But you might try the experiment of reducing the quantity you take at each dose by one half. Or you might try to do without it for twelve out of the twenty four hours—There will be no making out but by some such trials, whether the opium has really any thing to do with the pain in the head.

There can be no objection to the Blister. It may do you good—Try it by all means—I shall be glad if the relief it gives you, should make it unnecessary to lose any part of the benefit you derive from the opium by reducing its dose—

I am happy to consider myself quite well again—but the bitter weather demands a most inconvenient amount of care on my part to avoid becoming ill again—

Give my kind remembrance to your niece and believe me
My dear Madame
truly yours
P. M. Latham

iv. ALS from Peter Mere Latham, HM 543

36 Grosvenor Street—April 16. 1855
My dear Mrs. H. Martineau,

I presume that the pain which you describe is neuralgic. This is as much as to say "the pain is a pain"—and does not sound very wise. Well, but these pains, which do not come directly from disease, have often this good belonging to them, that they act as *natural counterirritants* keeping in check real disease, which already subsists in some other part. It would be a happy circumstance if this shd be the case with you. Let the hope that it may be so be your consolation.

I have written you a prescription for a local application—This may be gently rubbed upon the limb, following the course of the pain, with the hand—or a piece of lint may be laid upon the limb in the course of the pain, after it has been first moistened by the liniment—Try the effect of this proceeding, when the pain comes on—you may continue the use of the liniment either until the pain is abated by it, or until it produce (as it sometimes will) some smarting of the surface—you are at liberty to manage your opiate remedy as to time and quantity, in any way you please—For I suspect that experience has taught you by this time great dexterity in its use—

Give my kind remembrance to your excellent nurse—and believe me
My dear Mrs. Martineau
Very truly yours
P.M. Latham

v. ALS from Peter Mere Latham, HM 548

36 Grosvenor St
August 11.1855
Saturday Night
My dear Mrs. Martineau—
I find your letter upon my return to Town and to business. You are right in believing the enlargement of your person so far as the *abdomen* is concerned (pardon my technicality) not to be dropsical. When you were in Town I once (you may remember) examined this part by pressure and then I found it enlarged and hard. My belief was that this enlargement and hardness were due to a tumour, which by gradual growth and increase had at length filled the whole abdomen,—and so was no longer distinguishable as such—It very often happens that what is at first recognized as a round, hard, circumscribed substance and quite free from pain will seem to disappear. But so far from disappearing it has been increasing all the while—And as it has increased it has lost its distinctness, because it has now come to fill the abdomen, in which it once was a distinct movable Tumour—Such Tumours usually have their growth from an appendage of the uterus, the ovary—their increase is often so absolutely without pain that the patient's own attention would not be called to them at all but from finding that the Abdomen has become so preposterously large—

I do not think that any of your symptoms which I witnessed or those which have since been reported to me can be due to aneurism. But pray at any time tell me, or ask me whatever you like about yourself, and I will answer you as well and truly as I can—I hope you received my letter from Chepstow—
I remain
very truly yours
P.M. Latham

Appendix D: Harriet Martineau and Autobiographical Writing

1. From Volume One of *Harriet Martineau's Autobiography*. Ed. Maria Weston Chapman. Boston: Houghton, Osgood and Company, 1879.

Here closed the anxious period during which my reputation, and my industry, and my social intercourses were at their height of prosperity; but which was so charged with troubles that when I lay down on my couch of pain in my Tynemouth lodging, for a confinement of nearly six years, I felt myself comparatively happy in my release from responsibility, anxiety and suspense. The worst sufferings of my life were over now; and its best enjoyments and privileges were to come,—though I little knew it, and they were as yet a good way off.

FIFTH PERIOD.

TO THE AGE OF FORTY-THREE
SECTION I

The little volume which I wrote during my illness,—"Life in the Sick-room,"—tells nearly as much as it can be interesting or profitable for any body to hear about this period of my life. The shorter I can make my narrative of it, the better on all accounts. Five years seem a long time to look forward; and five years of suffering, of mind or body, seem sadly like an eternity in passing through them: but they collapse almost into nothingness, as soon as they are left behind, and another condition is fairly entered on. From the monotony of sick-room life, little beyond the general impression remains to be imparted, or even recalled; and if it were otherwise, I should probably say little of that dreary term, because it is not good to dwell much on morbid conditions, for any other purpose than scientific study, for the sake of the prevention or cure of the suffering in other cases. I am aware that the religious world, proud of its Christian faith as the "Worship of Sorrow," thinks it a duty and a privilege to dwell on the morbid conditions of human life; but my experience of wide extremes of health and sickness, of happiness and misery, leads me to a very different conclusion. For pathological purposes, there must be a study of morbid conditions; but that the study should be general,—that it should be enforced as a duty, and held up as a pleasure—seems to me one of those mistakes in morals which are aggravated and protracted by the mischievous influence of superstition.

Tracts and religious books swarm among us, and are thrust into the hands of every body by every body else, which describe the sufferings of illness, and generate vanity and egotism about bodily pain and early death,—rendering these disgraces of our ignorance and barbarism attractive to the foolish and the vain, and actually shaming the wholesome, natural desire for "a sound mind in a sound body."[1] The Christian superstition, now at last giving way before science, of the contemptible nature of the body, and its antagonism to the soul, has shockingly perverted our morals, as well as injured the health of Christendom: and every book, tract, and narrative which sets forth a sick-room as a condition of honour, blessing and moral safety, helps to sustain a delusion and corruption which have already cost the world too dear. I know too much of all this from my own experience to choose to do any thing towards encouragement of the morbid appetite for pathological contemplation,—physical or moral. My youthful vanity took the direction which might be expected in the case of a pious child. I was patient in illness and pain because I was proud of the distinction, and of being taken into such special pupilage by God; and I hoped for, and expected early death till it was too late to die early. It is grievous to me now to think what an amount of time and thought I have wasted in thinking about dying,—really believing as I did for many years that life was a mere preparation for dying: and now, after a pretty long life, when I find myself really about to die, the event seems to me so simple, natural, and, as I may say, negative in comparison with life and its interests, that I cannot but marvel at the quantity of attention and solicitude I lavished upon it while it was yet so far off as to require no attention at all. To think no more of death than is necessary for the winding up of the business of life, and to dwell no more upon sickness than is necessary for its treatment, or to learn to prevent it, seems to me the simple wisdom of the case,—totally opposite as this is to the sentiment and method of the religious world.

On the other hand, I do not propose to nourish a foolish pride by disguising, through shame, the facts of sickness and suffering. Pain and untimely death are, no doubt, the tokens of our ignorance, and of our sins against the laws of nature. I conceive our business to be to accept these consequences of our ignorance and weakness, with as little personal shame on the one hand as vanity or pride on the other. As far as any sickness of mine can afford warning, I am willing to disclose it; and I have every desire to acknowledge my own fault or folly in regard to it, while wholly averse to treat it as a matter of sentiment,—even to the degree in which I did it, sin-

---

1   For a comprehensive analysis of the Victorian investment in the idea of total health or wholeness—*mens sana in corpore sano*—see Bruce Haley's *The Healthy Body and Victorian Culture* (Cambridge, MA: Harvard University Press, 1978).

cerely enough, in "Life in the Sick-room," a dozen years ago. I propose, therefore, to be now as brief as I can, and at the same time, as frank, in speaking of the years between 1839 and 1845. — I have mentioned before, in regard to my deafness, that I have no doubt of its having been seriously aggravated by nervous excitement, at the age when I lived in reverie and vanities of the imagination; and that it was suddenly and severely increased by a sort of accident. That sort of accident was the result of ignorance in a person whom I need not point out: and thus it seems that my deafness is largely ascribable to disobedience to the laws of nature. And thus in regard to the disease which at this time was laying me low for so many years. It was unquestionably the result of excessive anxiety of mind, — of the extreme tension of nerves under which I had been living for some years, while the three anxious members of my family were, I may say, on my hands, — not in regard to money, but to care of a more important kind. My dear aunt, the sweetest of old ladies, was now extremely old, and required shielding from the anxiety caused by the other two. My mother was old, and fast becoming blind; and the irritability caused in her first by my position in society, and next by the wearing trial of her own increasing infirmity, told fearfully upon my already reduced health. My mother's dignified patience in the direct endurance of her blindness was a really beautiful spectacle: but the natural irritability found vent in other directions; and especially was it visited upon me. Heaven knows, I never sought fame; and I would thankfully have given it all away in exchange for domestic peace and ease: but there it was! and I had to bear the consequences. I was overworked, fearfully, in addition to the pain of mind I had to bear. I was not allowed to have a maid, at my own expense, or even to employ a workwoman; and thus, many were the hours after midnight when I ought to have been asleep, when I was sitting up to mend my clothes. Far worse than this, my mother would not be taken care of. She was daily getting out into the crowded streets by herself, when she could not see a yard before her. What the distress from this was to me may be judged of by the fact that for many months after my retreat to Tynemouth, I rarely slept without starting from a dream that my mother had fallen from a precipice, or over the banisters, or from a cathedral spire; and that it was my fault. These cares, to say nothing of the toils, had long been wearing me down, so that I became subject to attacks of faintness, on occasion of any domestic uneasiness; and two or three intimate friends, as well as some members of the family, urged my leaving home as frequently as possible, for my mother's sake as well as my own, as my return was always a joyful occasion to her. My habits and likings made this moving about a very irksome thing to me; and especially when arrangements had to be made about my work, — from which I had never any holiday. I loved, as I still love, the most monotonous life possible: but I took refuge in change, as the only relief from a pressure of trouble which was breaking me down,—I was not aware how rapidly. An internal disease was gaining ground for months or years before I was aware of it. A tumour was forming of a kind which usually originates in mental suffering; and when at last I broke down completely, and settled myself in a lodging at Tynemouth, I long felt that the lying down, in solitude and silence, free from responsibility and domestic care, was a blessed change from the life I had led since my return from America. My dear old aunt soon died: my mother was established at Liverpool, in the neighbourhood of three of her children; and the other claimant of my anxious care emigrated. It is impossible to deny that the illness under which I lay suffering for five years was induced by flagrant violations of the laws of nature: and I then failed to appropriate the comforts with which Christians deprave their moral sense in such a case, as I also felt unable to blame myself individually for my incapacity. No doubt, if I had felt less respect and less affection for my mother, I might have taken the management of matters more into my own hands, and should have felt her discontent with me less than I did; and again, if I had already found the supports of philosophy on relinquishing the selfish complacencies of religion, I should have borne my troubles with strength and ease. But, as it was, I was neither proud or vain of my discipline on the one hand, nor ashamed of it on the other, while fully aware that it was the result of fault and imperfection, moral and intellectual.

On my return from Italy, ill, my sister and her husband hospitably urged my taking up my abode with them, at least till the nature and prospects of my case were ascertained. After spending a month at a lodging in their neighbourhood in Newcastle-upon-Tyne, I removed to their hospitable house, where I was taken all possible care of for six months. They most generously desired me to remain: but there were various reasons which determined me to decline their kindness. It would have been clearly wrong to occupy their guest chamber permanently, and to impose restraints upon a healthy household: and, for my own part, I had an unspeakable longing for stillness and solitude. I therefore decided for myself that I would go to a lodging at Tynemouth, where my medical brother-in-law could reach me by railway in twenty minutes, while I was removed from the bustle and smoke of Newcastle by an interval of nine miles. With an affectionate reluctance and grudging, my family let me try this as an experiment,—all of them being fully convinced that I could not long bear the solitude and monotony, after the life of excitement and constant variety to which I had been accustomed for above seven years. I was right, however, and they were wrong. On the sofa where I stretched myself after my drive to Tynemouth, on the sixteenth of March, 1840, I lay for nearly five years, till obedience to a newly-discovered law of nature raised me up, and sent me forth into the world again, for another ten years of strenuous work, and almost undisturbed peace and enjoyment of mind and heart.

I had two rooms on the first floor in this house of my honest hostess, Mrs. Halliday, who little imagined, that March day, that the luck was happening to her of a lodger who would stay, summer and winter, for nearly five years. I had no servant with me at first; for I was not only suddenly cut off from my literary engagements, and almost from the power of work, but I had invested £1,000 of my earnings in a deferred annuity, two years before;—a step which seemed prudent at the time, and which I still consider to have been so; but which deprived me of immediate resources. It was not long before two generous ladies, (sisters) old friends of mine, sent me, to my amazement, a bank-note for £100, saying that my illness had probably interfered with certain plans which they knew I entertained. The generosity was of a kind impossible to refuse, because it extended through me to others. I took the money, and applied it as intended. I need hardly say that when my working days and my prosperity returned, I repaid the sum, which was, as I knew it would be, lodged in the hands of sufferers as needy as I was when it came to me.

I was waited upon in my lodging by a sickly-looking, untidy little orphan girl of fourteen,—untidy, because the state of her eyes was such that she could not sew, or have any fair chance for cleanliness. She was the niece and dependent of my hostess, by whom she was scolded without mercy, and, it seemed to me, incessantly. Her quiet and cheerful submission impressed me at once; and I heard such a report of her from the lady who had preceded me in the lodgings, and who had known the child from early infancy, that I took an interest in her, and studied her character from the outset. Her character was easily known; for a more simple, upright, truthful, ingenuous child could not be. She was, in fact, as intellectually incapable as morally indisposed to deception of any kind. This was "the girl Jane"[1] who recovered her health by mesmerism in companionship with me, and whom I was required by the doctors, and by the Athenaeum, to "give up" as "an impostor," after five years' household intercourse with her, in addition to my indirect knowledge of her, through my neighbour, from the age of three. I may mention here that my unvarying good opinion of her was confirmed after the recovery of both by the experience of her household qualities for seven years, during which period she lived with me as my cook, till she emigrated to Australia, where she has lived in high credit from the beginning of 1853 till now. This Jane, destined to so curious an experience, and to so discreditable a persecution, (which she bore in the finest

---

1   Jane Arrowsmith.

spirit) was at the door of my Tynemouth lodging when I arrived: and many were the heartaches I had for her, during the years that her muscles looked like dough, and her eyes like.........I will not say what. I suffered from the untidiness of my rooms, I own; and I soon found that my Norfolk notions of cleanliness met with no response at Tynemouth. Before long, I was shifted from purgatory to paradise in this essential matter. An uncle and some cousins, who had always been kind to me, were shocked to find that I was waited upon by only the people of the house; and they provided me with a maid, who happened to be the cleanliest of her sex. She remained with me during the whole of my illness: and never, in all that time, did I see a needless grain of dust on the furniture, nor a speck on the window panes that was not removed next morning.

For the view from my window, and the details of my mode of life as an invalid I must refer all who wish to know my Tynemouth self to "Life in the Sick-room." They will find there what the sea and shore were to me, and how kind friends came to see me, and my family were at my call; and for what reasons, and how peremptorily, I chose to live alone. One half year was rendered miserably burdensome by the cheating intrusion of an unwelcome and uncongenial person who came, (as I believed because I was told) for a month, and stayed seven, in a lodging next door. More serious mischiefs than the immediate annoyance were caused by this unwarrantable liberty taken with my comfort and convenience; and the suffering occasioned by them set me back in health not a little: but with the exception of that period, I obtained the quiet I so needed and desired.

During the first half of the time, I was able to work,—though with no great willingness, and with such extreme exhaustion that it became at length necessary to give up every exertion of the kind. "Deerbrook" had come out in the spring of 1839, just before my illness declared itself. That conception being wrought out and done with, I reverted to the one which I had held in abeyance, through the objections made to it by my friend Mrs. ———, whom alone I consulted in such matters, and on whose knowledge of books and taste in literature I reposed my judgment. Now that she was far away, my affections sprang back to the character and fortunes of Toussaint L'Ouverture.[1] I speedily made up my mind to present that genuine hero with his actual sayings and doings (as far as they were extant) to the world. When I had been some time at Tynemouth, finding my strength and spirits declining, I gave up the practice of keeping a diary, for two reasons which I now think good and sufficient;—first, that I found it becoming a burden; and next, that a diary, kept under such circumstances,

---

1   The subject of her novel *The Hour and the Man* (1841). Martineau stressed Toussaint L'Ouverture's heroic status as the symbolic figure of black liberty in French colonial Haiti.

must be mainly a record of frames and feelings,—many of them morbid, and few fit for any but pathological uses: but I cannot be sorry that I continued my journal for some months, as it preserves the traces of my progress in a work which I regard with some affection, though, to say the truth, without any admiration whatever. I find, in the sickly handwriting of that spring of 1840, notices of how my subject opened before me, and of how, as I lay gazing upon the moon-lit sea, in the evenings of April and May, new traits in the man, new links between the personages, and a clearer perception of the guiding principle of the work disclosed themselves to me...

To finish the subject of my authorship during this period, I will now tell how my anonymous volume, "Life in the Sick-room," came into existence, and how I, who never had a secret before or since, (as far as I can now remember) came to have one then. — In the book itself it is seen what I have to say on the subject of sympathy with the sick. When I had been living for above three years alone (for the most part) and with merely the change from one room to another,—from bed to sofa,—in constant uneasiness, and under the depression caused both by the nature of my disease and by heavy domestic cares, I had accumulated a weight of ideas and experiences which I longed to utter, and which indeed I needed to cast off. I need not repeat (what is amply explained in the book) that it was wholly my own doing that I lived alone, and why such was my choice; and the letters which I afterwards received from invalids satisfied me, and all who saw those letters, that my method was rational and prudent. It was not because I was destitute of kind nurses and visitors that I needed to pour out what was in my mind, but because the most perfect sympathy one can meet with in any trial common to humanity is reached by an appeal to the whole mind of society. It was on the fifteenth of September, 1843, that this mode of relief occurred to me, while I lay on my sofa at work on my inexhaustible resource, fancy-work. I kept no diary at that time; but I find inserted under that date in a note-book, "A new and imperative idea occurred to me,— 'Essays from a Sick-room.'" This conception was certainly the greatest refreshment I had during all those heavy years. During the next few days, while some of my family were with me, I brooded over the idea; and on the nineteenth, I wrote the first of the Essays. I never wrote any thing so fast as that book. It went off like sleep. I was hardly conscious of the act, while writing or afterwards,—so strong was the need to speak. I wrote the Essays as the subject pressed, and not in the order in which they stand. As I could not speak of them to any body, I suspended the indulgence of writing them while receiving the visits which I usually had in October,—preparatory to the long winter solitude; and it was therefore November when I finished my volume. I wrote the last Essay on the fourth. It was now necessary to tell one person;—viz, a publisher. I wrote confidentially to Mr. Moxon who, curiously enough, wrote to me on the same day, (so that our letters crossed,) to ask whether I was not able, after so long an interval of rest, to promise him some work to publish. My letter had a favourable reception; he carefully considered my wishes, and kept my secret, and I corrected my last proof on the twenty-sixth of November. On the seventh of December, the first news of the volume being out arrived in the shape of other letters than Mr. Moxon's. I was instantly and universally detected, as I had indeed supposed must be the case. On that day, my mother and eldest sister came over from Newcastle to see me. It was due to them not to let them hear such a fact in my history from the newspapers or from strangers; so, assuring them that it was the first time I had opened my lips on the subject, and that Mr. Moxon was the only person who had known it at all, I told them what I had done, and lent them my copy to take home. They were somewhat hurt, as were one or two more distant friends, who had no manner of right to be so. It proved to me how little reticence I can boast of, or have the credit for, that several friends confidently denied that the book was mine, on the ground that I had not told them a word about it,—a conviction in which I think them perfectly justified. There could not be a stronger proof of how I *felt* that book than my inability to speak of it except to my unknown comrades in suffering. My mother and sister had a special trial, I knew, to bear in discovering how great my suffering really was; and I could not but see that it was too much for them, and that from that time forward they were never again to me what they had been.

What the "success" of the book was, the fact of a speedy sale of the whole edition presently showed. What my own opinion of it is, at the distance of a dozen years, it may be worth while to record. My note-book of that November says that I wrote the Essays from the heart, and that there never was a truer book as to conviction. Such being the fact, I can only now say that I am ashamed, considering my years and experience of suffering, that my state of mind was so crude, if not morbid, as I now see it to have been. I say this, not from any saucy elevation of health and prosperity, but in an hour of pain and feebleness, under a more serious and certainly fatal illness than that of 1843, and after ten intervening years of health and strength, ease and prosperity. All the facts in the book, and some of the practical doctrine of the sick-room, I could still swear to: but the magnifying of my own experience, the desperate concern as to my own ease and happiness, the moaning undertone running through what many people have called the stoicism, and the total inability to distinguish between the metaphysically apparent and the positively true, make me, to say the truth, heartily despise a considerable part of the book. Great allowance is to be made, no doubt, for the effect of a depressing malady, and of the anxieties which caused it, and for an exile of years from fresh air, exercise, and change of scene. Let such allowance be made; but the very demand shows that the book is morbid,—or that part of it which needs such allowance. Stoical! Why, if I had been stoical I should not have written the book at all: —not *that* book; but if any, one wholly clear of the dismal self-consciousness which I then thought it my business to detail. The fact is, as I now see, that I was lingering in the metaphysical stage of mind, because I was not perfectly emancipated from the *débris* of the theological. The day of final release from both was drawing nigh, as I shall have occasion to show: but I had not yet ascertained my own position. I had quitted the old untenable point of view, and had not yet found the one on which I was soon to take my stand. And, while attesting the truth of the book on the whole,—its truth as a reflexion of my mind of that date,—I still can hardly reconcile with sincerity the religious remains that are found in it. To be sure, they are meagre and incoherent enough; but, such as they are they are compatible, I fear, with only a metaphysical, and not a positive order of sincerity. I had not yet learned, with decision and accuracy, what *conviction* is. I had yet no firm grasp of it; and I gave forth the contemporary persuasions of the imagination, or narratives of old traditions, as if they had been durable convictions, ascertained by personal exertion of my faculties. I suffered the retribution of this unsound dealing,—the results of this crude state of mind,—in the latent fear and blazoned pain through which I passed during that period; and if any one now demurs to my present judgment, on the score of lapse of time and change of circumstances, I would just remind him that I am again ill, as hopelessly, and more certainly fatally than I was then. I cannot be mistaken in what I am now feeling so sensibly from day to day,—that my condition is bliss itself in comparison with that of twelve years ago; and that I am now above the reach (while my brain remains unaffected by disease) of the solicitudes, regrets, apprehensions, self-regards, and inbred miseries of various kinds, which breathe through these Sick-room Essays, even where the language appears the least selfish and cowardly. I should not now write a sick-room book at all, except for express pathological purposes: but if I did, I should have a very different tale to tell. If not, the ten best years of my life—the ten which intervened between the two illnesses,—would have been lost upon me.

Before I dismiss this book, I must mention that its publisher did his duty amply by it and me. I told him at first to say nothing to me about money, as I could not bear to think of selling such an experience while in the midst of it. Long after, when I was in health and strength, he wrote that circumstances had now completely changed, and that life was again open before me; and he sent me a cheque for £75. On occasion of another edition, he sent me £50 more.

2. From Harriet Martineau's self-written obituary. Retitled as "An Autobiographic Memoir" for the *Daily News* and reprinted in Volume Two of *Harriet Martineau's Autobiography*. Maria Weston Chapman, Editor. Boston: Houghton, Osgood and Company, 1879.

On the publication of "Deerbrook," in April, 1839, she went abroad with a party of friends, partly to escort an invalid cousin, and partly for rest and refreshment to herself. She was not aware of the extent of her own illness; and she was brought home on a couch from Venice in June, in a state of health so hopeless that she left London and settled herself at Tynemouth, on the Northumberland coast, within reach of family care and tendance. There she remained, a prisoner to the couch, till the close of 1844. During her illness she wrote her second novel ("The Hour and the Man"), the four volumes of children's tales called "The Playfellow," and "Life in the Sick-Room;" originating also, in concert with the present Countess of Elgin and Mr. Knight, the series since so well known as "The Weekly Volume." Of her recovery the public heard at the time much more than she desired and approved. At the instigation of several of her friends, and especially of her medical attendant, she made trial of mesmerism, for the purpose of obtaining some release from the use of opiates. To her own surprise and that of others, the treatment procured her a release from the disease itself, from which several eminent men had declared recovery to be impossible. In five months she was perfectly well. Meantime, doctors and strangers in various parts of the kingdom had rushed into print, without her countenance or her knowledge; and the amount of misrepresentation and mischief soon became so great as to compel her to tell the story as it really happened. The commotion was just what might have been anticipated from the usual reception of new truths in science and the medical art. That she recovered when she ought to have died was an unpardonable offence. According to the doctors who saw her enter society again from the beginning of 1845, she was in a state of infatuation, and, being as ill as ever in reality, would sink down in six months. When, instead of so sinking down, she rode on a camel to Mount Sinai and Petra, and on horseback to Damascus,[1] they said she had never been ill. To the charge that it had been "all imagination," her reply was that, in that case, it was the doctor's imagination and not hers that was involved; for they had told her, and not she them, what and how serious her illness was. To the friends who blamed her for publishing her experience before the world was ripe for it, her reply was, first, that she had no option; and next, that it is hard to see how the world is to get ripened if experimenters in new departments of natural philosophy conceal their

---

1   This journey is the basis for Martineau's *Eastern Life, Present and Past* (1848).

experience. The immediate consequence of the whole business — the extension of the practice of mesmerism as a curative agent, and especially the restoration of several cases like her own — abundantly compensated Harriet Martineau for an amount of insult and ridicule which would have been a somewhat unreasonable penalty on any sin or folly which she could have committed. As a penalty on simply getting well when she was expected to die, the infliction was a curious sign of the times...

From the early part of 1852 she had contributed largely to the "Daily News," and her "Letters from Ireland" in the summer of that year were written for this paper. As her other works left her hands the connection with the paper became closer, and it was never interrupted except for a few months at the beginning of her last illness, when all her strength was needed for her Autobiography. When she had finished that task she had the work printed, and the engravings prepared for it under her own supervision, partly to avoid delay in its appearance (because any good that it could do would be best done immediately after her death), but chiefly to spare her executors all responsibility about publishing whatever may be found in the Memoir. Her last illness was a time of quiet enjoyment to her, soothed as it was by family and social love, and care, and sympathy, and, except for one heart-grief, — the loss in 1864 of her niece Maria, who was to her as a daughter, — free from anxiety of every kind, and amused by the constant interest of regarding life and its affairs from the verge of the horizon of existence. Her disease was deterioration and enlargement of the heart, the fatal character of which was discovered in January, 1855. She declined throughout that and subsequent years, and died —

Appendix E: Harriet Martineau and Florence Nightingale

1. Selected correspondence with Florence Nightingale. [Florence Nightingale Papers: Reprinted with permission of the British Library, BL Add 45,788.]

Ambleside
Janry 19/60

Dear Miss Nightingale

I have almost shrunk from writing to you about your "Notes" &c because I felt so strongly about them that it was difficult to speak without an apparent extravagance which one wd not offer to *you*. This is a work of genius, if ever I saw one; & it will operate accordingly. Maria[1] & I had devoured it before night; & I feel confident that it will be the same with a multitude of people, though all have not exactly the keen interest in the subject that M. & I have. The book will be, as "D. News" says (I don't know who wrote that) "a revelation." It is as fresh as if nobody had ever before spoken of nursing. It is so real & so intense, that it will, I doubt not, create an order of nurses before it has finished its work. — I want to be *doing*, to help the diffusion of the book. I wrote to the Edr of "D. News" that I wanted to treat it more broadly than can be done in a newspaper notice: &, as I knew he would, he at once got it done in decisive style. Meantime, we (Maria & I) have written (confidentially) to the Editor of the "Edinburgh Review" (who is in Paris) asking whether he is at all likely to be able to have an article on the broad subject of the Relation of the Well to the Sick,—on the text of these "Notes." *Entre nous*, I am engaged to write an article for him this quarter on another topic; but I shd not mind the delay of a quarter if he wd allow me to do what I wish. His hands are always full,—his programme bursting with articles: but he so honours all that you do that I don't despair. I have also written strongly to the Times reviewer about the "Notes," & I have little doubt of a good help to the circulation thence. Maria is writing to friends who have money, to show them what good they may do by putting this little book into every house where there are women of any good quality at all. — Maria longs, I know, to nurse you. I do think you wd find her as near to your standard of a nurse as anybody in Europe. O! how we [quibbled?] over that section "Chattering Hopes & Advices." How true it is! & how dreary! I gratefully admit that I

---

1   Maria Martineau, Harriet Martineau's beloved niece, served as her aunt's companion and attendant from 1858 until 1864, when she died of typhoid fever.

suffer very little indeed from that sort of plague. Maria wards it off, in fact. But in my former long illness I knew too well what it was: & now, there is a visitor occasionally who counts, or who relieves his or her own feelings in the ways you know so well. One good lady,— so kind otherwise! regularly says in autumn "Good bye now. I hope to find you quite well in the spring." And every second or third visit, she begins "Well, now — I want you to see another physician &c &c. I am persuaded, as you have gone on so long, that you might get well on some other plan &c &c &c." My dear cousin, Mrs. Turner, said one day "She will never say that again. She is now really impressed by what I told her,— that your being alive now is, according to your doctors, owing to your perfect quiet & monotony &c." However, just before Xmas my kind visitor went over the ground again, in the regular way. We are hoping she will read the "Notes."

If you will not for a moment think it needful to reply, I will add a thing or two. — I see no reference in any of your books to an important precautionary method which it is possible may not have come under your study;— that of putting beds North & South (the patient's head to the North.) The reason cannot be stated with any scientific precision but it is supposed to belong to the relation between the human electric current & the current of terrestrial magnetism. However that may be, the fact seems to be indisputable that in cases of extreme exhaustion or irritability, the position of the patient makes the difference between sleep & sleeplessness,— & therefore at times between life & death. You may see a pretty full statement of facts on this matter in Treatise III of Reichenbach's "Researches on Magnetism."[1] The head to the South is next best to the right position. The distress when the patient lies East & West is often very great — in puerperal cases, in nervous fevers & insanity, & in great feebleness of any kind. For several years, I always took a pocket compass when going to any Lunatic Asylum or hospital: & now that two of my nephews are "about to marry" I have given them a hint to set the beds the right way at first,— however little it matters to the healthy which way they lay their heads. I have now *privately* advised them to get the "Notes" before furnishing their houses & they will do it. — By the way, you wd approve Catherine of Russia's apartment in some respects: — bedposts (if there must be any) of purple glass; & the walls porcelain.

I will not trouble you further, except just to say, for truth's sake, that I go much further than you in approbation of Homeopathic treatment,— in the hand of not only amateurs but the profession. I have been watching it for 23 years; & I am as sure as I can be of anything future that it will supersede any

---

1   Charles von Reichenbach, author of *Physico-physiological researches on the dynamics of magnetism, electricity, heat, light, crystallization, and chemism in their relations to Vital Force.*

other principle & method known. There is much yet to learn in it: but that it is true as far as it goes, I am persuaded must be seen by all who really & effectually study it. There is a dreadful paucity of qualified practitioners, though they increase by hundreds every year. In Birmingham there are only two,—though "there is practice for a dozen," as the departmental chemist declares. Now that Town Councils vote money, as at Liverpool, for the support of Homeopathic Dispensaries, we are more in the way of a due supply of skill. I need not tell you that the "globules" for ever fastened on by the rival school are not a primary or essential part of the theory or practice.

I do wish I knew how you were. I will write to Julia soon. She has been *so* welcome at Nottingham!

As for me,—my special suffering of late has been from tic, from which I have not been free one day or night since the 24th of October. —Maria has however obtained sleep for me, in the very midst of the pain—by (*unknown to me at first*) mesmerizing my pillows, bed, nightclothes, & it was like a miracle. We cannot apply it directly by mesmerizing *me*, from the danger of congestion; or the pain wd soon be sent to the night about. But it is reduced since I got sleep. The doctor is too glad & relieved to quarrel with the means.

I am most gratefully your H. Martineau

30 Old Burlington St.
London W
Feb 8/60

Dear Miss Martineau

Many many thanks for your note of the 5th, which I should have answered before, but that I was unable to write.

Nothing would be more generally useful (or, by me, more desired) than that *you* should treat in your broad way the "mutual relations of the sick & well."

Your book, though it must be some 18 years since I read it—stays by my memory, as everything you write does. And I believe I could repeat it pretty nearly all, as I could nearly all your "Deerbrook" & much of your "Political Economy" Tales—

But I want to say one thing. I do believe there is not the smallest chance of anything you write not being discovered. If therefore you will not think me wholly impertinent & like my own "chattering" advisers, I would say, do not write anything which you do not wish to have known is by you. The article will be remarked, questions will be asked, and I never knew anything that people *wished* to know (of this kind) that did *not* at last "leak out." If a Review Article does not fall dead,—and depend upon it this will not people always ask, whose is it? And people always find out. Ultimately every body will know that you have written it—

You will say (& say truly) that you have great literary experience & I have none—Still I cannot help telling you, in return for your generous confidence, of what I believe will be the case.

So far from wishing to deter you from writing the Article, it would very much deter me from writing this, if I thought I should—

But—*whatever you write will be known.*
I am so glad to hear that you are something easier.
Ever yours sincerely & gratefully
F. Nightingale

I quite agree with you that *how to be ill* is a necessary complement of *how to nurse.* One is not complete without the other. — But, on the whole, I think the first duty better performed, generally, than the second. I thought—at the time (& I think so still) that you are a little hard upon the sick in your book. Because I am a Patient myself I think I am *not the less* inclined to be hard upon the sick too, as you were for the same reason. But I think a Patient's gratitude to a really good nurse is almost painfully intense. There is one thing, however, in which all my experience in sending out Nurses, as well as that of all Institutions which do send out Nurses, convinces me that (tho families of the sick perhaps oftener than) the sick themselves lamentably fail—and that is in expecting nurses to "sit up" night after night without any proper provision for quiet & regular sleep during the day. One is always obliged to *make a bargain for* one's nurses in this respect.

On the other hand, I do think that any aversion the Patient manifests or feels (unmanifested) towards the Nurse is generally the Nurses's own fault not the Patient's.

I have seen an expression of real terror pass across a Patient's face, whenever a Nurse came into the room who, he was sure, would tumble over the fire-irons.

I have seen Patients, scarcely able to crawl, get out of bed before such a Nurse came into the room, & put out of the way every thing she could throw down, hide every thing they were likely to want, (not because they had not a right to have it but because she was sure, in "putting things to rights," to put it out of their reach) and shut the window, because she was sure to leave the door open behind her (putting them into a thorough draught).

On the other hand, again, this is my painful experience & one which many medical men will corroborate. I am always asked to send a Nurse because the friends of the Patient are "worn out" with "sitting up" or to have the servants "running up & down stairs." I am never asked to send a nurse that the Patient may be *better nursed*.

I do believe this is the root of all—And the Nurses are made "to run up & downstairs" & "to sit up" till they are unfit for anything. — this being the avowed object a Nurse is there for—*not to nurse*

FN

Please not to think this letter requires an answer—

We have had a terrible loss in our poor "Director General" (of the Army Medl Dep.) To us it is irreparable. —

Private
May 2/66
Stationery: 35 South Street
Park Lane
London. W.

Dear friend

I cannot help saying one word—Your note gives the most convincing evidence against yourself—viz that your work in life is not necessarily over for ever. It may be a reason of mere temporary mental exhaustion such as is inevitably the lot of those who are suffering from both severe exertion & illness & grief. I do not say this wd give you pleasure. I am afraid, if it is true, it is just the thing to give you pain. I am afraid that to live is with you little more than an effort & a suffering, as with me. But I cannot help thinking that a period of complete mental rest might restore for a time the mental power. And I can hardly help hoping that it may be that you will once more enlighten public opinion & public feeling in England. Else, I am sure, the painfulness & the desolateness of a bereaved & infirm life is not what one could wish, a friend, like you.

I saw the other day a letter from a man resigning work for the same reasons you do. But his own letter, poor man, was the best proof that the step must be taken at once & for ever—quite the reverse of yours—

I could not but say these few words, at the risk of displeasing you—tho' I am not able to write more today. Otherwise I should have put it off till I could write more. For I have so much I should like to tell you, if I could. You will know that we have been rather in a fever lately, because Ministers were hovering between "in" & "out." On the whole, we are glad they stay "in." The Public Health Service is going to be organized in India. The reasons connected with the peculiar forms of Indian Government—new to me but not to you who have gone so deeply into Indian Govt....

I have much to write in answer to your—but not now—

Please burn this.
ever yours
living or dying
F. Nightingale

Ambleside
May 13/67

Dear friend

It is an immense time since I wrote to you. The reason why is easily told. One does not wish to send dismal letters to invalid friends; & this dreary Spring has been full of anxiety & trouble, to us—as to many other people. I will say nothing of family illnesses—very alarming at the time—wh have passed away: & of remaining troubles the only one that I need speak of regards myself chiefly. If there was an old woman in England securely & comfortably provided for in a moderate way, we shd have said it was myself; & now—when I cannot work, nor stir, nor alter my way of living, I find myself likely to be deprived (for the present, with wh alone I have any concern) of nearly two-thirds of my income. It is the Railway panic[1] wh causes this; & a most strange perplexity it is for a careful body like me. It comes up in my confused & broken nights disagreeably; but we are not much troubled by it by daylight. — And it *may* not happen,— I being a holder, not of Shares, but of Preferential stock. And I have money enough in bank & in hand till November; & I don't often look so far forward as that. And I cd raise a loan on good security; & I have plenty of friends eager to help me. But I wish to keep my independence, if possible. We all believe that there will be no loss of capital,— that there will be a complete recovery, sooner or later; & if so, my legatees will get what I have left them: but I don't expect, myself, to touch either principal or interest. — How many, almost as helpless, are set fast at present,—& in a worse way, as being Shareholders! I have heard of some—widows with young children, spinsters with narrow incomes, old people & the like, who don't know wh way to turn. The anxiety among my family & friends is that I shd not drop the very few things that it is possible to drop,— the *Times*, the Mudie box,[2] wine &c. & I have promised to go on with them for the six months. By that time, if I am not past all wants, we shall probably be able to form some notion what we ought to do.

---

1   The collapse of the railway securities market in late 1845 is often referred to as "the Railway Panic." Its aftermath was long-lasting, and in 1866 and 1867 tightening credit produced a series of bankruptcies.
2   Founded in 1842, Mudie's circulating library enabled people with subscriptions to have their borrowed books delivered.

Nobody need fear my attempting to write again. I never wrote (nor suppressed) a line for the sake of money; & I shd certainly not begin now, if ever so able: but I am utterly unable. At least I believe so. —My condition is odd,—& especially in contrast with you,—so unable as *you* are to bear opiates. The bowels continue to be the trouble; & I try in vain to get out of the practice of having two washings-out, & two opiate enemas daily, in addition to all I had before by the mouth. They make me very much more comfortable than I was till my doctor ordered this bold stroke; but I expect to pay for it; & it is a very thin disguise of various failures that I become more & more sensible of. The cold of this strange Spring (not bitter as in the Midland counties) has served me so well that I was ashamed—hearing & seeing how everybody else suffered by it: & now, my turn is coming. With the first warm days, my strength runs out like water from a leak. I hope I may think of it as good for you,—as far as good is yet possible. I have heard nothing distinct of you for a long time. Julia Smith has been at Liverpool,—amazing my sister,—& in truth overwhelming her—with her energy,—in the schools &c. I hear of her often—always as looking old, worn, & over-energizing. The old story! I have often wondered whether she seems, more or less, that she might do all she does, & more, without wear & tear, if she cd introduce order into her thoughts & ways. But, unhappily, she despises order—steadiness—regularity, as the ways & means of small & low minds,—& bad even for them. But in saying all this I am only groaning over a dismal waste of life & power,—*not* finding fault. I do honour & admire & love her that I *can* only mourn, & not blame. It is a case of constitutional liability,—so ingrained in her constitution that she wishes to be as she is, in regard to that class of conditions. There is some-thing fearful in passing into old age with an incapacity for repose, or even for any stationary form of energy. What an exquisite moral nature, hers is!—in my experience, one of the most awakening & moving disclosures I have been blessed within my whole life. I always tell myself that she *must* have been happier than I can see that she ever has been.

But what am I about to write all this to you who, if it is true, must know it so much better than I can!

How doleful all public affairs have been looking,—abroad & at home! All those mightily religious Governmts & Courts abroad, what a temper of heathen barbarism they have been showing, on every possible occasion!

—How I have run on! & now I am dining & writing at once. Do you savour the boiled beef?—or the custard?—Cow-keeping & poultry ditto give us such custards & other good things! I hope we shall not have to make such a change as giving up *that*....

Dear friend, I must say Good-bye, & send this as it is,— without a glance at it. I hope I may hear how you go on from somebody, some day. — My household are well. Ever your affectionate H. Martineau

2. From Florence Nightingale's *Notes on Nursing: What It Is, And What It Is Not.* **London, 1860.**

XII. CHATTERING HOPES AND ADVICES

The sick man to his advisers.

"My advisers! Their name is legion.

Somehow or other, it seems a provision of the universal destinies, that every man, woman, and child should consider him, her, or itself privileged especially to advise me. Why? That is precisely what I want to know." And that is what I have say to them. I have been advised to go to every place extant in and out of England — to take every kind of exercise by every kind of care, carriage — yes, and even swing (!) and dumb-bell (!) in existence; to imbibe every different kind of stimulus that ever has been invented. And this when those *best* fitted to know, viz., medical men, after long and close attendance, had declared any journey out of the question, had prohibited any kind of motion whatever, had closely laid down the diet and drink. What would my advisers say, were they the medical attendants, and I the patient left their advice, and took the casual adviser's? But the singularity in Legion's mind is this: it never occurs to him that everybody else is doing the same thing, and that I the patient *must* perforce say, in sheer self-defence, like Rosalind, "I could not do with all."[1]

"Chattering Hopes" may seem an odd heading. But I really believe there is scarcely a greater worry which invalids have to endure than the incurable hopes of their friends. There is no one practice against which I can speak more strongly from actual personal experience, wide and long, of its effects during sickness observed both upon others and upon myself. I would appeal most seriously to all friends, visitors, and attendants of the sick to leave off this practice of attempting to "cheer" the sick by making light of their danger and by exaggerating their probabilities of recovery.

Far more now than formerly does the medical attendant tell the truth to the sick who are really desirous to hear it about their own state.

How intense is the folly, then, to say the least of it, of the friend, be he even a medical man, who thinks that his opinion, given after a cursory observation, will weigh with the patient, against the opinion of the medical attendant, given, perhaps, after years of observation, after using every help to

---

1   Probably an allusion to Rosalind in Shakespeare's *As You Like It*.

diagnosis afforded by the stethoscope, the examination of pulse, tongue, &c.; and certainly after much more observation than the friend can possibly have had.

Supposing the patient to be possessed of common sense,—how can the "favourable" opinion, if it is to be called an opinion at all, of the casual visitor "cheer" him,—when different from that of the experienced attendant? Unquestionably the latter may, and often does, turn out to be wrong. But which is most likely to be wrong?

The fact is, that the patient[1] is not "cheered" at all by these well-meaning, most tiresome friends. On the contrary, he is depressed and wearied. If, on the one hand, he exerts himself to tell each successive member of this too numerous conspiracy, whose name is legion, why he does not think as they do,—in what respect he is worse,—what symptoms exist that they know nothing of,—he is fatigued instead of "cheered," and his attention is fixed upon himself. In general, patients who are really ill, do not want to talk about themselves. Hypochondriacs do, but again I say we are not on the subject of hypochondriacs.

If, on the other hand, and which is much more frequently the case, the patient says nothing, but the Shakespearian "Oh!" "Ah!" "Go to!" and "in good sooth!" in order to escape from the conversation about himself the sooner, he is depressed by want of sympathy. He feels isolated in the midst of friends. He feels what a convenience it would be, if there were any single person to whom he could speak simply and openly, without pulling the string upon himself of this shower-bath of silly hopes and encouragements; to whom he could express his wishes and directions without that person persisting in saying, "I hope that it will please God yet to give you twenty years," or, "You have a long life of activity before you." How often we see at the end of biographies or of cases recorded in medical papers, "after a long

---

1 Nightingale's original footnote here reads: "There are, of course, cases, as in first confinements, when an assurance from the doctor or experienced nurse to the frightened suffering woman that there is nothing unusual in her case, that she has nothing to fear but a few hours' pain, may cheer her most effectually. This is advice of quite another order. It is the advice of experience to utter inexperience. But the advice we have been referring to is the advice of inexperience to bitter experience; and, in general, amounts to nothing more than this, that *you* think *I* shall recover from consumption because somebody knows somebody somewhere who has recovered from fever.

I have heard a doctor condemned whose patient did not, alas! recover, because another doctor's patient of a *different* sex, of a *different* age, recovered from a *different* disease, in a *different* place. Yes, this is really true. If people who make these comparisons but did know (only they do not care to know), the care and preciseness with which such comparisons require to be made, (and are made,) in order to be of any value whatever, they would spare their tongues. In comparing the deaths of one hospital with those of another, any statistics are justly considered absolutely valueless which do not give the ages, the sexes, and the diseases of all the cases. It does not seem necessary to mention this. It does not seem neces-

illness A. died rather suddenly," or, "unexpectedly both to himself and to others." "Unexpectedly" to others, perhaps, who did not see, because they did not look; but by no means "unexpectedly to himself," as I feel entitled to believe, both from the internal evidence in such stories, and from watching similar cases; there was every reason to expect that A. would die, and he knew it; but he found it useless to insist upon his own knowledge to his friends.

In these remarks I am alluding neither to acute cases which terminate rapidly nor to "nervous" cases.

By the first much interest in their own danger is very rarely felt. In writings of fiction, whether novels or biographies, these death-beds are generally depicted as almost seraphic in lucidity of intelligence. Sadly large has been my experience in death-beds, and I can only say that I have seldom or never seen such. Indifference, excepting with regard to bodily suffering, or to some duty the dying man desires to perform, is the far more usual state.

The "nervous case," on the other hand, delights in figuring to himself and others a fictitious danger.

But the long chronic case, who knows too well himself, and who has been told by his physician that he will never enter active life again, who feels that every month he has to give up something he could do the month before—oh! spare such sufferers your chattering hopes. You do not know how you worry and weary them. Such real sufferers cannot bear to talk of themselves, still less to hope for what they cannot at all expect.

So also as to all the advice showered so profusely upon such sick, to leave off some occupation, to try some other doctor, some other house, climate, pill, powder, or specific; I say nothing of the inconsistency—for these advisers are sure to be the same persons who exhorted the sick man not to believe his own doctor's prognostics, because "doctors are always mistaken," but to believe some other doctor, because "this doctor is always right." Sure also are these advisers to be the persons to bring the sick man fresh occupation, while exhorting him to leave his own....

3. From *Quarterly Review*. 107 (April 1860): 392-422.[1]

Art. V. *Notes on Nursing: What It Is, and What It Is Not*. By Florence Nightingale. London. 1860. *Life in the Sick Room*. Essays, by an Invalid. London. Third Edition. 1849.

---

sary to say that there can be no comparison between old men with dropsies and young women with consumptions. Yet the cleverest men and the cleverest women are often heard making such comparisons, ignoring entirely sex, age, disease, place—in fact, *all* the conditions essential to the question. It is the merest *gossip*."

1   This review by Harriet Martineau appeared anonymously.

This little book of Miss Nightingale's is a work of genius, according to the conscious or unconscious testimony of a miscellaneous multitude of readers. Homely people, attracted by the homely title, and seeing before them a pamphlet in cloth of eighty pages, take it up as housewives take up a receipt-book,—to get hints about some details of management. It is not surprising that they do not lay it down till they come to the end; for, as many of us have observed, no woman knows how to lay down a receipt-book, or to be civil to visitors when interrupted in reading a Guide to Nursing: but the countenance and voice with which ladies, doctors, and maidservants speak of Miss Nightingale's "Notes," testify to some extraordinary quality in her remarks. All readers say nearly the same thing. They always thought they knew a good deal about nursing; but now they see that they had a very imperfect idea of what nursing is—that it is an art grounded on science. If such is not their expression, such is their meaning. They have all their lives tried to make their household patients as comfortable as they could; they have been liberal in advice and criticism about other people's nursing; and now they discover that they have too often been ignorant and unobservant, thoughtless and conceited. This is not our judgment of them: it is the verdict they pronounce on themselves.

There is another class, not practically concerned with nursing, which renders a graver and more pathetic testimony in another way—the healthful of both sexes who have been wont to speak confidently about sickness and the sick, but who now find that they have been not only ignorant and thoughtless, like their contrite neighbours the nurses, but frequently unjust and tormenting. Here, again, we are not offering our own opinion on their conduct, but simply expressing their voluntary confessions. The book, in fact, under its humble title and pretensions, opens to us a wide field of morals, and some new tracks of philosophy. The actual subject of these eighty pages is nothing less than the relation of the Well to the Sick....

The grand interest of Miss Nightingale's book is its disclosure of the relation which is seldom expressly and seriously thought of—that between the Healthy and the Sick. The corresponding relation—that between the Sick and the Healthy—was treated of nearly twenty years ago in the little book which we have coupled with Miss Nightingale's at the head of this article, for the sole reason, that, in this one respect, each is the counterpart of the other. "Life in the Sick-room" is simply the almost involuntary utterance by a sufferer of the thoughts and emotions belonging to the peculiar and ill-understood condition of protracted disease, in sharp contrast with the condition and ways of healthy people. Miss Nightingale's "Notes" are a disclosure of what is requisite for a proper understanding of the sick and their case. From the two together philosophical observers, and benevolent members of households, may learn a good deal that is new about a relation dating from the closing of the gate of Eden upon the pair who had left behind their unbroken health of body and mind, and the unity of spirit which belongs to it.

At the outset, in a very short preface, Miss Nightingale indicates the purpose of her "Notes." They are not a set of instructions how to nurse, rules by which nurses may teach themselves their art; they are hints for thought. Every woman must, some time or other in her life, "have the charge of somebody's health." "I do not pretend to teach her how," says Miss Nightingale, "I ask her to teach herself; and for this purpose I venture to give some hints." These hints presently disclose some matters as nearly concerning the men of the nation as any mother, wife, or sister of charity in the land.

When we come to look into the matter, it seems doubtful whether any clear understanding exists among us as to the meaning of health, sickness, and nursing. Pascal knew more than most men about a condition of permanent ill health; and his report is, that the condition of the invalid is so radically different from that of the healthy man, as to constitute a distinct phase of life. He says that the man in health cannot at all tell what he should do, or think, or desire, if he were ill; and when he is ill, he is in a transformed condition, with thoughts and feelings accommodated to the malady; and, we may add, therefore incomprehensible to his friends. The real evil, Pascal says, is in the contrariety introduced into the invalid's condition by fears and desires suggested by disorder within, or interference from without,—the passions of the state in which he is not being thrust in among those of the state in which he is. If this be the truth of the sick man's condition, his friends have a good deal to learn and to consider before they meddle with his mind and his ways. Do they set themselves to such a study when they have illness in the house, or when they go and witness it elsewhere? The writers of these two books think that people in general do not. Every reader of the "Notes" will probably be of their opinion, after seeing what are the needs of a state of sickness; and every reader of the Sick-room Essays, after learning what are its experiences.

Of the essential nature of disease we know no more than of the essential nature of anything else; but modern science has led us a step higher than our fathers in our understanding of the matter. It teaches us that the largest proportion of what we call disease is a process of cure. This must be understood before we can estimate the true function of nursing...

Here we are guided to the right view of nursing. What is it to be a nurse? From the imperfection of our knowledge there is a mischievous imperfection in our terms. In a large sense, Miss Nightingale calls every person a nurse who has in charge somebody's health, whether perfect or impaired. The office of a nurse, in this view, is "to put the constitution in such a state as that it will have no disease, or that it can recover from disease." (*Preface*.)...

"True nursing ignores infection, except to prevent it." And Miss Nightingale, being a true nurse, ignores it with a thoroughness which will be most consolatory to as many as can believe her. "Now, do tell us," she asks, "why must a child have measles?" She does not believe that there is any occasion for the process of going through the diseases of childhood, as they are called, or the diseases of adult life either. Measles, whooping-cough, scarlet-fever, small-pox, are all, in her opinion, avoidable misfortunes. She pleads nature's *laws* for preserving the health of houses against man's *opinion* that certain diseases are inevitable; and, for the children's sake, urges a trial of obedience to those laws rather than submission to that opinion. Here reference to small-pox especially is most impressive, coming as it does from so accurate an observer of facts...

Hitherto we have looked only at the antecedent relations of the Healthy to the Sick. In the question of forecast about illness, and of forming ideas about the nature and conditions of maladies, there is little controversy — at any rate till the concrete practice is arrived at. People may be careless or ignorant; but nobody disputes the desirableness of avoiding illness, and of lessening its degree, if the thing can really be done. No opposition of interests or contrariety of moods takes place thus far. When all parties are well together, they feel and think alike; they are wise with the same wisdom, or scornful with the same scorn, or careless with the same levity, or grave with the same foreboding. It is when the illness arrives that they begin to part off, and a special relation arises between the sick and the well. The sick man passes into a new condition, in which his friends are unable to follow him: it is a thing which cannot be done. The impossibility is illustrated in the Sick-room Essays — in the testing form of a comparison of the feelings of the patient himself in a season of pain and one of ease...

The two books before us are in remarkable accord in treating the conditions of health and sickness as radically distinct; and this testimony is the more valuable from the one speaking from the side of health and other from that of sickness. The Nurse represents the sound, and the Invalid the sick. It is perhaps a natural consequence that the one is strongly impressed by the shortcomings, and the other by the advantages of the healthy. The commonest criticism that we have heard on each is, that the Nurse is very severe on the nurses and friends, and that the Invalid is hard upon the invalids. It happens to be one of the particulars in which we most honour Miss Nightingale's brave book, that, with the most intense and considerate and learned compassion for the sick, she joins an unflinching and outspoken rebuke of such sins towards them as are owing to ignorance or carelessness. The only question is, are the faults and shortcomings she exposes remediable or not? If they are, her severity is righteous; and we have every hope that her exposition of what nursing is, and what it ought to be, will soon produce results that will justify her opinion of nursing as it commonly has been. As to the other case, in which the Invalid is charged with "stoicism," the question is simply, whether invalids are the better or the worse, in character and peace of mind, for keeping their sufferings out of other people's way, and for regarding their own condition as a lowly one in comparison with that of health. If it be true that egotism is the besetting moral danger of the sick-room, such a view as the following may be safer and more true than the less "stoical" one which many readers have desired...

Natural as it is to many invalids to desire to be, and even to live alone, there can be no doubt that the longing is intensified by sufferings like these—sufferings caused by the insuperable difference between the states of health and sickness. A constant sufferer from asthma, which ended fatally after a course of painful years, said, in a confidential mood, that her life would be relieved of half its pains if she could live alone, or (and she gently intimated) if she could persuade her devoted family to leave her at times in peace and quiet. There is a passage in the Invalid's Essays which shows that this desire does not always spring from selfishness, and is not necessarily a sign of unreasonableness....

Miss Nightingale's repeated testimony to the "shyness" of invalids, their modesty about giving trouble, and their almost painful gratitude to their nurses, should go a long way with persons who think that "a little self-control" is all that is necessary to place the patient on the same level with themselves. Her vivid indications of what it is to a weak patient to transact business may set such critics thinking, and her own exquisite considerateness may open to them a new view of their duty...

What then is to be done if there is this impassable gulf between the experience of the sick and the well? It is a great thing to have brought complacent persons to this point—of inquiring what can be done. It is clear that there is something—that there is everything to be done by the healthy for the sick. The lives saved that have been despaired of, the alleviation of suffering which astonishes the sufferer himself, the ingenuity in resource which at once delights and amuses the patient, the intensity of gratitude which makes the sick man kiss the passing shadow of his nurse upon his pillow, the success which follows the ministrations of individuals in private homes and in hospitals, all indicate the truth that, though the sensations of health and sickness are insuperably different, no difficulties from this cause need be insuperable. What are the resources? Those who cannot, by possibility, feel with the sick, must ascertain the facts of their patient's feelings as well as of his malady. That which cannot be known by sympathy must be learned by observation. Perhaps it is necessary to read Miss

Nightingale's "Notes" to form a conception of the frequent lack of this quality in the sick-room. And yet it is little more than we might anticipate upon reflection. It is a subject of remark in every-day life if we meet with a person capable of quick and accurate observation, and especially if the faculty is exercised among obscure and unfamiliar classes of facts. Not only is it antecedently improbable that such a faculty should be found in any household which illness happens to visit, but there is the further difficulty that the observers are prepossessed with the associations and the impressions of health. The consequence is, that the patient overhears the strangest accounts given to the doctor of what he has been doing or experiencing since the last visit. He could contradict every statement of how much he has slept, how much he has eaten, when he was feverish, and whether he has been faint. Now and then he may feel moved and enabled to tell his own story; but this seldom happens. The doctor must needs believe the nurse rather than the patient when they contradict each other; and it seldom happens that the sick have energy to protest and argue. They perforce give up everything, and let others do with them what they will. It is asserted, for instance, that the patient has had a good night, when he knows that he has not dozed more than an hour from sunset to sunrise. Miss Nightingale says the same answer has been given about two persons, one of whom woke occasionally in each night of nine or ten hours, and another who did not sleep at all for five nights and days, and died in consequence. Another patient, who has pulled his food about a little, but eaten none, hears it reported that he has taken his food much as usual. He may even hear that he had a comfortable evening or morning, because the nurse had amused herself by talking to him without perceiving that he was too faint to reply or to stop her. Some nurses, as Miss Nightingale shows us, can tell by the eye, within a quarter of an ounce, how much food the patient has actually eaten, and precisely how many hours he slept last night, and how much he has dozed, and whether any qualm of faintness passed over him while he lay silent. Others give only vague reports, or, if they attempt details, get monstrously wrong. Many an educated lady might say of herself what an ungrammatical nurse honestly admitted: — "I knows I fibs dreadful," says Miss Nightingale's candid acquaintance; "but believe me, Miss, I never finds out I have fibbed until they tells me so." It would be curious to ascertain how a conviction of fibbing was received by thirteen persons mentioned in the "Notes," who "concurred" in declaring that a fourteenth went to a distant chapel every morning at seven o'clock during a period of, as it happened, absolute confinement to his bed...

Thus far we have followed Miss Nightingale in her views of the duty of the healthy in regard to precluding sickness in their dwellings; in regard to establishing an understanding between themselves and the sick by observation and a careful process of learning; in regard to the external, bodily charge of the sick; and in regard to the proper treatment of nurses. There remains another phase of the relation, as important as any, and on which Miss Nightingale speaks with particular force and pathos. The section on "Chattering Hopes and Advices" will do more for the invalid class, in the relief of their minds and nerves, than perhaps all the rest of her pleadings together. She speaks as a nurse, and not as a moralist or mental philosopher; but it is not conceivable that any analysis of human emotions from the professor's chair could better develop a new sense of the relation of mind to mind than Miss Nightingale's disclosure of the effects of imperfect sympathies in the Healthy towards the Sick...

Let us take the invalid's foibles first. Readers of Miss Nightingale's "Notes" exclaim, "Is the fault, then all on one side? Are patients never exacting, never petulant, never mistaken as to the moral treatment which is good for them?" What says the Invalid of the faults and foibles of the sick? More than we can quote here. There is a whole chapter on some of the moral perils and penalties of invalidism: and the supposition throughout the book is that the sick are inferior to the healthy, as living in impaired and vitiated conditions. It is quite certain that the proneness to fetishism is as great on the one side as the other; that men must be very wise before they surmount the liability to attribute their own experience to others, and thus to judge precipitately for everybody. The sick not only ache in every limb when they see from the window the running and leaping of boys and the heavy tasks done by men, but they fail to sympathise in the fun and frolic of life, and are apt to require from everybody the composure which is the highest condition practicable for them. Because they are "virtuous" perforce, there ought to be "no more cakes and ale." Where such narrowness exists, it is more of a fault than in the healthy, because the invalid has had experience of being well, whereas the well have seldom had experience of the sick man's state. So says the invalid; and the generous Nurse herself, with all her intense compassion and thoroughgoing championship of the sick, admits, *en passant*, the weaknesses of her protégés. "If you knew," she says, "how unreasonably sick people suffer from reasonable causes of distress, you would take more pains about all these things."...

After all is said, the fact remains which is a mere truism—that the sick are in a morbid condition, and cannot possibly, by any effort or any discipline, see things at all times from the ordinary point of view. When the healthy, on the other hand, not only fail to find the standpoint for viewing the condition of the sick, but do not seek it—rather striving to impose on the sick their pain in seeing pain—the fault of want of sympathy becomes as grave as it appears in the "Notes" before us...

Thus much is indeed in the power of all; while the genius of sympathy may be the gift of very few. Those must be obtuse or selfish who inflict the grosser hardships exposed by our Invalid and Nurse; but a world of pain may be inflicted by the mere ignorance on the part of kind-hearted friends that they and the sick have different points of view, and different sensations, mental as well as bodily. This may be, and continually is, learned by persons not naturally gifted with the insight which is a part of sympathy of the highest kind. The testimonies borne by both the authorities before us to much noble and genial service rendered by the Healthy to the Sick show what is possible to others than heaven-born nurses...

Others than would-be nurses may, however, profit by these disclosures. The healthiest and kindliest of us must sooner or later have relations with those who are ill. There have been occasions on which we have probably hurt somebody's feelings, and therefore somebody's health, in a sick-room. After reading this book, we ought never to do it again. Whenever we hear of the 100,000 needless deaths which annually occur in England we should henceforth remember that many more would be reported if we could learn the amount of blight inflicted, at moments critical for the heart and brain, by our imperfect sympathies.

As for the faults of the book,—we must leave it to medical critics to assert their objections to Miss Nightingale's opinions about open windows at night, the facts of the origin of contagion, and other professional questions. For our part, we have only one thing to regret; and that is the distribution of some of the matter of the book, and especially the arbitrary division between the text and the notes. Some of the best things in the work are scattered through the latter, where it is not easy to find them; and notes upon "Notes" are an awkward form of instruction.

Miss Nightingale vitally served many thousands of sick and wounded sufferers during her days of health. She may serve more by this strong and tender work of her mind and heart, now that she has strength to nurse no longer. Her form may never again be seen bending over the beds of sufferers; but, for generations to come, her shadow may pass over their pillows, blessing and beloved as the hospitals at Scutari.[1]

---

1   During the Crimean War years of 1854-1856, Nightingale was in charge of military hospitals at Scutari in Turkey; there she struggled with the myriad health problems resulting from crowded conditions and inadequate sanitation.

Appendix F: Harriet Martineau and Health Writing

1. Harriet Martineau's "Letter to the Deaf," from *Tait's Edinburgh Magazine* (April 1834): 174-179.

My Dear Companions,

The deafness under which I have now for some years past suffered, has become, from being an almost intolerable grievance, so much less of one to myself and my friends, than such a deprivation usually is, that I have often of late longed to communicate with my fellow-sufferers, in the hope of benefiting, by my experience, some to whom the discipline is newer than to myself.

I have for some time done what I could in private conversation; but it never occurred to me to print what I had to say, till it was lately not only suggested to me, but urged upon me as a duty. I adopt this method as the only means of reaching you all; and I am writing with the freedom which I should use in a private letter to each of you. It does not matter what may be thought of anything I now say, or of my saying it in this manner, by those who do not belong to our fraternity. I write merely for those who are deeply concerned in the subject of my letter. The time may come when I shall tell the public some of our secrets, for other purposes than those which are now before me. At present I address only you; and as there is no need for us to tell our secrets to one another, there may be little here to interest any but ourselves. I am afraid I have nothing to offer to those of you who have been deaf from early childhood. Your case is very different from mine, as I have reason to know through my intimacy with a friend who became deaf at five years old. Before I was so myself, I had so prodigious a respect for this lady, (which she well deserves,) that if she could have heard the lightest whisper in which a timid girl ever spoke, I should not have dared to address her. Circumstances directed her attention towards me, and she began a correspondence, by letter, which flattered me, and gave me courage to converse with her when we met, and our acquaintance grew into an intimacy which enabled me at last to take a very bold step;—to send her a sonnet, in allusion to our common infirmity; my deafness being then new, and the uppermost thing in my mind day and night. I was surprised and mortified at her not seeming to enter into what I had no doubt in the world must touch her very nearly; but I soon understood the reason. When we came to compare our experiences, we were amused to find how differently we felt, and had always felt, about our privation. Neither of us, I believe, much envies the other, though neither of us pretends to strike the balance of evil. She had suffered the most privations, and I the most pain.

Nothing can be more different than the two cases necessarily are. Nine-tenths of my miseries arose from false shame; and, instead of that false shame, the early deaf entertain themselves with a sort of pride of singularity: and usually contrive to make their account of this, as of other infirmities, by obtaining privileges and indulgences, for which they care much more than for advantages which they have never known and cannot appreciate. My friend and I have principles, major and minor, on which our methods of managing our infirmity are founded; but some of the minor principles, and all the methods, are as different as might be expected from the diversity of the experience which has given rise to them. Nothing can be better for her than her own management, and, of course, I think the same of my own for myself, or I should change it. Before I dismiss this lady, I must mention that I am acquainted with several deaf ladies; so that no one but herself and our two families can know whom I have been referring to....

The first thing to be done is to fix upon our principle. This is easy enough. To give the least possible pain to others is the right principle: how to apply it requires more consideration. Let me just observe, that we are more inexcusable in forsaking our principle here than in any other case, and than the generality of people are in the generality of cases. Principles are usually forsaken from being forgotten,—from the occasion for them not being perceived. We have no such excuse while beginning to act upon our principle. We cannot forget,—we cannot fail to perceive the occasion, for five minutes together, that we spend in society. By the time that we become sufficiently at ease to be careless, habit may, if we choose, have grown up to support our principle, and we may be safe.

Our principle requires that we should boldly review our case, and calmly determine for ourselves what we will give up, and what struggle to retain. It is a miserable thing to get on without a plan from day to day, nervously watching whether our infirmity lessens or increases, of choosing to take for granted that we shall be rid of it; or hopelessly and indolently giving up every thing but a few selfish gratifications, or weakly refusing to resign what we can no longer enjoy. We must ascertain the probability for the future, if we can find physicians humane enough to tell us the truth: and where it cannot be ascertained, we must not delay making provision for the present. The greatest difficulty here arises from the mistaken kindness of friends. The physician had rather not say, as mine said to me, "I consider yours a bad case." The parent entreats to be questioned about any thing that passes; brothers and sisters wish that music should be kept up; and, what is remarkable, every body has a vast deal of advice to give, if the subject be fairly mentioned; though every body helps, by false tenderness, to make the subject too sacred an one to be touched upon. We sufferers are the persons to put an end to all this delusion and mismanagement. Advice must go for nothing with us in a case where nobody is qualified to advise. We must cross-question our physician, and hold him to it till he has told us all. We must destroy the sacredness of the subject, by speaking of it ourselves; not perpetually and sentimentally, but, when occasion arises, boldly, cheerfully, and as a plain matter of fact. When every body about us gets to treat it as a matter of fact, our daily difficulties are almost gone; and when we have to do with strangers, the simple, cheerful declaration, "I am very deaf," removes almost all trouble. Whether there was ever as much reluctance to acknowledge defective sight as there now is defective hearing,—whether the mention of spectacles was ever as hateful as that of a trumpet is now, I do not know; but I was full as much grieved as amused lately at what was said to me in a shop where I went to try a new kind of trumpet: "I assure you, Ma'am," said the shopkeeper, "I dread to see a deaf person come into my shop. They all expect me to find them some little thing that they may put into their ears, that will make them hear every thing, without any body finding out what is the matter with them."

Well, what must be given up, and what may be struggled for?

The first thing which we are disposed to give up is the very last which we ought to relinquish—society. How many good reasons we are apt to see,—are we not?—why we should not dine out; why it is absurd to go into an evening party; why we ought to be allowed to remain quiet up stairs when visitors are below! This will not do. Social communication must be kept up through all its pains, for the sake of our friends as well as for our own. It can never be for the interest of our friends that we should grow selfish, or absorbed in what does not concern our day and generation, or nervous, dependent, and helpless in common affairs. The less able we become to pick up tidings of man and circumstance, the more diligently we must go in search of the information. The more our sympathies are in danger of contraction, the more must we put ourselves in the way of being interested by what is happening all about us. Society is the very last thing to be given up; but it must be sought, (and I say it with deep sympathy for those of you to whom the effort is new,) under a bondage of self-denial, which annihilates for a time almost all the pleasures. Whatever may be our fate,—whether we may be set down at the end of a half circle, where nobody comes to address us, or whether we may be placed beside a lady who cannot speak above her breath, or a gentleman who shouts till every body turns to see what is the matter; whether one well meaning friend says across the room, in our behalf, "do tell that joke over again to—," and all look to see how we laugh when they have done; or another kind person says, "how I wish you could hear that song,"—or "that harp in the next room," or "those sweet nightingales," if we happen to be out of doors,—

whether any or all these doings and sayings befal us, we must bravely go on taking our place in society.

Taking our place, I say. What is our place? It is difficult to decide. Certainly, not that of chief talker any more than that of chief listener. We must make up our minds for a time to hold the place that we may chance to be put into,—to depend on the tact and kindness of those near us. This is not very pleasant; but if we cannot submit to it for a while, we cannot boast much of our humility, nor of our patience. We must submit to be usually insignificant, and sometimes ridiculous. Do not be dismayed, dear companions. This necessity will not last long, and it is well worth while undergoing it. Those who have strength of mind to seek society under this humiliation, and to keep their tempers through it, cannot long remain insignificant there. They must rise to their proper place, if they do but abstain from pressing beyond it. It is astonishing how everything brightens sooner or later. The nightingales and the harp will be still out of the question, but they will be given up almost without pain, because it is a settled matter to every body present that they *are* out of the question. Friends will have discovered that jokes are not the things to be repeated; and that which is repeated will be taken as coming in due course, and will at length consist of all that has been really worth hearing of what has been said. Other people may laugh without occasioning a nervous distortion on your countenance; and it is quite certain that if your temper have stood your trial, you will never pass an evening without meeting with some attention which will touch, some frank kindness which will elevate your feelings, and send you home wiser and happier than you came forth.

This can only be, however, if you have stood your trial well, if you bring an open temper and an open countenance. It is a matter of wonder that we are addressed so much as we are; and if, in addition to the difficulty of making us hear, we offer the disagreeableness of (not a constrained, that will be pitied, but) a frowning countenance, we may betake ourselves to the books of prints on the table, but may as well give up all hope of conversation. As a general rule, nothing can be worse than for people to think at all about their countenances; but in our case it is worth while, for a time, and to a certain extent. I was kindly told, a few years ago, that many people wished to converse with me, but that I looked as if I had rather not be spoken to. Well I might; for I then discovered that in trying to check one bad habit, I had fallen into another. I had a trick of sighing, to cover which I used to twist my fingers out of joint, (and so do you, I dare say,) and the pain of this process very naturally made me frown. My friend's hint put me on my guard. Instead of twisting my fingers, I recalled my vow of patience, and this made me smile; and the world has been a different place to me since. Some such little rule as turning every sigh into a smile will help you over a multitude of difficulties, and save you, at length, the trouble of thinking about either smiling or sighing.

It has always been my rule *never* to ask what is going forward; and the consequence has well compensated all I had to go through from the reproaches of kind friends, who were very anxious that I should trouble them in that way. Our principle plainly forbids the practice; and nothing can therefore justify it. There is at first no temptation, for we had then rather miss the sayings of the wise men of Greece, than obtain them by such means; but the practice once begun, there is no telling where it will stop. Have we not seen—it sickens me to think of it—restless, inquisitive, deaf people, who will have every insignificant thing repeated to them, to their own incessant disappointment, and the suffering of every body about them, whom they make, by their appeals, almost as ridiculous as themselves. I never could tolerate the idea of any approach to the condition of one of these. I felt, besides, that it was impossible for me to judge of what might fairly be asked for, and what had better be let pass. I therefore obstinately adhered to my rule; and I believe that no one whom I have met in any society, (and I have seen a great deal,) has been enabled to carry away more that is valuable, or to enjoy it more thoroughly than myself. I was sure that I might trust to the kindness of my neighbours, if I was but careful not to vex and weary it; and my confidence has been fully justified. The duty extends to not looking as if you wanted to be amused. Your friends can have little satisfaction in your presence, if they believe that when you are not conversing you are no longer amused. "I wonder every day," said a young friend to me, when I was staying in a large well-filled country house, "what you do with yourself during our long dinners, when we none of us talk with you, because we have talked so much more comfortably on the lawn all the morning. I cannot think how you help going to sleep." "I watch how you help the soup," was my inconsiderate reply—I was not aware how inconsiderate, till I saw how she blushed every day after on taking up the ladle. I mentioned the soup only as a specimen of my occupations during dinner. There were also the sunset lights and shadows on the lawn to be watched, and the never ceasing play of human countenances,—our grand resource when we have once gained ease enough to enjoy them at leisure. There were graceful and light-headed girls, and there was an originality of action in the whole family which amused me from morning till night. The very apparatus of the table, and the various dexterities of the servants, are matters worth observing when we have nothing else to do. I never yet found a dinner too long, whether or not my next neighbour might be disposed in a tête-a-tête—never, I mean, since the time when every social occupation was to me full of weariness and constraint....

I think it best for us to give up also all undertakings and occupations in which we cannot mark and check our own failures;——teaching any thing which requires ear, preaching, and lecturing, and music. I gave up music, in opposition to much entreaty, some reproach, and strong secret inclination; because I knew that my friends would rather put up with a wrong bass in my playing, and false time in my singing, than deprive me of a resource. Our principle clearly forbids this kind of indulgence; therefore, however confident we may be of our musical ear, let us be quite sure that we shall never again be judges of our own music, or our own oratory, and avoid all wish of making others suffer needlessly by our privations. Listen to no persuasions, dear companions, if you are convinced that what I have said is right. No one *can* judge for you. Be thankful for the kind intentions of your friends; but propose to enjoy their private eloquence instead of offering your own in public; and please yourselves with their music, as long as you can, without attempting to rival it. These are matters in which we have a right to be obstinate, if we are sure of the principle we go upon; for we are certainly much better able to judge what will be for the happiness of our friends, in their common circumstances, than they can be of ours, in our uncommon ones.

How much less pain there is in calmly estimating the enjoyments from which we must separate ourselves, of bravely saying, for once and for ever, "Let them go," than in feeling them waste and dwindle, till their very shadows escape from our grasp! With the best management, there is quite enough, for some of us, of this wasting and dwindling, when we find, at the close of each season, that we are finally parting with something, and at the beginning of each that we have lost something since the last. We miss first the song of the skylark, and then the distant nightingale, and then one bird after another, till the loud thrush itself seems to have vanished; and we go in the way of every twittering under the eaves, because we know that that will soon be silenced too. But I need not enlarge upon this to you. I only mean to point out the prudence of lessening this kind of pain to the utmost, by making a considerable effort at first; and the most calculating prudence becomes a virtue, when it is certain that as much must at best be gone through as will afflict our friends, and may possibly overpower ourselves, our temper and deportment, if not our principles and our affections. I do not know how sufficiently to enforce these sacrifices being made with frankness and simplicity; and nothing so much needs enforcing. If our friends were but aware how cruel an injury is the false delicacy which is so common, they would not encourage our false shame as they do. If they have known anything of the bondage of ordinary false shame, they may imagine something of our suffering in circumstances of irremediable singularity. Instead of putting the singularity out of sight, they should lead us to acknowledge it in words, prepare for it in habits, and act upon it in social intercourse. If they will not assist us here, we must do it for ourselves. Our principle, again, requires this. Thus only can we save others from being uneasy in our presence, and sad when they think of us. That we can thus alone make ourselves sought and beloved is an inferior consideration, though an important one to us, to whom warmth and kindliness are as peculiarly animating as sunshine to the caged bird. This frankness, simplicity, and cheerfulness, can only grow out of a perfect acquiescence in our circumstances. Submission is not enough. Pride fails at the most critical moment. Nothing short of acquiescence will preserve the united consistency and cheerfulness of our acknowledgement of infirmity. Submission will bemoan it while making it. Pride will put on indifference while making it. But hearty acquiescence cannot fail to bring forth cheerfulness. The thrill of delight which arises during the ready agreement to profit by pain — (emphatically the joy with which no stranger intermeddleth) — must subside like all other emotions; but it does not depart without leaving the spirit lightened and cheered; and every visitation leaves it in a more genial state than the last.

And now, what may we struggle for? I dare say the words of the moralist lie as deep down in your hearts as in my own: "We must not repine, but we may lawfully struggle!" I go further, and say that we are bound to struggle. Our principle requires it. We must struggle for whatever may be had, without encroaching on the comfort of others. With this limitation, we must hear all we can, for as long as we can. Yet how few of us will use the helps we might have! How seldom is a deaf person to be seen with a trumpet! I should have been diverted, if I had not been too much vexed, at the variety of excuses that I have heard on this head since I have been much in society. The trumpet makes the sound disagreeable; or is of no use; or is not wanted in a noise, because we hear better in a noise; nor in quiet, because we hear very fairly in quiet; or we think our friends do not like it; or we ourselves do not care for it, if it does not enable us to hear general conversation; or — a hundred other reasons just as good. Now, dear friends, believe me these are but excuses. I have tried them all in turn, and I know them to be so. The sound soon becomes anything but disagreeable; and the relief to the nerves, arising from the use of such a help, is indescribable. None but the totally deaf can fail to find some kind of trumpet that will be of use to them, if they choose to look for it properly, and give it a fair trial. That it is not wanted in a noise is usually true; but we are seldom in a noise; and quiet is our greatest enemy, (next to darkness, when the play of the countenance is lost to us.) To reject a tête-à-tête in comfort because the same means will not afford us the pleasure of general conversation, is not very wise. Is it? As for the fancy, that our friends do not like it, it is a mistake, and a serious mistake. I can speak confidently of this. By means of galvanism,[1] (which I do not, from my own experience, recommend,) I once nearly recovered my hearing for a few weeks. It was well worth while being in a sort of nervous fever during those weeks, and more deaf than ever afterwards, for the enlightenment which I gained during the interval on various subjects, of which the one that concerns us now, is,—the toil that our friends undergo on our account. This is the last topic on which I should speak to you, but for the prevalent unwillingness in our fraternity to use such helps as much as their own nerves. Of course, my friends could not suddenly accommodate their speech to my improved hearing; and I was absolutely shocked when I found what efforts they had been making for my sake. I vowed that I would never again bestow an unkind thought on their natural mistakes, or be restive under their inapplicable instructions; and, as for carrying a trumpet, I liked it no better than my brethren till then; but now, if it would in any degree ease my friends that I should wear a fool's cap and bells, I would do it. Any of you who may have had this kind of experience, are, I should think, using trumpets. I entreat those of you who have not been so made aware of your state, to take my word for what you are obliging your friends to undergo. You know that we can be no judges of the degree of effort necessary to make us hear. We might as well try to echo the skylark. I speak plainly, it may seem harshly; but I am sure you would thank me ere long if I could persuade you to encounter this one struggle to make the most of your remnant of one of God's prime blessings....

What else may we struggle for? For far more in the way of knowledge than I can now even intimate. I am not going to make out, as some would have me, that we lose nothing after all; that what we lose in one way we gain in another, and so on; pursuing a line of argument equally insulting to our own understandings, and to the wisdom and benignity of Him who framed that curious instrument, the ear, and strung the chords of its nerves, and keeps up the perpetual harmonies of the atmosphere for its gratification. The ear was not made that men should be happier without it. To attempt to persuade *you* so, would above all be folly. But, in some sense, there is a compensation to us, if we choose to accept it; and it is to improve this to the utmost that I would urge you and stimulate myself. We *have* some accomplishments which we may gratefully acknowledge, while the means by which we gain them must prevent our being proud of them. We are good physiognomists—good perceivers in every way, and have (if we are not idle) rather the advantage over others in the power of abstract reasoning. This union of two kinds of power, which in common cases are often cultivated at the expense of each other, puts a considerable amount of

---

[1] An application of electricity to stimulate the nerves.

accurate knowledge within easier reach of us than of most other people. We must never forget what a vast quantity we must forego, but neither must we lose sight of whatever is peculiarly within our power. We have more time; too, than anybody else: more than the laziest lordling, who does nothing but let his ears be filled with nonsense from morning till night. The very busiest of our fraternity has, I should think, time every day for as much thought as is good for him, between the hours of rising and of rest.

Your affectionate sister,
Harriet Martineau.
March 16, 1834.

2. "Miss Martineau on Mesmerism." From *The Athenaeum* **23 November 1844. Reprinted as "Letter I" of** *Letters on Mesmerism.* **London: Edward Moxon, 1845.**

Tynemouth, Nov. 12.

It is important to society to know whether Mesmerism is true. The revival of its pretensions from age to age makes the negative of this question appear so improbable, and the affirmative involves anticipation so vast, that no testimony of a conscientious witness can be unworthy of attention. I am now capable of affording testimony; and all personal considerations must give way before the social duty of imparting the facts of which I am in possession.

Those who know Mesmerism to be true from their own experience are now a large number; many more, I believe, than is at all supposed by those who have not attended to the subject. Another considerable class consists of those who believe upon testimony: who find it impossible not to yield credit to the long array of cases in many books, and to the attestation of friends whose judgment and veracity they are in the habit of respecting. After these there remain a good many who amuse themselves with observing some of the effects of Mesmerism, calling them strange and unaccountable, and then going way and thinking no more about them; and lastly, the great majority who know nothing of the matter, and are so little aware of its seriousness as to call it a "bore," or to laugh at it as nonsense or a cheat.

If nonsense, it is remarkable that those who have most patiently and deeply examined it, should be the most firmly and invariably convinced of its truth. If it is a cheat, it is no laughing matter. If large numbers of men can, age after age, be helplessly prostrated under such a delusion as this, under a wicked influence so potential over mind and body, it is one of the most mournful facts in the history of man.

For some years before June last, I was in the class of believers upon testimony. I had witnessed no mesmeric facts whatever; but I could not doubt the existence of many which were related to me without distrusting either the understanding, or the integrity, of some of the wisest and best people I knew. Nor did I find it possible to resist the evidence of books, of details of many cases of protracted bodily and mental effects. Nor, if it had been possible, could I have thought it desirable or philosophical to set up my negative ignorance of the functions of the nerves and the powers of the mind, against the positive evidence of observers and recorders of new phenomena. People do not, or ought not, to reach my years without learning that the strangeness and absolute novelty of facts attested by more than one mind is rather a presumption of their truth than the contrary, as there would be something more familiar in any devices or conceptions of men; that our researches into the powers of nature, of human nature with the rest, have as yet gone such a little way that many discoveries are yet to be looked for; and that, while we have hardly recovered from the surprise of the new lights thrown upon the functions and texture of the human frame by Harvey, Bell,[1] and others, it is too soon to decide that there shall be no more as wonderful, and presumptuous in the extreme to predetermine what they shall or shall not be.

Such was the state of my mind on the subject of Mesmerism six years ago, when I related a series of facts, on the testimony of five persons whom I could trust, to one whose intellect I was accustomed to look up to, though I had had occasion to see that great discoveries were received or rejected by him on other grounds than the evidence on which their pretensions rested. He threw himself back in his chair when I began my story, exclaiming, "Is it possible that you are bit by that nonsense?" On my declaring the amount of testimony on which I believed what I was telling, he declared, as he frequently did afterwards, that if he saw the incidents himself, he would not believe them; he would sooner think himself and the whole company mad than admit them. This declaration did me good; though, of course, it gave me concern. It showed me that I must keep my mind free, and must observe and decide independently, as there could be neither help nor hindrance from minds self-exiled in this way from the region of evidence. From that time till June last, I was, as I have said, a believer in Mesmerism on testimony.

The reason why I did not qualify myself for belief or disbelief on evidence was a substantial one. From the early summer of 1839, I was, till this autumn, a prisoner from illness. My recovery now, by means of mesmeric

---

1   William Harvey (1578-1657), English physician and anatomist, and Charles Bell (1774-1842), Scottish anatomist and surgeon.

treatment alone, has given me the most thorough knowledge possible that Mesmerism is true.

This is not the place in which to give any details of disease. It will be sufficient to explain briefly, in order to render my story intelligible, that the internal disease, under which I suffered, appears to have been coming on for many years; that after warnings of failing health, which I carelessly overlooked, I broke down, while travelling abroad, in June 1839;—that I sank lower and lower for three years after my return, and remained nearly stationary for two more, preceding last June. During these five years, I never felt wholly at ease for one single hour. I seldom had severe pain; but never entire comfort. A besetting sickness, almost disabling me from taking food for two years, brought me very low; and, together with other evils, it confined me to a condition of almost entire stillness,—to a life passed between my bed and my sofa. It was not till after many attempts at gentle exercise that my friends agreed with me that the cost was too great for any advantage gained: and at length it was clear that even going down one flight of stairs was imprudent. From that time, I lay still; and by means of this undisturbed quiet, and such an increase of opiates as kept down my most urgent discomforts, I passed the last two years with less suffering than the three preceding. There was, however, no favourable change in the disease. Everything was done for me that the best medical skill and science could suggest, and the most indefatigable humanity and family affection devise: but nothing could avail beyond mere alleviation. My dependence on opiates was desperate. My kind and vigilant medical friend,—the most sanguine man I know, and the most bent upon keeping his patients hopeful,— avowed to me last Christmas, and twice afterwards, that he found himself compelled to give up all hope of affecting the disease,—of doing more than keeping me up, in collateral respects, to the highest practicable point. This was no surprise to me; for when any specific medicine is taken for above two years without affecting the disease, there is no more ground for hope in reason than in feeling. In June last, I suffered more than usual, and new measures of alleviation we resorted to. As to all the essential points of the disease, I was never lower than immediately before I made trial of Mesmerism.

If, at any time during my illness, I had been asked, with serious purpose, whether I believed there was no resource for me, I should have replied that Mesmerism might perhaps give me partial relief. I thought it right—and still think it was right—to wear out all other means first. It was not, however for the reason that the testimony might be thus rendered wholly unquestionable,—though I now feel my years of suffering but a light cost for such result;—it was for a more personal reason that I waited. Surrounded as I was by relations and friends, who, knowing nothing of

Mesmerism, regarded it as a delusion or an imposture,— tenderly guarded and cared for as I was by those who so thought, and who went even further than myself in deference for the ordinary medical science and practice, it was morally impossible for me to entertain the idea of trying Mesmerism while any hope was cherished from other means.

If it had not been so, there was the difficulty that I could not move, to go in search of aid from Mesmerists; and to bring it hither while other means were in course of trial was out of the question. After my medical friend's avowal of his hopelessness, however, I felt myself not only at liberty, but in duty bound, to try, if possible, the only remaining resource for alleviation. I felt then, and I feel now, that through all mortification of old prejudices, and all springing up of new, nobody in the world would undertake to say I was wrong in seeking even recovery by any harmless means, when every other hope was given up by all: and it was not recovery that was in my thoughts, but only solace. It never presented itself to me as possible that disease so long and deeply fixed could be removed; and I was perfectly sincere in saying, that the utmost I looked for was release from my miserable dependence on opiates. Deep as are my obligations to my faithful and skilful medical friend, for a long course of humane effort on his part, no one kindness of his has touched me so sensibly as the grace with which he met my desire to try a means of which he had no knowledge or opinion, and himself brought over the Mesmerist under whom the first trial of my susceptibility was made.

Last winter, I wrote to two friends in London, telling them of my desire to try Mesmerism, and entreating them to be on the watch to let me know if any one came this way of whose aid I might avail myself. They watched for me; and one made it a business to gain all the information she could on my behalf; but nothing was actually done, or seemed likely to be done, when in June a sudden opening for the experiment was made, without any effort of my own, and on the 22nd I found myself, for the first time, under the hands of a Mesmerist.

It all came about easily and naturally at last. I had letters,— several in the course of ten days,— one relating a case in which a surgeon, a near relative of mine, had, to his own astonishment, operated on a person in the mesmeric sleep without causing pain;— one from an invalid friend, ignorant of Mesmerism, who suggested it to me as a *pis aller*;[1]— and one from Mr. and Mrs. Basil Montagu,[2] who, supposing me an unbeliever, yet related to me the case of Ann Vials, and earnestly pressed upon me the expediency of a

---

1   Worst, as in last-ditch alternative.
2   Personal friends of Martineau, the Montagus introduced her also to Henry Atkinson.

trial:—and, at the same time, Mr. Spencer T. Hall[1] being at Newcastle lecturing, my medical friend went out of curiosity, was impressed by what he saw, and came to me very full of the subject. I told him what was in my mind; and I have said above with what a grace he met my wishes, and immediately set about gratifying them.

At the end of four months I was, as far as my own feelings could be any warrant, quite well. My Mesmerist and I are not so precipitate as to conclude my disease yet extirpated, and my health established beyond all danger of relapse; because time only can prove such facts. We have not yet discontinued the mesmeric treatment, and I have not re-entered upon the hurry and bustle of the world. The case is thus not complete enough for a professional statement. But, as I am aware of no ailment, and am restored to the full enjoyment of active days and nights of rest, to the full use of my powers of body and mind; and as many invalids, still languishing in such illness as I have recovered from, are looking to me for guidance in the pursuit of health by the same means, I think it right not to delay giving a precise statement of my own mesmeric experience, and of my observation of some different manifestations in the instance of another patient in the same house. A further reason against delay is, that it would be a pity to omit the record of some of the fresh feelings and immature ideas which attend an early experience of mesmeric influence, and which it may be an aid and comfort to novices to recognise from my record. And again, as there is no saying in regard to a subject so obscure, what is trivial and what is not, the fullest detail is likely to be the wisest; and the earlier the narrative the fuller, while better knowledge will teach us hereafter what are the non-essentials that may be dismissed.

On Saturday, June 22nd, Mr. Spencer Hall and my medical friend came, as arranged, at my worst hour of the day, between the expiration of one opiate and the taking of another. By an accident the gentlemen were rather in a hurry,—a circumstance unfavourable to a first experiment. But result enough was obtained to encourage a further trial, though it was of a nature entirely unanticipated by me. I had no other idea than that I should either drop asleep or feel nothing. I did not drop asleep, and I did feel something very strange. Various passes were tried by Mr. Hall; the first that appeared effectual, and the most so for some time after, were passes over the head, made from behind,—passes from the forehead down to the back of the head, and a little way down the spine. A very short time after these were tried, and twenty minutes from the beginning of the *séance*, I became sensi-

---

1   Spencer T. Hall is described by Martineau's biographer R.K. Webb as an "itinerant lecturer" whose purported successes as a mesmerist were well known (Webb 226).

ble of an extraordinary appearance, most unexpected, and wholly unlike anything I had ever conceived of. Something seemed to diffuse itself through the atmosphere,—not like smoke, nor steam, nor haze,—but most like a clear twilight, closing in from the windows and down from the ceiling, and in which one object after another melted away, till scarcely anything was left visible before my wide-open eyes. First, the outlines of all objects were blurred; then a bust, standing on a pedestal in a strong light, melted quite away; then the opposite bust; then the table with its gay cover, then the floor, and the ceiling, till one small picture, high up on the opposite wall, only remained visible,—like a patch of phosphoric light. I feared to move my eyes, lest the singular appearance should vanish; and I cried out, "O! deepen it! deepen it!" supposing this the precursor of the sleep. It could not be deepened, however; and when I glanced aside from the luminous point, I found that I need not fear the return of objects to their ordinary appearance while the passes were continued. The busts reappeared, ghost-like, in the dim atmosphere, like faint shadows, except that their outlines, and the parts in the highest relief, burned with the same phosphoric light. The features of one, an Isis with bent head, seemed to be illumined by a fire on the floor, though this bust has its back to the windows. Wherever I glanced, all outlines were dressed in this beautiful light; and so they have been, at every *séance*, without exception to this day; though the appearance has rather given way to drowsiness since I left off opiates entirely. This appearance continued during the remaining twenty minutes before the gentlemen were obliged to leave me. The other effects produced were, first, heat, oppression and sickness, and, for a few hours after, disordered stomach; followed, in the course of the evening, by a feeling of lightness and relief, in which I thought I could hardly be mistaken.

On occasions of a perfectly new experience, however, scepticism and self-distrust are very strong. I was aware of this beforehand, and also, of course, of the common sneer—that mesmeric effects are "all imagination." When the singular appearances presented themselves, I thought to myself,— "Now, shall I ever believe that this was all fancy? When it is gone, and when people laugh, shall I ever doubt having seen what is now as distinct to my waking eyes as the rolling waves of yonder sea, or the faces round my sofa?" I did a little doubt it in the course of the evening: I had some misgivings even so soon as that; and yet more the next morning, when it appeared like a dream.

Great was the comfort, therefore, of recognising the appearances on the second afternoon. "Now," thought I, "can I again doubt?" I did, more faintly; but, before a week was over, I was certain of the fidelity of my own senses in regard to this, and more.

There was no other agreeable experience on this second afternoon. Mr. Hall was exhausted and unwell, from having mesmerized many patients; and I was more oppressed and disordered than on the preceding day, and the disord\. continued for a longer time: but again, towards night, I felt refreshed and relieved. How much of my ease was to be attributed to Mesmerism, and how much to my accustomed opiate, there was no saying, in the then uncertain state of my mind.

The next day, however, left no doubt. Mr. Hall was prevented by illness from coming over, too late to let me know. Unwilling to take my opiate while in expectation of his arrival, and too wretched to do without some resource, I rang for my maid, and asked whether she had any objection to attempt what she saw Mr. Hall do the day before. With the greatest alacrity she complied. Within one minute the twilight and phosphoric lights appeared; and in two or three more, a delicious sensation of ease spread through me,—a cool comfort, before which all pain and distress gave way, oozing out, as it were, at the soles of my feet. During that hour, and almost the whole evening, I could no more help exclaiming with pleasure than a person in torture crying out with pain. I became hungry, and ate with relish, for the first time for five years. There was no heat, oppression, or sickness during the *séance*, nor any disorder afterwards. During the whole evening, instead of the lazy hot ease of opiates, under which pain is felt to lie in wait, I experienced something of the indescribable sensation of health, which I had quite lost and forgotten. I walked about my rooms, and was gay and talkative. Something of this relief remained till the next morning; and then there was no reaction. I was no worse than usual; and perhaps rather better.

Nothing to me is more unquestionable and more striking about this influence than the absence of all reaction. Its highest exhilaration is followed, not by depression or exhaustion, but by a further renovation. From the first hour to the present, I have never fallen back a single step. Every point gained has been steadily held. Improved composure of nerve and spirits has followed upon every mesmeric exhilaration. I have been spared all the weaknesses of convalescence, and carried through all the usually formidable enterprises of return from deep disease to health with a steadiness and tranquillity astonishing to all witnesses. At this time, before venturing to speak of my health as established, I believe myself more firm in nerve, more calm and steady in mind and spirits, than at any time of my life before. So much, in consideration of the natural and common fear of the mesmeric influence as pernicious excitement,—as a kind of intoxication.

When Mr. Hall saw how congenial was the influence of this new Mesmerist, he advised our going on by ourselves, which we did till the 6th of September. I owe much to Mr. Hall for his disinterested zeal and kindness. He did for me all he could; and it was much to make a beginning, and put us in the way of proceeding.

I next procured, for guidance, Deleuze's "Instruction Pratique sur le Magnétisme Animal."[1] Out of this I directed my maid; and for some weeks we went on pretty well. Finding my appetite and digestion sufficiently improved, I left off tonics, and also the medicine which I had taken for two years and four months, in obedience to my doctor's hope of affecting the disease,— though the eminent physician who saw me before that time declared that he had "tried it in an infinite number of cases, and never knew it avail." I never felt the want of these medicines, nor of others which I afterwards discontinued. From the first week in August, I took no medicines but opiates; and these I was gradually reducing. These particulars are mentioned to show how early in the experiment Mesmerism became my sole reliance.

On four days, scattered through six weeks, our *séance* was prevented by visitors or other accidents. On these four days, the old distress and pain recurred; but never on the days when I was mesmerized.

From the middle of August (after I had discontinued all medicines but opiates), the departure of the worst pains and oppressions of my disease made me suspect that the complaint itself,— the incurable, hopeless disease of so many years,— was reached; and now I first began to glance towards the thought of recovery. In two or three weeks more, it became certain that I was not deceived; and the radical amendment has since gone on, without intermission.

Another thing, however, was also becoming clear: that more aid was necessary. My maid did for me whatever, under my own instruction, goodwill and affection could do. But the patience and strenuous purpose required in a case of such long and deep-seated disease can only be looked for in an educated person, so familiar with the practice of Mesmerism as to be able to keep a steady eye on the end, through all delays and doubtful incidents. And it is also important, if not necessary, that the predominance of will should be in the Mesmerist, not the patient. The offices of an untrained servant may avail perfectly in a short case,— for the removal of sudden pain, or a brief illness; but, from the subordination being in the wrong party, we found ourselves coming to a stand.

This difficulty was abolished by the kindness and sagacity of Mr. Atkinson, who had been my adviser throughout.[2] He explained my posi-

---

1 Jean Philippe Francois Deleuze (1753-1835).

2 Henry G. Atkinson, a phreno-mesmerist, who with Martineau would later author *Letters on the Laws of Man's Nature and Development* (London: John Chapman, 1851).

tion to a friend of his—a lady, the widow of a clergyman, deeply and practically interested in Mesmerism—possessed of great mesmeric power, and of those high qualities of mind and heart which fortify and sanctify its influence. In pure zeal and benevolence, this lady came to me, and has been with me ever since. When I found myself able to repose on the knowledge and power (mental and moral) of my Mesmerist, the last impediments to my progress were cleared away, and I improved accordingly.

Under her hands the visual appearances and other immediate sensations were much the same as before; but the experience of recovery was more rapid. I can describe it only by saying, that I felt as if my life were fed from day to day. The vital force infused or induced was as clear and certain as the strength given by food to those who are faint from hunger. I am careful to avoid theorizing at present on a subject which has not yet furnished me with a sufficiency of facts; but it can hardly be called theorizing to say (while silent as to the nature of the agency) that the principle of life itself— that principle which is antagonistic to disease—appears to be fortified by the mesmeric influence; and thus far we may account for Mesmerism being no specific, but successful through the widest range of diseases that are not hereditary, and have not caused disorganization. No mistake about Mesmerism is more prevalent than the supposition that it can avail only in nervous diseases. The numerous cases recorded of cure of rheumatism, dropsy, cancer, and the whole class of tumours,—cases as distinct, and almost as numerous as those of cure of paralysis, epilepsy, and other diseases of the brain and nerves, must make any inquirer cautious of limiting his anticipations and experiments by any theory of exclusive action on the nervous system. Whether Mesmerism, and, indeed, any influence whatever, acts exclusively through the nervous system, is another question.

A few days after the arrival of my kind Mesmerist, I had my foot on the grass for the first time for four years and a half. I went down to the little garden under my windows. I never before was in the open air, after an illness of merely a week or two, without feeling more or less overpowered; but now, under the open sky, after four years and a half spent between bed and a sofa, I felt no faintness, exhaustion, or nervousness of any kind. I was somewhat haunted for a day or two by the stalks of the grass, which I had not seen growing for so long (for, well-supplied as I had been with flowers, rich and rare, I had seen no grass, except from my windows); but at the time, I was as self-possessed as any walker in the place. In a day or two, I walked round the garden, then down the lane, then to the haven, and so on, till now, in two months, five miles are no fatigue to me. At first, the evidences of the extent of the disease were so clear as to make me think that I had never before fully understood how ill I had been. They disappeared, one by one; and now I feel nothing of them.

The same fortifying influence carried me through the greatest effort of all,—the final severance from opiates. What that struggle is, can be conceived only by those who have experienced, or watched it with solicitude in a case of desperate dependence on them for years. No previous reduction can bridge over the chasm which separates an opiated from the natural state. I see in my own experience a consoling promise for the diseased, and also for the intemperate, who may desire to regain a natural condition, but might fail through bodily suffering. Where the mesmeric sleep can be induced, the transition may be made comparatively easy. It appears, however, that opiates are a great hindrance to the production of the sleep; but even so, the mesmeric influence is an inestimable help, as I can testify. I gave all my opiates to my Mesmerist, desiring her not to let me have any on any entreaty; and during the day I scarcely felt the want of them. Her mesmerising kept me up; and, much more, it intercepted the distress,—obviated the accumulation of miseries under which the unaided sufferer is apt to sink. It enabled me to encounter every night afresh,—acting as it does in cases of insanity, where it is all important to suspend the peculiar irritation—to banish the haunting idea. What further aid I derived in this last struggle from Mesmerism in another form, I shall mention when I detail the other case with which my own became implicated, and in which, to myself at least, the interest of my own has completely merged.

It will be supposed that during the whole experiment, I longed to enjoy the mesmeric sleep, and was on the watch for some of the wonders which I knew to be common. The sleep never came: and except the great marvel of restored health, I have experienced less of the wonders than I have observed in another. Some curious particulars are, however, worth noting.

The first very striking circumstance to me, a novice, though familiar enough to be practiced, was the power of my Mesmerist's volitions, without any co-operation on my part. One very warm morning in August, when every body else was oppressed with heat, I was shivering a little under the mesmeric influence of my maid,—the influence, in those days, causing the sensation of cold currents running through me, from head to foot. "This cold will not do for you, ma'am," said M., "O!" said I, "it is fresh, and I do not mind it:" and immediately my mind went off to something else. In a few minutes, I was surprised by a feeling as of warm water trickling through the channels of the late cold. In reply to my observation, that I was warm now, M. said, "Yes, ma'am, that is what I am doing." By inquiry and observation, it became clear to me, that her influence was, generally speaking, composing, just in proportion to her power of willing that it should be so. When I afterwards saw, in the case I shall relate, how the volition of the Mesmerist caused immediate waking from the deepest sleep, and a supposition that the same glass of water was now wine—now porter, &c., I became too much familiarised with the effect to be as much astonished as many of my readers will doubtless be.

Another striking incident occurred in one of the earliest of my walks. My Mesmerist and I had reached a headland nearly half a mile from home, and were resting there, when she proposed to mesmerise me a little — partly to refresh me for our return, and partly to see whether any effect would be produced in a new place, and while a fresh breeze was blowing. She merely laid her hand on my forehead, and, in a minute or two the usual appearances came, assuming a strange air of novelty from the scene in which I was. After the blurring of the outlines, which made all objects more dim than the dull gray day had already made them, the phosphoric lights appeared, glorifying every rock and headland, the horizon, and all the vessels in sight. One of the dirtiest and meanest of the steam tugs in the port was passing at the time, and it was all dressed in heavenly radiance — the last object that any imagination would select as an element of a vision. Then, and often before and since, did it occur to me that if I had been a pious and very ignorant Catholic, I could not have escaped the persuasion that I had seen heavenly visions. Every glorified object before my open eyes would have been a revelation; and my Mesmerist, with the white halo round her head, and the illuminated profile, would have been a saint or an angel.

Sometimes the induced darkening has been so great, that I have seriously inquired whether the lamp was not out, when a few movements of the head convinced me that it was burning as brightly as ever. As the muscular power oozes away under the mesmeric influence, a strange inexplicable feeling ensues of the frame becoming transparent and ductile. My head has often appeared to be drawn out, to change its form, according to the traction of my Mesmerist; and an indescribable and exceedingly agreeable sensation of transparency and lightness, through a part or the whole of the frame, has followed. Then begins the moaning, of which so much has been made, as an indication of pain. I have often moaned, and much oftener have been disposed to do so, when the sensations have been the most tranquil and agreeable. At such times, my Mesmerist has struggled not to disturb me by a laugh, when I have murmured, with a serious tone, "Here are my hands, but they have no arms to them:" "O dear! what shall I do? here is none of me left!": the intellect and moral powers being all the while at their strongest. Between this condition and the mesmeric sleep there is a state, transient and rare, of which I have had experience, but of which I intend to give no account. A somnambule[1] calls it a glimmering of the lights of somnambulism and clairvoyance. To me there appears nothing like a

---

1   A sleep-walker.

glimmering in it. The ideas that I have snatched from it, and now retain, are, of all ideas which ever visited me, the most lucid and impressive. It may be well that they are incommunicable—partly from their nature and relations, and partly from their unfitness for translation into mere words. I will only say that the condition is one of no "nervous excitement," as far as experience and outward indications can be taken as a test. Such a state of repose, of calm translucent intellectuality, I had never conceived of; and no reaction followed, no excitement but that which is natural to every one who finds himself in possession of a great new idea.

Before leaving the narrative of my own case for that of another, widely different, I put in a claim for my experiment being considered rational. It surely was so, not only on account of my previous knowledge of facts, and of my hopelessness from any other resource, but on grounds which other sufferers may share with me;—on the ground that though the science of medicine may be exhausted in any particular case, it does not follow that curative means are exhausted;—on the ground of the ignorance of all men of the nature and extent of the reparative power which lies under our hand, and which is vaguely indicated by the term "Nature;"—on the ground of the ignorance of all men regarding the very structure, and much more, the functions of the nervous system;—and on the broad ultimate ground of our total ignorance of the principle of life,—of what it is, and where it resides, and whether it can be reached, and in any way beneficially affected by a voluntary application of human energy.

It seemed to me rational to seek a way to refreshment first, and then to health, amidst this wilderness of ignorance, rather than to lie perishing in their depths. The event seems to prove it so. The story appears to me to speak for itself. If it does not assert itself to all,—if any should, as is common in cases of restoration by Mesmerism,—try to account for the result by any means but those which are obvious, supposing a host of moral impossibilities rather than admit a plain new fact, I have no concern with such objectors or objections.

In a case of blindness cured, once upon a time, and cavilled at and denied, from hostility to the means, an answer was given which we are wont to consider sufficiently satisfactory: "One thing I know, that whereas I was blind, now I see."[1] Those who could dispute the fact after this must be left to their doubts. They could, it is true, cast out their restored brother; but they could not impair his joy in his new blessing, nor despoil him of his far higher privileges of belief in and allegiance to his benefactor. Thus, whenever, under the Providence which leads on our race to knowledge and power, any new blessing of healing arises, it is little to one who enjoys it

1 John 9:25.

what disputes are caused among observers. To him, the privilege is clear and substantial. Physically, having been diseased, he is now well. Intellectually, having been blind, he now sees. For the wisest this is enough. And for those of a somewhat lower order, who have a restless craving for human sympathy in their recovered relish of life, there is almost a certainty that somewhere near them there exist hearts susceptible of simple faith in the unexplored powers of nature, and minds capable of an ingenuous recognition of plain facts, though they be new, and must wait for a theoretical solution.

HARRIET MARTINEAU

Appendix G: Additional Examples of Sickroom Literature

1. From *Letters from a Sick Room*. Boston: Massachusetts Sabbath School Society, 1845. From Chapter II, "Employments."

How many have I pitied, as they sat listless and languid in the room from which they could not move, when I have heard them complain of the sickly air which they must ever breathe, of the tiresome walls upon which they must ever gaze, the sameness of every thing within their view. And they *were* to be pitied. He who has never been deprived of the exquisite pleasure of *walking*, of lifting the window *himself* to inhale the fresh air, of varying his position at every sensation of uneasiness, can never know the value of the blessings he enjoys. He may tender his sympathy, and gratefully is it received. He may *conceive* the weariness of reclining hours, and weeks, and months, in one almost unchangeable posture, to be altered at least only with the assistance of others, and may picture to himself all the monotony of such an existence, and all this he can better understand than the inexpressible sensation which *motion* produces, the thrill of delight which pervades the whole frame of one who goes forth for the first time beyond the limits of the landscape he has been so long obliged to trace.

But there is a moral energy (I hardly know by what other name to call it) which can in some measure supply this want of physical strength. There is much that can be done to abstract thought from ourselves, and enable us to forget slight pain, and promote contentment and cheerfulness.

Any exertion of mind is often feared by friends and even prohibited by physicians, when the body is weak; but after a few trials and a little experience I heeded not such prohibitions, though I am usually conscientiously scrupulous in complying with the requests, and attending to the prescriptions of those who I have employed to counsel and direct me. If I have no confidence in them I will not employ them; but it is certainly gross injustice to disregard their injunctions, for how can any change be ascribed to its right cause, unless all orders have been complied with? how can any different mode of treatment be decided upon, unless that already adopted has been faithfully tried?

But with the advice that my mind should only be employed on light reading,—stories that kept my eyes fixed without requiring any thought, I obstinately refused to comply. In some things, to a reasonable and thinking being, experience is the best teacher. The restlessness and lassitude of body, to say nothing of the dissatisfaction to an immortal mind which is produced by spending day after day in doing nothing when employment is possible, is sufficient to protract the season of helplessness. No severe mental application ever left me at night so exhausted as a day of listless inactivity, when the hours had been spent in pondering upon my utter dependence, my inability in any way to take care of myself, and the prospect of being ever thus obliged to rely on the kindness of others.

Method is necessary to the success of any important undertaking, and with a well-digested system much intellectual labor may be accomplished in the midst of many discouragements. The seasons will come when racking pain will so steal away the strength, and unhinge the nerves, that all connected thought must be dispensed with, but if the plan is rightly formed, when the necessary portion of strength returns, we can begin where we left off, and pursue the course till the same cause again interrupts.

A young lady, whose state of health during many months prohibited all exercise and precluded even the use of the needle, determined to make herself acquainted with the political history of our country, and began with the history of the revolution, its causes and its effects, proceeding with the interesting details concerning the formation of the federal government, and the lives and writings of the great men to whom we owe our blessed institutions. Many a ponderous folio did she examine, when others, with more strength, would have thought themselves only able to turn the pages of a light magazine; and instead of attempting to learn the nature of man by tracing a few facts woven into a tissue of falsehoods, she studied the authentic history of mankind. It was labor, but of a healthy and invigorating kind, producing no unnatural excitement to enfeeble the intellect and debase the passions. The acquisition of useful knowledge was her object, and she was afterwards called to a station which, without this addition to her store, she could not have filled with credit to herself or benefit to others.

I consider it as sinful for us to sit idle all day long, or to be engaged only in useless and frivolous pursuits, as it is for those who are in health. To be sure, recovery is the one thing to be desired, and whatever will promote this, may be considered useful. The idea that we may indulge in any species of amusement because enduring so many privations, no immortal, responsible being ought for a moment to admit. There may be employments which it would be wrong to undertake,— which would prolong sickness, cause additional expense, and increase the trouble and anxiety of friends; we should do nothing that would seem to be tampering with life and health.

When the head is diseased, all mental activity and excitement must be avoided; then we can only aim to regulate thought, to fix it upon proper objects, to keep the heart right, and submit uncomplainingly to what God has appointed. Under all circumstances this is a duty, and is it any easy matter? He who has watched the operations of his own heart for one day can find an answer. Every imagination of the heart of man is evil, every thought is mixed with sin. But the grace of God can purify every fountain of corruption, and strength from on high enable us to walk in the ways of truth and righteousness.

I pity those who feel as if deprived of all enjoyment because they are not able to ride, to walk, to meet assemblies of their friends; but I pity them for considering these their highest sources of happiness...

If the mind has been early trained to labor and systematic effort, a course of study must be no frightful project for an invalid. Desultory reading will not be likely to prove permanently beneficial, nor the gratification of an appetite, which devours every thing that comes in its way, without time for digestion....

2. From *Devotions for the Sick Room, and For Times of Trouble*. Compiled from Ancient Liturgies and The Writings of Holy Men. By Robert Brett. London: Joseph Masters, 1843.

"A Prayer That The Affliction May Be Profitable"

O Merciful Lord, who usest Thy rod in anger as well as in love, and expectest that we should be bettered by every correction; with the compassions of a Father look upon me, teach me to call my ways to remembrance, and find out the accursed thing that has brought this affliction upon me; and make me so sensible of my manifold provocations, and so sincerely to lament, and abhor, and forsake them, that this correction may appear the effect of Thy love and pity, and by a serious and hearty repentance, a lively faith, and a just affiance in Thy mercy, fit me for the night in which no man can work; that if Thou thinkest fit to spare me, I may live an example of one bettered by Thy judgment; or else reap the benefits of Thy Fatherly correction in an entire submission to Thy will here, and being received to Thy glory hereafter, for Jesus Christ's sake. Amen. —*Inett.*

"On Taking Physic"

O Lord, without whom all my endeavours are but vain, give Thy blessing to the means now used for my recovery, and (if it be Thy blessed will,) make them so effectual for that end, that I may live, and be an instrument of Thy glory, and better prepared for the coming of my Lord. Amen. —*New Manual.*

"A Prayer for Patience"

O God, who hast told us, that in this world we shall have tribulation; grant that my present affliction may work patience, and that I may be submissive under Thy chastisements. And, forasmuch as I suffer no more than the common lot of sinful men, strengthen me, O Lord, that no pains or sufferings may ever drive me from Thee; but rather work in me a contempt for this world, the mortification of my lusts, and a patient abiding of the cross; so that I may finish my course with joy, and at last rest from all my labours and sorrows, with Thy redeemed people. Grant this, O most gracious Father, for the sake of Thy beloved Son Jesus Christ our Lord. Amen.

"On Want of Sleep"

O Righteous Lord, Thou holdest mine eyes waking, and in the night season I take no rest. I seek sleep, to ease my pains, and to recruit my spirits; but I find it not: but, O merciful God, let it not always fly from me; let my wearied eyes at length lay hold of it, and make my sleep sweet unto me. Consider my weariness, which calls aloud for rest; and my weakness, which greatly needs refreshment. While Thou keepest me awake, let me commune with my own heart, and search out my spirit; let me remember Thee on my bed, and meditate on Thee in the night-watches: let the consideration of Thy tender mercies be my comfort, till thy goodness sees fit to give sleep to my eyes, and refreshment to my sorrows, through my dearest Lord and Saviour Jesus Christ. Amen. —*Kettlewell*.

"Prayers and Ejaculations for Resignation"

Grant, gracious Lord, that I may never dispute the reasonableness of Thy will; but ever close with it, as the best that can happen. Prepare me always for what Thy providence shall bring forth. Let me never murmur, be dejected, or impatient, under any of the troubles of this life; but ever find rest and comfort in this: this is the will of my Father, and of my God. Grant this for Jesus Christ's sake. Amen.

O my crucified King and Saviour, let my submission to whatever afflictions shall befal me, for Thy sake, or by Thy appointment, be to me a pledge and an assurance of my fidelity to Thee, and conformity to Thy sufferings. Amen. —*Bishop Wilson*.

Grant, O God, that I may always accept of the punishment of my sins with resignation to Thy good pleasure. Remember me, O Lord, in this day of trouble; keep me from all excess of fear, concern, and sadness. Grant me a humble and a resigned heart, that with perfect content I may ever acquiesce in all the methods of Thy grace, that I may never frustrate the designs of Thy mercy.

4. From *Occasional Poems: By an Invalid*. Birmingham: H.C. Langbridge, MDCCCXLVIII [1848].

"SONNET. CONSOLATION. 1840"

Fain would I seek some interval from grief
    In cherished Studies — but it cannot be;
      The charm is lost — the spell dissolved for me:
And yet I court such respite, cold and brief;
For O! I dare not look upon the past;
    I dare not meet the deep-felt misery
      That fills my heart in every thought of Thee,
And tells of all thou wert, all I have lost.
Yet are there moments when my lot I bless,
    Moments too brief, when in the high-wrought mind,
      Each fond regret seems lost, each grief resign'd
For feelings of more hallow'd tenderness.
One solace high and pure is then mine own,
Thou art at rest — I suffer, but *alone*.

"SONNET. RESIGNATION. 1840."

I Murmur not, but with patient heart,
    And calm, to present misery resign;
      Blessings beyond all price had long been mine;
I knew them frail, and felt that I must part
With all: still trembling while I priz'd them most,
    And conscious that on Earth the purest Light
      Still casts the deepest Shadow: thus aright
I read my lot — but O! how vain the boast
    Of mind or heart prepar'd, that lot to meet
      In all its unimagin'd bitterness!
      Its soul-felt desolation! Not the less
I check each sigh, and with obedient feet
Pursue my path! To cheer its darkest hour
One Light is beaming still — still blooms one peerless
Flower.

SONNET. THE INFLUENCE OF SICKNESS

The vernal Flowers are blooming, the soft wind
    Plays on my feverish cheek; o'er all the Scene
I gaze, and feel with calm, tho' saddened mind,
    How many Springs are past, how few remain.
Life has been full of good; but while I bless
    Its youthful hours, with varied pleasures fraught,
I prize with deeper, holier, thankfulness,
    Lessons of mind and heart, by suffering taught.
I prize those years of Trial, when arise
    Habits of calm endurance, and the power
To hail each transient sunbeam as it flies,
    To cull along the Waste each scatter'd flower: —
And when the flower shall fade, the light depart,
To wait for their return, with firm undoubting heart

Works Cited and Recommended Reading

1. Bibliography, Biography, and Letters

Arbuckle, Elisabeth S., ed. *Harriet Martineau's Letters to Fanny Wedgwood*. Stanford, CA: Stanford UP, 1983.

Greenhow, T.M. *Medical Report of the Case of Miss H—— M——*. London: Samuel Highley, 1845.

——. "Termination of the Case of Miss Harriet Martineau." *British Medical Journal* (14 April 1877): 449-450.

Horne, R.H. *A New Spirit of the Age*, 2 vols. London: Smith, Elder & Co., 1844.

Martineau, Harriet. *Harriet Martineau's Autobiography, With Memorials by Maria Weston Chapman*. Two Volumes. Boston: Houghton, Osgood and Company, 1877.

Miller, Mrs. Florence Fenwick. *Harriet Martineau*. London: W.H. Allen & Co., 1884. Reprint. Port Washington, NY: Kennikat Press, 1972.

Oliphant, Margaret. "Harriet Martineau." *Blackwood's Edinburgh Magazine* 121 (1877): 472-96.

Pichanick, Valerie Kossew. *Harriet Martineau: The Woman and Her Work*. Ann Arbor: U of Michigan P, 1980.

Rivlin, Joseph B. *Harriet Martineau: A Bibliography of her Separately Printed Books*. New York: The New York Public Library, 1847.

Sanders, Valerie, ed. *Harriet Martineau: Selected Letters*. Oxford: Clarendon Press, 1990.

Simcox, G.A. "Miss Martineau." *Fortnightly Review* CXXIV (April 1877): 516-37.

Smiles, Samuel. "Harriet Martineau." *Brief Biographies*. Chicago: Belford, Clarke, and Co. 1883. 499-510.

Thomas, Gillian. "Harriet Martineau." *Dictionary of Literary Biography*. 55 (1987) 168-75.

——. *Harriet Martineau*. Boston: Twayne, 1985.

Webb, R.K. *Harriet Martineau: A Radical Victorian*. New York: Columbia UP, 1960.

Wheatley, Vera. *The Life and Work of Harriet Martineau*. London: Secker & Warburg, 1957.

Yates, Gayle Graham. *Harriet Martineau on Women*. New Brunswick, NJ: Rutgers UP, 1985.

2. Cultural History and Literary Criticism

Broughton, Trev Lynn. "Making the Most of Martyrdom: Harriet Martineau, Autobiography, and Death." *Literature and History* 2, 2 (1993): 24-45.

Cooter, Roger. "Dichotomy and Denial: Mesmerism, Medicine and Harriet Martineau." *Science and Sensibility: Gender and Scientific Enquiry, 1780-1945.* Ed. Marina Benjamin. Oxford: Basil Blackwell, 1991. 144-73.

David, Deirdre. *Intellectual Women and Victorian Patriarchy: Harriet Martineau, Elizabeth Barrett Browning, George Eliot.* Ithaca: Cornell UP, 1987.

Frawley, Maria. "'A Prisoner to the Couch': Harriet Martineau, Invalidism, and Self- Representation." *The Body and Physical Difference: Discourses of Disability.* Eds. David T. Mitchell and Sharon L. Snyder. Ann Arbor, MI: U of Michigan P, 1997. 174-88.

Freedgood, Elaine. "Banishing Panic: Harriet Martineau and the Popularization of Political Economy." *Victorian Studies* 39,1 (Autumn 1995): 33-53.

Haley, Bruce. *The Healthy Body and Victorian Culture.* Cambridge: Harvard UP, 1978.

Hawkins, Anne Hunsaker. *Reconstructing Illness: Studies in Pathography.* West Lafayette, IN: Purdue UP, 1995.

Hobart, Ann. "Harriet Martineau's Political Economy of Everyday Life." *Victorian Studies* 37.2 (Winter 1994): 223-52.

Hoecker-Drysdale, Susan. *Harriet Martineau: First Woman Sociologist.* New York: Berg, 1992.

Hunter, Shelagh. *Harriet Martineau: The Poetics of Moralism.* Brookfield, VT: Scolar Press, 1995.

Logan, Deborah Anna. *The Hour and the Woman: Harriet Martineau's "Somewhat Remarkable" Life.* Dekalb, IL: Northern Illinois UP, 2002.

Myers, Mitzi. "Harriet Martineau's Autobiography: The Making of a Female Philosopher." *Women's Autobiography.* Ed. Estelle C. Jelinek. Bloomington and London: Indiana UP, 1980. 53-70.

Oppenheim, Janet. *"Shattered Nerves": Doctors, Patients, and Depression in Victorian England.* Oxford: Oxford UP, 1991.

Orazem, Claudia. *Political Economy and Fiction in the Early Works of Harriet Martineau.* Anglo-American Studies Series. New York: Peter Lang, 1999.

Pelatson, Timothy. "Life Writing." *A Companion to Victorian Literature and Culture.* Ed. Herbert F. Tucker. Oxford: Blackwell, 1999. 356-72.

Peterson, Linda H. "Harriet Martineau: Masculine Discourse, Female Sage." *Victorian Sages and Cultural Discourse*. Ed. Thais Morgan. New Brunswick, NJ: Rutgers UP, 1990. 171-86.

———. "The Polemics of Piety: Charlotte Elizabeth Tonna's Personal Recollections, Harriet Martineau's Autobiography, and the Ideological Uses of Spiritual Autobiography." *Traditions of Victorian Women's Autobiography: The Poetics and Politics of Life Writing*. Charlottesville, VA, and London: UP of Virginia, 1999. 43-79.

———. "Sage Writing." *A Companion to Victorian Literature and Culture*. Ed. Herbert F. Tucker. Oxford: Blackwell, 1999. 373-87.

Poovey, Mary. "Scenes of an Indelicate Character: The Medical 'Treatment' of Victorian Women." *The Making of the Modern Body: Sexuality and Society in the Nineteenth Century*. Eds. Catherine Gallagher and Thomas Laqueur. Berkeley, CA: U of California P, 1987. 137-68.

Porter, Roy. *Health For Sale: Quackery in England 1660-1850*. Manchester: Manchester UP, 1989.

Porter, Roy, and Dorothy Porter. *In Sickness and In Health: The British Experience 1650-1850*. London: Fourth Estate, 1988.

Postlethwaite, Diana. "Mothering and Mesmerism in the Life of Harriet Martineau." *Signs* 14, 3 (1989): 583-609.

Roberts, Caroline. The Woman and the Hour: Harriet Martineau and Victorian Ideologies. Toronto: U of Toronto P, 2002.

Ryall, Anka. "Medical Body and Lived Experience: The Case of Harriet Martineau." *Mosaic* 33, 4 (2000): 35-53.

Sanders, Valerie. *Reason over Passion: Harriet Martineau and the Victorian Novel*. New York: St. Martin's Press, 1986.

Showalter, Elaine. *The Female Malady: Women, Madness, and English Culture, 1830-1980*. New York: Penguin, 1985.

Sontag, Susan. *Illness as Metaphor*. New York: Farrar, Straus, and Giroux, 1989.

Vrettos, Athena. *Somatic Fictions: Imagining Illness in Victorian Culture*. Stanford, CA: Stanford UP, 1995.

Winter, Alison. "Harriet Martineau and the Reform of the Invalid." *The Historical Journal* 38, 3 (1995): 597-616.

———. *Mesmerized. Powers of Mind in Victorian Britain*. Chicago and London: U of Chicago P, 1998.

Woolf, Virginia. "On Being Ill." *The Moment and Other Essays*, 948. Reprinted in *Collected Essays*. 4 Vols. Ed. L. Woolf. London: Chattos & Windus, 1969. 193-203.